Slouching Towards Bethlehem

Also by Graeme Carlé and published by Emmaus Road
Publishing, New Zealand:

Eating Sacred Cows
A Closer Look at Tithing

Because of the Angels
Unveiling 1 Corinthians 11:2-16

The Red Heifer's Ashes
Mysteries of Ancient Israel

Born of the Spirit
A study guide for new believers

The Revelation Series:

1. Dancing in the Dragon's Jaws
The Mystery of Israel's Survival

2. Slouching Towards Bethlehem
The Rise of the Antichrists

3. Gotta Serve Somebody
The Mystery of the Marks & 666

4. Silencing the Witnesses
Jerusalem and The Ascent of Secularism

5. Threshing Hour
Armageddon & Babylon the Great

6. Back in 7
The Seven Seals, Trumpets & Bowls

7. Kingdom Come
Justice for All

Slouching Towards Bethlehem

The Rise of the Antichrists

Graeme Carlé

First published 2012, revised 2018, 2020, 2025
Book design and production by Peter Aranyi
Illustrations by Alyssa McClelland
Cover design by Richard Westmoreland
Author photo by Samantha Ives

ISBN 978-0-9582746-8-5

2020-53

Unless otherwise stated, all Scripture quoted is from the NEW AMERICAN STANDARD BIBLE®, Copyright ©1995 The Lockman Foundation. Used with permission.

Emmaus Road Publishing
PO Box 38 823 Howick, Auckland 2014 New Zealand
www.emmausroad.org.nz

Contents

Figures

"But I say to you, love your enemies and pray for those who persecute you, so that you may be sons of your Father who is in heaven; for He causes His sun to rise on the evil and the good, and sends rain on the righteous and the unrighteous"

                    - Jesus of Nazareth (Matt 5:44-45)

For our struggle is not against flesh and blood, but against the principalities, against the powers, against the world forces of this darkness, against the spiritual forces of wickedness in the heavenly places.   - Paul of Tarsus (Eph 6:12)

Dedication

To Bruce Hamilton
(1933 - 2020)
who first challenged me to read, appreciate and think.

Thanks

To family and friends for their love, support and often painstaking feedback, especially Arthur Amon, Benjamin & Dolly Pan, Chris & Mali Gabriel, David & Louise Lee, Errol Francis, Kristin Herman, Lyssie McClelland, Marie Shaw, Mohan Herath, Olivia & Neil Ladyman, Peter & Lynne Maddison, Peter & Miriam Woolston, Peter & Susan Ridley, Richard Westmoreland, Rory Cavanagh, Ross & Jenny Shaw, Simone & Steve Varney, Tom Gillooly and Western Suburbs Christian Fellowship. As for Peter Aranyi, to painstaking add incredibly patient.

Foreword

If you are like me, you often wonder about the future, about where we are heading.

Science fiction is often optimistic, imagining utopias created by the wonders of scientific innovation, ever-improving technology and new ways for the good guys to beat the bad guys. *Star Trek* boldly took us all over the universe, conquering enemies, solving problems and healing broken relationships; in *Back to the Future* and *Star Wars,* our heroes overcome all obstacles.

However, sci-fi can also be bleakly dystopian: cautionary tales warning us of the consequences if we continue to live as we do or ignore particular trends. H.G. Wells, one of sci-fi's first great thinkers and writers, wrote both utopian and dystopian novels, beginning optimistically with *A Modern Utopia* (1905), *The World Set Free* (1914), *Men Like Gods* (1923) and *The Shape of Things to Come* (1933). He believed fervently in an inevitable World State, hoping it would be democratic, but literally finished writing with his bleak *Mind at the End of its Tether* (1946) and penning his own epitaph as: "I told you so. You *damned* fools".[1]

George Orwell (aka Eric Blair) always feared the worst as he considered the impact of the 20th Century's totalitarian regimes. His *Animal Farm,* an allegory of the Russian Revolution, has all the animals taking over a farm from a tyrannical farmer only to find themselves worse off under the regime of the Bolshevik pigs. Extrapolating on that, in 1948 he penned his most famous work, *1984,* and created a whole new vocabulary for us: 'Big Brother' – the dictator who watches everyone; 'Thought Police' – those who punish 'thoughtcrime'

---

1 Italics in the original, Wells's preface to the 1941 edition of *The War in the Air,* www.telelib.com/authors/W/WellsHerbertGeorge/prose/warintheair/warinair-pref1941.html, 24 May, 2011.

i.e. dissent; 'Newspeak' – the state's way of using language to erase the past.

In 1932, Aldous Huxley's remarkable *Brave New World*, set in London in the year 2540 A.D., projected the effects of scientific breakthroughs, especially in human reproductive technology and recreational drugs, but within a luxurious, tragically unaware, totalitarian society.

This fear of totalitarianism, the State controlling the totality of our lives, was, of course, well-founded.

Just a few years earlier, Benito Mussolini had set out to make Italy a wonderful example of what Fascism could achieve, distilling his philosophy into:

> *Tutto nello Stato, niente al di fuori dello Stato, nulla contro lo Stato* (Everything in the State, nothing outside the State, nothing against the State)

Imagine how this would appeal to any autocrat who could get his hands on the controls, and Adolf Hitler was watching carefully.

Political theorist Hannah Arendt sought to explain in *The Origins of Totalitarianism* (1951) that its roots are the natural forces of racism, bureaucracy and mankind's overwhelming desire to dominate. 19th Century philosopher Friedrich Nietzsche saw its roots as philosophical, predicting that "the death of God" would ultimately lead to us all being forced to accept totalitarian government.

However, W.B. Yeats wrote in 1920 of a chilling supernatural origin in his poem, *The Second Coming*:[2]

> Turning and turning in the widening gyre
> The falcon cannot hear the falconer;
> Things fall apart; the centre cannot hold;

---

2 William Butler Yeats won the Nobel Prize for Literature in 1923 and, in regard to the supernatural, he was an occultist and spiritualist. Sadly, the profound insight he expresses in this poem did not seem to extend to the rest of his beliefs.

          Slouching Towards Bethlehem

Mere anarchy is loosed upon the world,
The blood-dimmed tide is loosed, and everywhere
The ceremony of innocence is drowned;
The best lack all conviction, while the worst
Are full of passionate intensity.
Surely some revelation is at hand;
Surely the Second Coming is at hand.
The Second Coming! Hardly are those words out
When a vast image out of *Spiritus Mundi* [3]
Troubles my sight: somewhere in sands of the desert
A shape with lion body and the head of a man,
A gaze blank and pitiless as the sun,
Is moving its slow thighs, while all about it
Reel shadows of the indignant desert birds.
The darkness drops again; but now I know
That twenty centuries of stony sleep
Were vexed to nightmare by a rocking cradle,
And what rough beast, its hour come round at last,
Slouches towards Bethlehem to be born?

Forty-eight years later, acclaimed journalist Joan Didion published *Slouching Towards Bethlehem: Essays*,[4] a collection of observations that captured the mood of 1960s America. Her title essay described San Francisco's drug-dazed Haight-Ashbury but she saw both the counter-culture and the 'straight' celebrity-culture as falling apart because 'the centre cannot hold'. However, she made no attempt at all to identify what, or why anything, is 'slouching towards Bethlehem'.

This book seeks to identify 'what rough beast, its hour come round at last' is about to be born, and why.

We will also consider how close these pioneer thinkers and writers came to the Biblical revelation and how we should respond.

---

3 Latin, spirit of the world.
4 First published 1968. New York; Farrar, Straus and Giroux, 1990.

Introduction

In our previous study of Revelation's chapter 12, *Dancing in the Dragon's Jaws*, we saw how the dragon, Satan, hates and tries to destroy the woman, Israel, and her coming child, the Messiah. The last verse of that chapter tells us that when the dragon fails, he turns to attack 'the rest of her offspring' i.e. every follower of the Messiah, whether Jew or Gentile. What we are about to see now in chapter 13 are details of that attack, how the dragon uses invisible principalities and powers in the so-called secular political and social realm in every generation, including ours.

We saw that the dragon's seven heads symbolise seven great Gentile empires' power over Israel. The angel's interpretation, "five have fallen, one is, the other has not yet come" (Rev 17:10), describes the five successive empires during the two thousand years before Christ (Egypt, Assyria, Babylonia, Medo-Persia and Greece) and the sixth which was ascendant in John's time (Rome). As for the seventh with its ten horns, we simply noted it was "not yet come" when John was writing in about 96 A.D.

In this study, we will identify that seventh head and also the two beasts i.e. wild animals which the dragon uses to dominate all the nations, the whole world, and to persecute Christians. For those of us living in the West and mostly free of persecution, this may seem academic. However, like Tolkien's hobbits living in the Shire, we need to become aware of the bigger picture, because it is about to affect us all.

To the first beast, the dragon gives 'his power and his throne and great authority' (Rev 13:2) and to the second, all the authority of the first beast (v. 12) but more importantly, the speech of a dragon (v. 11). However, despite the dragon giving the beasts his authority, ultimately it is God who allows them to function, even though they blaspheme 'His name and His tabernacle, that is, those who dwell in heaven' (v. 6). It is God who gives the first beast the right 'to wage war with the saints and to overcome them' (v. 7). The vision of Revelation 13, therefore, is to explain one of the great mysteries of the Bible: *why, and for how long, does God allow the persecution and martyrdom of His people?*

This was hugely relevant to John and the saints of his day: John was himself in exile on Patmos (Rev 1:9); his brother James had been killed by Herod (Acts 12:2); Paul had been jailed for years before he and Peter were martyred in about 67 A.D. Many thousands of believers had been, or were about to be, slaughtered in the Roman circuses. Accordingly, John heard the souls of the martyrs in heaven crying out:

> "How long, O Lord, holy and true, will you refrain from judging and avenging our blood on those who dwell on the earth?"
> (Rev 6:10)

They are not questioning God's faithfulness or power but they do not understand why He is waiting and when He will act. This vision is to tell us why and when – He will let these beasts act for 'forty two months' (Rev 13:5), the same period of time that Israel, the woman, was in the wilderness. He is patiently waiting until the end of 'the partial hardening of Israel' and of "the times of the Gentiles" which, as we saw in our previous study, extends from the 1st Century right up to our times.

We established that timing can be identified, according to Jesus Himself, by the status of Jerusalem:

> "…and they will fall by the edge of the sword, and will be led captive into all the nations; and Jerusalem will be trampled under foot by the Gentiles until the times of the Gentiles are fulfilled" (Luke 21:24)

In other words, since Jerusalem was captured and destroyed in 70 A.D., "the times of the Gentile are fulfilled" only when

Israel finally regains sovereignty over their historic capital. This brings it right into our times because Israel recaptured most of Jerusalem in 1967. Here is this vision's special relevance to us today – if we are wise, we will want to know as much as we can about these beasts since they are still on the loose:

(i)   What exactly are they?

(ii)   What have they been doing?

(iii)   What will they do next?

(iv)   How and when will they come to their end?

This revelation will therefore help us to properly understand some of the most terrible events of the last century and, lastly, how we should live in our day.

We will finish this study of Revelation 13 at verse 15, leaving verses 16-18, and therefore the infamous mark of the beast, to be examined in Book 3. That mark needs to be considered at the same time as the mark of God (Rev 14:1) as well the consequences (Rev 14:9-12). In that study, you will see for yourself that, contrary to much of what is thought and taught today,[5] the mark of the beast is not a future event based around our shopping. It has actually been around for the last two thousand years. Accordingly, instead of waiting for it to come, we should have been recognising it happening right before our eyes.

However, let us not get ahead of ourselves. Before we can properly understand the second beast's mark, we need to correctly understand the two beasts. Given that the Old Testament will again provide us with the keys, we really should pray:

---

5 For example, in the largest Christian publishing phenomenon of our time, the 65 million copies of the *Left Behind* sixteen-book series by Tim LaHaye & Jerry B. Jenkins; Wheaton, Illinois; Tyndale, 1995-2007.

                              Slouching Towards Bethlehem

Open my eyes, that I may behold wonderful things from
Your law; I am a stranger in the earth; do not hide Your
commandments from me (Psa 119:18-19)

Text of Revelation 13

1. And he [the dragon] stood on the sand of the seashore. And
I saw a beast coming up out of the sea, having ten horns and
seven heads, and on his horns were ten diadems, and on his
heads were blasphemous names.
2. And the beast which I saw was like a leopard, and his feet
were like those of a bear, and his mouth like the mouth of a lion.
And the dragon gave him his power and his throne and great
authority.
3. And I saw one of his heads as if it had been slain, and his
fatal wound was healed. And the whole earth was amazed and
followed after the beast;
4. and they worshiped the dragon, because he gave his
authority to the beast, and they worshiped the beast, saying,
"Who is like the beast, and who is able to wage war with him?"
5. And there was given to him a mouth speaking arrogant words
and blasphemies; and authority to act for forty-two months was
given to him.
6. And he opened his mouth in blasphemies against God, to
blaspheme His name and His tabernacle, that is, those who
dwell in heaven.
7. And it was given to him to make war with the saints and to
overcome them; and authority over every tribe and people and
tongue and nation was given to him.
8. And all who dwell on the earth will worship him, everyone
whose names have not been written from the foundation of the
world in the book of life of the Lamb who has been slain.
9. If anyone has an ear, let him hear.
10. If anyone is destined for captivity, to captivity he goes; if
anyone kills with the sword, with the sword he must be killed.
Here is perseverance and the faith of the saints.
11. And I saw another beast coming up out of the earth; and he
had two horns like a lamb, and he spoke as a dragon.
12. And he exercises all the authority of the first beast in his

presence. And he makes the earth and those who dwell in it to worship the first beast, whose fatal wound was healed.

13. And he performs great signs, so that he even makes fire come down out of heaven to the earth in the presence of men.

14. And he deceives those who dwell on the earth because of the signs which it was given him to perform in the presence of the beast, telling those who dwell in the earth to make an image to the beast who had the wound of the sword and has come to life.

15. And there was given to him to give breath to the image of the beast, that the image of the beast might even speak and cause as many as do not worship the image of the beast to be killed.

1

The First Beast
'Out of the Sea'

> And he [the dragon] stood on the sand of the seashore. And
> I saw a beast coming up out of the sea, having ten horns and
> seven heads, and on his horns were ten diadems, and on his
> heads were blasphemous names (Rev 13:1)

Having been cast down from heaven to 'the earth and the sea' (Rev 12:12), the dragon stands on the seashore as the first beast emerges from the sea on to the earth. As we saw in our earlier study, the Greek word for beast (*therion*) is a generic term for dangerous wild animals, being used another thirty six times in Revelation. For example, in Revelation 6:8, people are being killed by 'wild beasts'. This was the time of the Colosseum and the Roman circuses, which routinely featured criminals and Christians facing *damnatio ad bestias* (i.e. execution by wild animals).

Obviously no ordinary wild animal, this fierce, deadly, and blaspheming enemy of God and His people must first be understood *as it was in the 1st Century* by the original hearers of John's message. Only when we have that established can we respond properly today.

Why does it come up out of the sea? 'The sea' is the Mediterranean, which in those days was usually called the Great Sea, in comparison to the Sea of Galilee, the Dead Sea and the Red Sea. Later in his vision, when John sees a horrible woman sitting on 'many waters', "the waters" are interpreted by an angel as meaning "peoples and multitudes and nations and tongues" (Rev 17:15). The first beast, then, arises from 'all the nations' i.e. the Gentiles, as will be confirmed next.

Like the dragon (Rev 12:3), this beast has seven heads and ten horns but is a composite of other animals:

> And the beast which I saw was like a leopard, and his feet were like those of a bear, and his mouth like the mouth of a lion. And the dragon gave him his power and his throne and great authority (Rev 13:2)

'Like a Leopard..., a Bear... And a Lion'

As bizarre as this beast may seem to us, 1st Century Jewish Christians would have readily understood this image because these three animals had featured, in reverse order, six hundred and fifty years earlier in a then very well-known vision of Daniel's. The reverse order is because Daniel saw them in about 550 B.C.[6] as affecting Israel's future whereas John was looking back from about 100 A.D. at Israel's past.

Daniel had a dream about the coming of four wild animals that would precede the coming of Israel's long-awaited Messiah:

> I was looking in my vision by night, and behold, the four winds of heaven were stirring up the great sea. And four great beasts were coming up from the sea, different from one another. The first was like a lion… a second one, resembling a bear… another one like a leopard (Dan 7:2-6)

Note the first three are 'like a lion.., a bear.., and a leopard' and also come up from 'the great sea', the Mediterranean. They appear one after another and are each given 'dominion' (Dan 7:6 & 12). The fourth beast which follows them is not like any particular animal but Daniel goes on:

> After this… a fourth beast, frightening and terrifying, and very strong. And it had great iron teeth; it devoured and broke in pieces, and stamped the rest with its feet. And it was different from all the beasts before it and it had ten horns (Dan 7:7)

---

6 Date of Daniel 7:1, *The Zondervan Pictorial Encyclopedia of the Bible*, edit. Merrill C. Tenney, 1977, Vol 1, pp. 515-516.

Slouching Towards Bethlehem

After this beast, Messiah appears:

> I kept looking in the night visions and behold, with the clouds of
> heaven, one like a Son of Man was coming and He came up to
> the Ancient of Days and was presented before Him.
> And to Him was given dominion, glory and a kingdom that all
> the peoples, nations and men of every language might serve
> Him. His dominion is an everlasting dominion which will not
> pass away; and His kingdom is one which will not be destroyed
> (Dan 7:13-14)

Remember, it was Jesus' quoting of this prophecy that caused
the high priest and the Sanhedrin to sentence Him to death
for blasphemy. The high priest had asked Him if He was the
Messiah and He replied:

> "… I tell you, hereafter you will see THE SON OF MAN SITTING
> AT THE RIGHT HAND OF POWER and COMING ON THE CLOUDS OF
> HEAVEN".
> Then the high priest tore his robes and said, "He has
> blasphemed! What further need do we have of witnesses?
> Behold, you have now heard the blasphemy; what do you
> think?" They answered, "He deserves death!"
> (Matt 26:64-66, capitals in NASB to show Old Testament
> quotations)

Daniel is then given the interpretation of the beasts:

> 17. "These great beasts, which are four in number, are four kings
> who will arise from the earth.
> 18. "But the saints of the Highest One will receive the kingdom
> and possess the kingdom forever, for all ages to come"
> (Dan 7:17-18)

The beasts then are 'four kings' (v. 17), and as we saw in Book
1,[7] in Jewish thinking 'king' can denote not only a single
individual but also a kingdom and a dynasty of kings or
emperors.[8] These 'four kings' are earthly and temporal and they

---

7 *Dancing in the Dragon's Jaws*, Auckland; Emmaus Road Publishing,
2011, p. 25.
8   e.g. Dan 2:37-44, 5:31, 7:22-23.

are to be superseded by the heavenly and eternal Kingdom and 'the saints' (v. 18), i.e. God's people, will 'receive' and 'possess' it forever.

Daniel also carefully notes that even though the first three beasts, the ones like a lion, a bear and a leopard, lose 'their dominion', they are going to reappear at a later time:

> As for the rest of the beasts, their dominion was taken away, but an extension of life was granted to them for an appointed period of time (Dan 7:12)

As we will see, this 'extension of life... for an appointed period of time' is the time of Revelation chapter 13, comprises "the times of the Gentiles", and is therefore the last 2,000 years.[9]

Identifying Daniel's Four Beasts

These 'four kings' are not specifically identified in Daniel 7, but they did not need to be because they already had been, some fifty years earlier. In 604 B.C.,[10] both the Babylonian king Nebuchadnezzar and Daniel had had identical dreams about these same four kingdoms and the Messianic kingdom. It was then that Daniel was given the divine interpretation and reason for the dreams:

> "O king, while on your bed your thoughts turned to what would take place in the future, and He who reveals mysteries has made known to you what will take place" (Dan 2:29)

So, like the rest of us, Nebuchadnezzar was wondering about the future and Daniel got to tell him. He began by explaining the four kingdoms for Nebuchadnezzar, the first being his own Babylonian Empire:

---

9 *Dancing in the Dragon's Jaws,* pp. 119-121.

10 Dan 2:1 according to *The Zondervan Pictorial Encyclopedia of the Bible,* edit. Merrill C. Tenney, 1977, Vol 4, p. 395.

Slouching Towards Bethlehem

> "You are the head of gold. And after you there will arise another
> kingdom [the Medo-Persians]… then another third kingdom
> [the Greeks] which will rule over all the earth. Then there will be
> a fourth kingdom [the Romans]…" (Dan 2:38-40)

Accordingly, in Daniel 7's parallel vision: the first beast, the lion, is the Babylonian Empire; the second, the bear, is the Medo-Persian; the third, the leopard, is the Greek and the fourth beast is the Roman Empire.

We will confirm their identities soon because they are very like stepping stones in a swamp where many have wandered off and sunk in confusion. We have to establish each step as rock solid before we seek the next. For example, *The New Oxford Annotated Bible* identifies the four beasts as Babylon, Media, Persia and Greece.[11] Its scholars have decided that the Book of Daniel is not supernatural or predictive so that 'the history recorded in these visions suggest that they were composed sometime before 164 B.C.' i.e. in the time of the Greeks. Their decision therefore rules out Rome as the fourth beast since it was not then significant and also locks these scholars into two more critical errors.

Firstly, they are using modern Gentile thinking to count the empires, overlooking the Jewish understanding recorded throughout Daniel that the Medes and the Persians comprised one empire, not two (Dan 5:28, 6:8, 6:12, 6:15). For example, in a vision dated about 551-552 B.C.,[12] Daniel sees the Medo-Persian Empire as another animal, this time as a ram with two horns, being overcome by a goat. An angel interprets for him:

> "The ram which you saw with the two horns represents the
> kings of Media and Persia. The shaggy goat represents the
> kingdom of Greece" (Dan 8:20-21)

---

11 Augmented 3rd Edition, New York; Oxford University Press, 2001, pp. 1258, 1267, Hebrew Bible.
12 *Zondervan NASB Study Bible,* p. 1240.

In Daniel 7 then, the second beast is Medo-Persia, the third is Greece and the fourth is Rome.

The second critical and surely most sobering error of these scholars is that they make Jesus Himself wrong in claiming He was fulfilling both Daniel 2 (Matt 21-42-44) and Daniel 7 (Matt 26:64-66) in the time of the Romans. According to their reasoning, He should have been in the time of the Greeks![13]

Although today we have to back-track to identify these 'four kings', remember how much easier it was for 1st Century Jewish believers. They already knew which was which, since their nation had historically experienced the first three (Babylonia 605-539 B.C., Medo-Persia 539-333 B.C., and Greece 333-165 B.C.) and their own daily experience was of the fourth: Rome. Rome had been ruling them since 63 B.C. when Pompey captured Jerusalem;[14] it was also John's own context in writing the Revelation in 95-96 A.D.

Why Did God Permit These Beasts?

Given the character of these beasts, why did God allow them to rise up? After all, for seven hundred years they ravaged and dominated His own nation of Israel as well as Messiah, His own Son, and His 1st Century friends and followers. While it is the dragon, Satan, who inspires these entities to hatred

---

13   Others today such as Walid Shoebat and Joel Richardson in *God's War on Terror (Islam, Prophecy and the Bible)* [Top Executive Media, 2008, p. 311] note some renowned medieval Jewish scholars such as Abraham ibn Ezra (1040-1164 A.D.) saw Daniel 7 differently:

> Rome is included in the third kingdom as relatives of the Greeks. The Romans are considered to be the Kittim mentioned in Numbers 24:24.
>
> In Genesis 10:4, Kittim are the sons of Yavan (Greece).

Ibn Ezra believed the fourth kingdom was the Arabic empire of Islam. However, this would mean Messiah has not yet come, which the rabbis were trying to prove, and therefore denying Jesus' claim of fulfilling Daniel 2 and 7.

14   www.jewishencyclopedia.com/view.jsp?artid=52&letter=B#172 and www.scaruffi.com/politics/neareast.html, 19 Feb, 2009.

and genocide, ultimately God *is* allowing it all to happen for this time. Why?

Almost one hundred and fifty years before Daniel, between 753 and 723 B.C.,[15] Hosea called Israel to turn back to God, warning that if they remained unfaithful, God would withdraw His protection, like a shepherd walking away from his flock and allowing wild predators to ravage them. Notice the particular animals Hosea predicted would attack them:

> "I have been the LORD your God since the land of Egypt;
> And you were not to know of any god except Me.
> I cared for you in the wilderness [like a shepherd], in the land of drought.
> As they [the flock of Israel] had their pasture, they became satisfied,
> And being satisfied, their heart became proud;
> Therefore they forgot Me.
> So I will be ***like a lion*** to them;
> ***Like a leopard*** I will lie in wait by the wayside.
> I will encounter them ***like a bear*** robbed of her cubs…"
> (Hos 13:4-8, emphasis added)

Accordingly, having warned Israel many times over hundreds of years previously, God finally allowed these Gentile empires, 'a lion, a leopard and a bear', to arise to bring judgement on His flock. Notice, He says "*I* will be like…" because He is the ultimate Judge and the penalties are from Him, even though the agents of destruction are directly inspired by Satan, the dragon.

---

15 *The Zondervan Pictorial Encyclopedia of the Bible*, edit. Merrill C. Tenney, 1977, Vol 5, p. 210.

John's First Beast

So, returning to Revelation 13, let us now consider the first beast of John's vision, which includes aspects of each of these three animals:

> ...And I saw a beast coming up out of the sea, having ten horns and seven heads, and on his horns were ten diadems, and on his heads were blasphemous names.
> 2. And the beast which I saw was like a leopard, and his feet were like those of a bear, and his mouth like the mouth of a lion. And the dragon gave him his power and his throne and great authority (Rev 13:1b-2)

So although John is seeing this beast in the time of the Roman Empire, its being 'like a leopard' links it to the preceding Greek Empire, its feet 'like those of a bear' links it to the earlier Medo-Persian Empire, and its mouth 'like the mouth of a lion', back further to the Babylonian Empire.

Just as today, to John's initial hearers each of these animals had clearly recognised characteristics as can be seen from their ancient Scriptures. The beast's body being like a leopard means it is capable of great speed,[16] ferocity [17] and stealth;[18] its feet being like a bear's means strength and power,[19] ferocity [20] and aggression,[21] while its claws can inflict great damage.[22] Of course, a lion is also ferocious,[23] stealthy [24] and destructive,[25] but 'the mouth of the lion', its roar, is particularly terrifying, instilling fear well beyond its immediate presence.[26] We can

---

16 Habbakuk 1:8
17 Isaiah 11:6
18 Jeremiah 5:6, Hosea 13:7
19 1 Samuel 17:37
20 2 Samuel 17:8, Proverbs 17:12
21 Proverbs 28:15, Isaiah 11:7
22 1 Samuel 17:37
23 Psalm 17:12, Isaiah 11:6
24 Psalm 10:9
25 Ezekiel 22:25
26 Amos 3:8, 1 Peter 5:8

today easily underestimate this effect, since the only time we hear a lion roaring it is usually on television or, if we see a live lion, it is safely behind strong bars. In John's day, however, the roar often preceded a face to face encounter. As Amos said:

John's first beast then, having features of all three, has speed, ferocity, stealth, aggression, deadly effect and the ability to instill great fear in all who hear it.

So what is it exactly? What has elements of each of these great Gentile kingdoms but is not one of them? In some way, it is made up of them all – Babylonia, Medo-Persia, Greece and Rome – and yet is something else. And how is it stealthy?

It is not one of them because it is not a political entity of flesh and blood – *it is the power structure at work behind the scenes which has developed a life or momentum of its own and gone wild.* Stealthy because it is invisible, it has elements of each of these 'flesh and blood' empires and was manifest in each of them as they sought to dominate the people of God, firstly the Jews and then in the time of the Romans, the Christians, whether Jews or Gentiles.

Authorities and Powers

> For our struggle is not against flesh and blood, but against the rulers, against the powers (Gk. *exousia*, authorities), against the world forces of this darkness, against the spiritual forces of wickedness in the heavenly places (Eph 6:12)

When Paul warns us here of the breadth of opposition we face as followers of Jesus, he includes not only spiritual personalities such as fallen angels and demons (Rom 8:38, 1 Tim 4:1) but also corrupt impersonal authority and power structures in our society. 'Authorities' are those with the legitimate 'right to enforce obedience';[27] 'powers' (Gk. *dynamis*, hence dynamite and dynamo) are those with the *ability* to enforce obedience. Because we are all fallible individuals, all of our collective endeavours are fallible, yet the structures themselves were created as good:

> For by Him all things were created, both in the heavens and on earth, visible and invisible, whether thrones or dominions or rulers or authorities – all things have been created through Him and for Him (Col 1:16)

Accordingly, we are to honour governments and governors:

> Every person is to be in subjection to the governing authorities (Gk. *exousia*) for there is no authority except from God, and those which exist are established by God. Therefore whoever resists authority has opposed the ordinance of God (Rom 13:1-2)

However, as with everything human, our structures go wrong when we allow them to fall or to be diverted from their original purpose. When it comes to the government, Paul explains its primary purpose is to be God's agent for justice and good order in society, including creating and maintaining infrastructure to facilitate commerce, health, education, transport and travel:

> 4. … it is a minister of God to you for good. But if you do what is evil, be afraid; for it does not bear the sword for nothing; for it is a minister of God, an avenger who brings wrath on the one who practices evil.
> 5. Therefore it is necessary to be in subjection, not only because of wrath, but also for conscience' sake.
> 6. For because of this you also pay taxes, for rulers are servants of God, devoting themselves to this very thing.
> 7. Render to all what is due them: tax to whom tax is due; custom to whom custom; fear to whom fear; honour to whom honour (Rom 13:4-7)

Notice, God has given the state 'the sword' (v. 4), the power of

---

27 *Concise Oxford Dictionary*, p. 58.

                                    Slouching Towards Bethlehem

life and death, since it alone has the right to enforce obedience on wrong-doers.[28] This is the Biblical mandate legitimising all states to have armed forces for defence and police forces to enforce justice and subdue any illegitimate use of force.

As believers then, we are all to work as "salt and light" (Matt 5:13-14) to keep all human authorities as honest and just as we can (Luke 3:14, 1 Tim 2:1-3). Take John the Baptist for example:

> And some tax collectors also came to be baptised, and they said to him, "Teacher, what shall we do?" And he said to them, "Collect no more than what you have been ordered to." Some soldiers were questioning him, saying, "And what about us, what shall we do?" And he said to them, "Do not take money from anyone by force, or accuse anyone falsely, and be content with your wages" (Luke 3:12-14)

He does not reject their roles but addresses the corresponding temptation in their hearts – the tax collectors are to be scrupulously honest and the soldiers are not to abuse their position or accept bribes.

Lastly, we will all need to be salt and light until 'all rule and all authority and power' except the kingdom of God is abolished at the Second Coming (1 Cor 15:24).

Thomas Hobbes's *Leviathan*

Just as Daniel and John spoke zoomorphically, describing particular empires as different animals, so too did English philosopher Thomas Hobbes. In 1651, he published his famous treatise, *Leviathan,* which is credited with laying the foundation for much of today's Western political philosophy and anthropology. Sub-titled *The Matter, Forme and Power of a Common Wealth Ecclesiasticall and Civil,* it argued for the

---

28 Sociologist Max Weber defines the state as an entity with a 'monopoly on the legitimate use of violence' i.e. coercive, physical force. *Politics as a Vocation,* 1920.

necessity of a 'social contract' between us all, to prevent a 'war of all against all' and without which life would be, in his often quoted phrase, 'solitary, poor, nasty, brutish and short'. To achieve this common benefit, Hobbes thought, mankind imitates the God who made us in His image by making another, 'an artificial man', in our own image:

> Art goes yet further, imitating that rational and most excellent work of Nature, man. For by art is created that great LEVIATHAN called a COMMONWEALTH, or STATE (in Latin, CIVITAS), which is but an artificial man, though of greater stature and strength than the natural, for whose protection and defence it was intended.[29]

In other words, he thought that mankind creates the State to organise, benefit and protect us all. Later, he describes how that is achieved:

> …if every man should say to every man: I authorise and give up my right of governing myself to this man, or to this assembly of men, on this condition; that thou [also] give up thy right to him, and authorise all his actions in like manner. This done, the multitude so united in one person is called a COMMONWEALTH; in Latin, CIVITAS. This is the generation [or, creation] of that great LEVIATHAN, or rather, to speak more reverently, of that mortal god to which we owe, under the immortal God, our peace and defence.[30]

Why then did Hobbes choose the name, *Leviathan*? Biblically, Leviathan is another name for the dragon:

> In that day the LORD will punish Leviathan the fleeing serpent,
> With His fierce and great and mighty sword,
> Even Leviathan the twisted serpent;
> And He will kill the dragon who lives in the sea (Isa 27:1)

---

29   Introduction of *Leviathan*, emphasis in original. http://oregonstate.edu/instruct/phl302/texts/hobbes/leviathan-contents.html, 14 Feb, 2011.
30   Ibid., Chapter XVII.

Slouching Towards Bethlehem

We examined this in Book 1, *Dancing in the Dragon's Jaws*, where we saw that 'the serpent of old' is also 'called the devil and Satan, who deceives the whole world' (Rev 12:9). In other words, Leviathan is a metaphorical name for Satan.[31] Isaiah here describes Leviathan as living 'in the sea' which is also a symbol of 'the abyss', i.e. the bottomless pit, the place of the dead (Rom 10:7, Rev 20:13) and of evil spirits (Luke 8:31, Rev 9:11).

However, Leviathan can also be translated literally as a whale (Psa 104:25-26) which can mean that Jonah was swallowed by a whale but 'it ain't necessarily so'[32] – the word describes any large denizen of the deep, natural or spiritual, whether whale, large shark, giant squid, or the dragon.[33]

Hobbes was a Bible-believing Christian but it seems he did not understand this. Accordingly, he took his metaphor from Job chapter 41, where Leviathan is the largest of sea creatures with overwhelming strength and power, to symbolise the State which is to benevolently unify or collectivise the will of all the people. To this, he thought, we owe 'our peace and defence'.

By way of contrast, he also wrote *Behemoth*,[34] taking this title from the other huge creature described in Job (Job 40:15-24), which Hobbes explained was his metaphor for the evil of civil war.[35]

So Hobbes thought that mankind creates the State as a means of organising, benefitting and protecting us all, as 'a mortal god… under the immortal God' and he named it Leviathan after the greatest of all God's creatures.

---

31 *Dancing in the Dragon's Jaws*, pp. 36-37.

32 For very different reasons than those given in 1935 by Ira Gershwin and DuBose Heyward in *Porgy and Bess*.

33 *Dancing in the Dragon's Jaws*, p. 37.

34 Subtitled, *The history of the causes of the civil wars of England, and of the counsels and artifices by which they were carried on from the year 1640 to the year 1660*, published posthumously in 1681.

35 *Part One - Behemoth, or the Epitome of the Civil Wars of England.*

When Good Governments Go Bad

What then are we to make of the state when, to complete Hobbes's zoomorphism, the animal goes feral or wild? When, for example, the state or the leader of the state lays claim to godhood?

In Nebuchadnezzar's case of self-glorifying, he was humbled when he temporarily lost his mind and became like 'a beast of the field'. God had warned him in a fearful dream, interpreted by Daniel, but he ignored it:

> Immediately the word concerning Nebuchadnezzar was fulfilled; and he was driven away from mankind and began eating grass like cattle, and his body was drenched with the dew of heaven until his hair had grown like eagles' feathers and his nails like birds' claws (Dan 4:33)

After 'seven times' i.e. years (Dan 4:16), his reason returned and he honoured Daniel's God as the Everlasting King (v. 34). Later, when Daniel dreamed of the four beasts, the one representing Babylon tells of Nebuchadnezzar's humbling in another way:

> The first was like a lion and had the wings of an eagle. I kept looking until its wings were plucked, and it was lifted up from the ground and made to stand on two feet like a man; a human mind also was given to it (Dan 7:4)

The Ishtar Gate, one of the eight gates of Nebuchadnezzar's renowned Hanging Gardens of Babylon, was decorated with winged lions.[36] Having exalted himself to the heavens, he became like an animal before coming back to his true place as a man.

What extraordinary grace God shows to this pagan emperor, loving him through to humility.

Accordingly, Paul urges us to pray for our political leaders:

---

36 Photos of these in Berlin's Pergamon Museum can be seen on www.flickr.com/photos/monceau/sets/72157625440142759/ and www. ancientreplicas.com/babylon/striding-lion.html.

> 1. First of all, then, I urge that entreaties and prayers, petitions and thanksgivings, be made on behalf of all men,
> 2. for kings and all who are in authority, so that we may lead a tranquil and quiet life in all godliness and dignity.
> 3. This is good and acceptable in the sight of God our Saviour,
> 4. who desires all men to be saved and to come to the knowledge of the truth (1 Tim 2:1-4)

This is astonishing because Paul had more reason than most of us to pray vindictively against our political leaders. He had lived through the madness of the reigns of Caligula (37-41 A.D.) and Claudius (41-54) and was here writing to Timothy while waiting to be judged and executed by Nero in about 66 A.D. Emperors are to be honoured as individuals for whom Christ died as well as supported by our prayers and taxes (Matt 22:21, Rom 13:1-7). The effect would then be like salt slowing down the inevitable corruption of meat and also bring respite from persecution.

The beast, however, will not ultimately be diverted, which returns us to John's first beast. While similar to Hobbes's Leviathan, John's is not just any manifestation of a State becoming corrupt – he is describing a spiritual corruption:

> And the dragon gave the beast his power and his throne and great authority (Rev 13:2b)

Behind the scenes of this beast, the dragon not only encourages its corruption but leads it to blasphemy.

Notice, the beast does not at this stage include Asian, African or American peoples; only those Middle Eastern empires that impinged on Israel. This beast is the 'principality and power' behind those Gentile kings, the 'world forces' ruling over Israel through the four empires.

However, it did not come to an end with them. John saw this beast in the Middle East in the 1st Century A.D. but, as we will see, it has continued to manifest itself to terrible effect anywhere it can throughout the last two thousand years.

Now in our day, it is making its final appearance, its ultimate culmination, as the dragon's seventh head.

Before we consider that, let us summarise what we have established so far.

Summary of the First Beast

John sees the dragon on the seashore while a great wild beast emerges from the sea, having features of three that are very familiar to him and his 1st Century Jewish listeners – a leopard, a bear and a lion:

(i) These particular animals had been predicted by Hosea almost a thousand years earlier, in eighth century B.C., as metaphors of God's coming judgement on the flock of Israel for their unfaithfulness.

(ii) Some two hundred years after Hosea, Daniel dreamed of four great beasts (Daniel 7, circa 550 B.C.), signifying four successive Gentile kingdoms, followed by the coming of Messiah. The first three were like a lion, a bear and a leopard and symbolised the Babylonian, Medo-Persian and Greek empires. The fourth beast was the Roman empire of John's day which saw the coming of Messiah and the beginning of His kingdom.

(iii) The animals' identities had been established fifty years earlier (Daniel 2, circa 600 B.C.) in two dreams of a statue and a growing stone which, Daniel was told, revealed four successive Gentile kingdoms and the coming of Messiah's kingdom. The first was the Babylonian empire which was followed by the Medo-Persian, Greek and Roman empires and, of course, the coming of Jesus as Messiah.

(iv) In the dreams recorded by Daniel, the fourth empire was to culminate in one somehow comprising ten (the statue's ten toes, the fourth beast's ten horns) in the time of Messiah's kingdom; in John's vision, the first beast also has ten horns as does the dragon of Revelation 12 and the beast of Revelation 17.

(v) John and his 1st Century Jewish listeners knew which was which and why these beasts attacked Israel because they highly valued their nation's historical and unfolding prophetic record: Hosea's warning in about 750 B.C., Nebuchadnezzar and Daniel's dreams of the statue in about 600 B.C. and Daniel's dream of the four beasts in about 550 B.C.

(vi) John's first beast, in the time of the fourth empire but with features of the previous three, is the 'principality and power' of these Gentile kings, the 'world forces' behind and above their empires.

(vii) These animal metaphors parallel what we established in our earlier study of Revelation chapter 12, where the dragon's seven heads were identified as a total of six Gentile empires that had dominated Israel (these four from Daniel plus the earlier two, Egypt and Assyria) with the seventh "yet to come" with its ten horns.

(viii) Turning now to governments, Paul warns us that as believers we face inevitable opposition from not only fallen spiritual and human beings but also from corrupt impersonal authority and power structures in our society. We are therefore to honour those in authority but work to keep them honest and just.

(ix) Hobbes's *Leviathan* is a useful illustration from 17th Century England. While his labelling is not helpful because it misapplies a name of the dragon, he uses the most powerful of all animals as a metaphor for the State as the most powerful of all human entities and defines its function and benefits.

(x) In this metaphor, when any good government goes bad, when it abandons or abuses its legitimate function, it is like a domesticated animal reverting to the wild.

(xi) This is the metaphor being used by John in Revelation 13. John shows how in his day, the State, the Roman Empire, was being influenced by the dragon to become blasphemous, persecuting and murdering the people of God. As we will see when we consider the beast's seventh head, this wild animal is still very much on the loose.

2

The Seventh Head
John's Future Empire

In order to establish the correct meaning and timing of the seventh head and its ten horns, we need to consider Revelation chapter 13 alongside Daniel chapters 2 and 7 as well as Revelation chapters 12 and 17. While this may seem complicated, the answers that emerge are surprisingly simple and consistent, confirming what John's original hearers in the 1st Century would have already understood. It will also help us avoid starting with our button in the wrong button hole as evident in *The New Oxford Annotated Bible:*

> The seven kings are Roman emperors… which interpreters have sought to identify with emperors from Julius Caesar to Domitian. [The] ten horns represent subordinate or client rulers.[37]

Those interpreters were never going to be successful because Domitian was the eleventh emperor.[38] The seven heads are not Roman emperors nor, as we will see, are the ten horns 'subordinate or client rulers' or Nero's provincial governors.[39]

In Revelation 12, we saw the diadems were on the seven heads, highlighting the six Gentile kingdoms of Israel's previous 2,000 years of history with the seventh yet to come. Here in Revelation 13, the diadems highlight the ten horns:

---

37 Augmented Third Edition, 2006, p. 442, NT.
38 www.roman-emperors.org/impindex.htm, 18 Aug, 2011.
39 David Chilton, *Paradise Restored: A Biblical Theology of Dominion,* Ft. Worth, TX; Dominion Press, 1985.

Just as we did with the seven heads, we find the ten horns'
meaning in the angel's interpretation of their third appearance
in Revelation:

So Revelation 13's ten diadems focus us on the "ten kings"
which were, in John's time, yet to come on the seventh head.
To help us identify them, we are given the testimonies of
three eyewitnesses of their coming – Nebuchadnezzar, Daniel
and John. This is because in the Scriptures 'every fact is to
be confirmed by the testimony of two or three witnesses'
(2 Cor 13:1) and, as in everyday courtrooms everywhere, we
will need to collate all of their evidence to get the complete
picture.

We will also see confirmed that they are contemporaneous
and not consecutive kings as others have thought, still trying
to match them up with the Caesars.[40]

The Testimony of Three Eyewitnesses

(i) In Daniel chapter 2

Nebuchadnezzar and Daniel have identical dreams of a statue
of a man with head of gold, breast and arms of silver, belly
and thighs of bronze, legs of iron, and feet with *ten toes* made
of a mixture of iron and clay i.e. pottery.

These metals are divinely interpreted (vv. 36-40) as being
successive empires starting from Babylon (gold) which would

---

40   For example, Jay Rogers on www.forerunner.com/daniel/X0023_
Notes_on_Daniel__par.html, 18 Aug, 2011.

---

make them Medo-Persia (silver), Greece (bronze) and Rome (iron). As for the feet of iron and pottery, that symbolises an ensuing "divided kingdom" (v. 41) of kings and kingdoms who mingle through marriage alliances, which necessarily makes them contemporaries, but they fail to "adhere to one another" i.e. hold together:

> "As the toes of the feet were partly of iron and partly of pottery, so some of the kingdom will be strong and part of it will be brittle. And in that you saw the iron mixed with common clay, they will combine with one another in the seed of men; but they will not adhere to one another, even as iron does not combine with pottery" (Dan 2:42-43)

Nebuchadnezzar and Daniel's dreams also foretell the end of these successive empires:

> "… a stone was cut out without hands, and it struck the statue on its feet of iron and clay and crushed them. Then the iron, the clay, the bronze, the silver and the gold were crushed all at the same time and became like chaff from the summer threshing floors; and the wind carried them away so that not a trace of them was found. But the stone that struck the statue became a great mountain and filled the whole earth" (Dan 2:34-35)

Daniel then interprets the stone's striking on the feet and toes:

> "As the toes of the feet… In the days of those [ten] kings the God of heaven will set up a kingdom which will never be destroyed, and that kingdom will not be left for another people; it will crush and put an end to all these kingdoms, but it will itself endure forever" (Dan 2:42-44)

Some six hundred years later, Jesus of Nazareth announced the arrival of this kingdom of stone:

> "Therefore I say to you, the kingdom of God will be taken away from you [unbelieving Jews] and given to a people producing the fruit of it [believing Jews and Gentiles]. And he who falls on this stone will be broken to pieces; but on whomever it falls, it will scatter him like dust" (Matt 21:43-44)

Remember in Daniel 7:18 where it is "the saints" who will "receive" and "possess" the kingdom of stone? Here Jesus says "the kingdom of God" is given to "a people" who are no longer only Jewish but fruitful believers in Him from any nation. We will return to this later.

Notice too, according to Jesus Himself, this kingdom of stone was arriving in the time of the Roman Empire so *the ten toes must also have existed at that time.*

(ii) In Daniel 7

Daniel sees four beasts rising out of the sea and the fourth beast has ten horns.

An angel explains to him that these horns are ten kingdoms which would "arise out of" the fourth beast (v. 24), the Roman Empire. Daniel then sees that an eleventh but *different* horn is to arise and gives us a very significant time-span for it:

> 24. "…and another will arise after them, and he will be different from the previous ones [the ten kings] and will subdue three kings.
> 25. "And he will speak out against the Most High and wear down the saints of the Highest One, and he will intend to make alterations in times and in law; and they will be given into his hand for *a time, times, and half a time*" (Dan 7:24-25, emphasis added)

So these two inspired interpretations tell us that the ten follow the Roman Empire and emerge from it. The ten are then dominated by another horn which is different from them and which wages war against the saints for a now very familiar period of time – "a time, times, and half a time" i.e. three and a half years.

At this point, therefore, we see the particular relevance of the key we gained in Book 1, *Dancing in the Dragon's Jaws* – the period of three and a half years is the prophetic device symbolising Elijah's two 'comings', "the times of the Gentiles"

Slouching Towards Bethlehem

and the 'partial hardening of Israel.' [41] So, while the time span of the ten kingdoms is not explicitly given, that of the eleventh and "different" horn is – he will "wear down the saints" who have been "given into his hands" (v. 25) for what we can now see have been *the last two millennia*.

(iii) In Revelation chapter 17

John sees a beast whose seventh head also has the ten horns. An angel then gives John the third explanation but with more details of their time:

> 12. "The ten horns which you saw are ten kings who have not yet received a kingdom, but they receive authority as kings with the beast for one hour.
> 13. These have one purpose and they give their power and authority to the beast.
> 14. These will wage war against the Lamb, and the Lamb will overcome them, because He is Lord of lords and King of kings, and those who are with Him are the called and chosen and faithful" (Rev 17:12-14)

Although Daniel saw the ten kings, or kingdoms, *beginning* as "a divided kingdom" (Dan 2:41) and that they "will not adhere to each other" (Dan 2:43), John sees them as *ending up* together in the last hour, when they finally have just the "one purpose" and through each giving "their power and authority to the beast" (Rev 17:13). The angel further explains:

> "For God has put it in their hearts to execute His purpose by having a common purpose, and by giving their kingdom to the beast, until the words of God will be fulfilled" (Rev 17:17)

---

41   i.e. assuming the reader has read Book 1. If not, what follows may remain locked away. In brief, this period is not literal but metaphorical and began with Israel's rejection of Jesus as Messiah in 30 A.D. and seems to have come to an end when the Jews recaptured Jerusalem in 1967 (Luke 21:24). The doubt of complete fulfillment arises from their handing back the Temple Mount to the Muslim authorities.

We can therefore deduce *the time of the end* of the ten horns:

(a)   We know their "one hour" as a unified kingdom had "not yet" begun (v. 12) when John was writing at the end of the 1st Century A.D.

(b)   We know when the "one hour" will end – it will be at the Second Coming, when the Lamb overcomes them as the returning "Lord of lords and King of kings" (v. 14), when at last "the words of God will be fulfilled" (v. 17). This is confirmed in Revelation 19 where the Lord Jesus Christ returns to defeat 'the beast and the kings of the earth and their armies' (Rev 19:19).

The ten toes/horns therefore have been around from the 1st Century and will be until the Lord returns.

"They Receive Authority… For One Hour"

It is usually assumed that the "one hour" means the ten only come into existence in that last hour but look more closely:

> "The ten horns which you saw are ten kings who have not yet received a kingdom, but they receive authority as kings with the beast for one hour" (Rev 17:12)

In other words, they existed in John's day around 100 A.D. as ten kings but not yet as "*a* kingdom". As "kings with the beast", i.e. on the seventh head, they are not due to rule in union until the last hour, the hour just before the kingdom of God comes in all its power and glory with the return of Jesus.

We also see this timing in Nebuchadnezzar's and Daniel's dream of the statue and the stone:

> …a stone was cut out without hands, and it struck the statue on its feet of iron and clay and crushed them… But the stone that struck the statue became a great mountain and filled the whole earth (Dan 2:34-35)

                     Slouching Towards Bethlehem

Daniel was told this means that "in the days of those kings, the God of heaven will set up a kingdom which will never be destroyed, and that kingdom will not be left for another people" (Dan 2:44). We know that Jesus set up "that kingdom" in the 1st Century and it has grown every day since, encircling the globe; we know it will continue to grow right up to the Second Coming when it will finally "fill the whole earth". At that time, and it can only be at that time, the kingdom of the ten horns/toes/kings/kingdoms will at last come to an end.

The ten kings have therefore also been around, though not unified, for the last two millennia. The seventh head is this kingdom of the ten, an alliance or confederacy of nations, which will become unified just before, and will be dealt with by, the Lord's Second Coming.

Guessing at the Ten

So, how can we identify or recognise them now?

I began to study these Scriptures when I became a follower of Jesus in 1973. I was taught to keep my eyes on Europe because it was changing from being a continent of continually warring nations to, in Winston Churchill's words, "a kind of United States of Europe". At the time, the European Economic Community (EEC), as it was then known, had six members and four countries were about to join. That would make the desired ten so I watched in eager anticipation for the EEC to become the ten horns confederacy.

However, at the last moment, Norway withdrew and only three joined. Then, while I and my friends were still getting over that disappointment, three more were added in, making twelve. In 2004, another ten joined and by January 1, 2007, the renamed European Union (EU), had become twenty seven with three more hoping to join,[42] so many will now have to

____

42 http://europa.eu/abc/12lessons/lesson_2/index_en.htm, 19th Feb, 2009.

leave to get it back down to ten. Given their present economic crisis, that could yet happen.

Other Christians in the 1970s had their eyes on the Oil Producing and Exporting Countries (OPEC). Created in 1960, there were originally five but expanded to ten in 1970. However, by 1973 OPEC had twelve member states and in 2007, thirteen.[43] Will these shrink back to become the "ten kings"?

Another possibility was the Arab League. Founded in 1945 with seven nations, by 1970 it consisted of thirteen nations, one of which was the PLO (Palestinian Liberation Organisation). It is openly antisemitic, suspending Egypt for signing a peace treaty with Israel. However, instead of shrinking to ten, by the end of that decade there were twenty one and, since 1989, twenty two.[44]

Some were looking suspiciously at the Group of Six (the G6), founded as a forum by France in 1975 for the six richest Gentile countries. However, it too grew to G7, to G8, to then trying to include five very large developing countries and renamed the G8 Plus 5. When, in September 2009, it was replaced by the G20, that summit discussed radical reform of the world's monetary system, creating a possibility of the legendary 'mark of the beast'. But twenty is not ten.

The last option I came across was the International Monetary Fund's G10 which in 1962 was ten nations arranging to borrow from each other (GAB - General Arrangements to Borrow). However, in 1998, the arrangement (NAB - New Arrangements to Borrow) expanded to 26 and in March, 2011, to 39 participants.[45]

43   www.opec.org/aboutus/history/history.htm, 19th Feb, 2009.
44   www.arabji.com/ArabGovt/ArabLeague.htm, 19th Feb, 2009.
45   www.imf.org/external/np/exr/facts/groups.htm, 31 Jan, 2012.

In the meantime, I had begun to question what I had been taught. I began to search the Scriptures again, having realised that in ancient Jewish thinking the numbers seven and ten can be ambiguous, having both literal and metaphorical meanings. I also saw that since there are literally seven heads, we can readily assume the same is true of the ten horns. But should we? What would John's original audience have actually heard and understood? How would this all look if 'ten' was a metaphor?

3

The Meaning of 'Ten'
Literal or Metaphorical?

What, for example, did Jacob mean when he complained that his rascally uncle Laban had cheated him and changed his wages "ten times" (Gen 31:7 & 31:41) over the twenty years he had worked for him? Or Job, when he accused his friends of insulting him "these ten times" (Job 19:3)? The three friends are recorded as having spoken five times between them at that stage. Did they really average two insults per speech, while Job sat there patiently counting them? Likewise, God rebuked the nation of Israel for testing Him "these ten times" by disobeying Him (Num 14:22) – was that really all? And Nehemiah wrote of people coming to warn him 'ten times' (Neh 4:12) before he responded to them.

In each case, ten times is possibly literal but far more likely metaphorical. This struck a chord with me because when I was a child, my mother used to tell me off for not responding until she had asked me to do something "sixteen times". I was always puzzled because it had seemed to me to have been at most only half a dozen. Obviously, she meant too many. What then would 'ten times' mean to 1st Century Jewish believers like John? Also obviously many or numerous, but, metaphorically, since the clear intention is to include every occasion, no matter how many that may have been, *it means all or 'the fulness'.* The Hebrew word for ten is *yod*, their tenth letter, as in most Semitic alphabets,[46] and is believed to come from an ancient pictograph of a hand, which is *yad* in Hebrew. This meaning of 'all' may therefore have come from using all

---

46 For example Phoenician, Aramaic, Syriac and Arabic.

                                        Slouching Towards Bethlehem

the fingers of our hands to count.[47]

If we now consider how God uses ten as a recurring theme in His designs, we see this same meaning emerges:

(i) Prior to the Exodus, there were ten plagues, judgements (Exo 8-12) to humble '*all* the Egyptians … [and] their gods' (Num 33:3-4).

(ii) The Ten Commandments represent all of the Mosaic Covenant (Deut 4:13) which actually consists of 613 commands for men[48] and 3 for women,[49] unfair as that may seem! Of course, all of the commandments were given initially to the men as the representatives of their households and always to be passed on as applicable to their wives and children (Deut 16:16 cf. 6:7).

(iii) The Tabernacle was covered by ten linen curtains. Linen typifies righteousness (Rev 19:8) so these curtains reveal the complete righteousness of Jesus, 'who knew no sin... that we might become the righteousness of God in Him' (2 Cor 5:21).

(iv) The Holy of Holies in the Tabernacle was ten cubits high, ten wide and ten long. Since the Tabernacle typified Jesus (John 1:14) in whom '*all the fulness* of Deity dwells in bodily form' (Col 2:9), this ten by ten by ten illustrates 'all the fulness' of God earlier dwelling in the Tabernacle of Moses.

(v) 'All the fulness' is also seen in the Temple of Solomon which contained ten lampstands, ten tables for the showbread and ten basins for washing the sacrifices. Its bronze sea from which the priests were to wash was ten cubits across, with decorations around the rim ten

---

47 www.jewishencyclopedia.com/articles/14314-ten, 13 Feb, 2012.
48 www.jewishencyclopedia.com/articles/4566-commandments-the-613, 7 Jan, 2012.
49 www.jewfaq.org/women.htm, 7 Jan, 2012.

to the cubit. The two cherubim who covered its holiest item, the Ark of the Covenant, were ten cubits high and their outspread wings were ten cubits wide.

(vi) The Passover lamb was set aside on the 10th day, to be sacrificed on the 14th of the first month. This prefigures Jesus as Messiah, coming in '*the fulness* of time' (Gal 4:4) for a three and a half year ministry before being sacrificed.

(vii) The most solemn day in Israel's calendar, Yom Kippur or the Day of Atonement, is on the 10th day of the seventh month (Lev 23:26), being the day when *all* the sin of Israel was to be dealt with.

(viii) Israel were to tithe, to set aside one tenth of their annual harvest (Deut 14:22-29) to be enjoyed at the Feast of Tabernacles, signifying that all they had came from the hand of God.

All of these literal tens establish a clear pattern, giving us the meaning of a metaphorical ten as numerous, all, every, complete, whole or 'the fulness'.

We see this too in the parables of Jesus: when He refers to the ten virgins waiting for the wedding feast (Matt 25:1ff), He clearly means all of His disciples; with the woman's ten silver coins (Luke 15:8), He is saying that regardless of how many she still has, she will always search for the one that is lost until she again has all of them; the master gives talents to ten servants (Luke 19:13) signifying God giving talents to all (1 Peter 4:10).

However, there is one particular instance in an Old Testament prophecy which not only again gives us this meaning of ten but also makes *a definitive connection with Gentile nations*:

> Thus says the LORD of hosts, "In those days ***ten men from all the nations*** will grasp the garment of a Jew saying, 'Let us go with you, for we have heard that God is with you'"
> (Zech 8:23, emphasis added)

This tells us that to God, "ten men" specifically represent "all the nations" or Gentiles.

Zechariah is, of course, restating what Abraham, patriarch of the nation of Israel, was promised one and a half thousand years earlier – that one day, through him, "all the families of the earth shall be blessed" (Gen 12:3). "Those days" began in the 1st Century when Jesus commanded His first disciples to "make disciples of all the nations" (Matt 28:19). In fact, Jesus said He would not return *until* His message had been taken to "all the nations" (Matt 24:14).

John therefore sees that ultimately around the heavenly throne there will be people 'purchased for God... from *every* tribe and tongue and people and nation' (Rev 5:9). Sadly, after "ten men from all the nations" join with all those in Israel who believe in Jesus, all those in "all the nations" who *do not* believe in Jesus will eventually become the seventh head with the ten horns, as we will see.

After Rome, Where?

Before we look at the future, however, we need to return to the 1st Century. We saw from Daniel 2's statue that the ten toes on feet of iron and clay, logically enough, come after the iron legs of the Roman Empire; from Daniel 7's four beasts, the ten horns grow out of the fourth beast which is also Rome. This is awkward timing for much end-time teaching today so it is often asserted that when Jesus was crucified, a kind of prophetic clock was paused and only restarted in our day. In response, Preterist teachers like David Chilton[50] and

---

50 *The Days of Vengeance: An Exposition of the Book of Revelation*, Fort Worth, Texas; Dominion Press, 1990.

others like N.T. Wright[51] argue against the insertion of this 2,000 year gap and insist it was all fulfilled by 70 A.D. However, there is simply no need for either the gap or the rush to fulfil everything.

Remember, Daniel's dreams and John's visions are telling us about what would happen to *Israel*. There was no stopping of a prophetic clock for Israel – all we need to understand is, where *exactly* did Israel go after the Romans destroyed Jerusalem? And there is no need to guess because Jesus Himself is specific:

> "...and they will fall by the edge of the sword, and will be led captive into all the nations; and Jerusalem will be trampled under foot by the Gentiles until the times of the Gentiles are fulfilled" (Luke 21:24)

They were "led captive into all the nations". The Roman domination of Israel was followed by the Jewish people having to accept the sovereignty of every nation on earth except their own. It is remarkable that they even made it to Australia and New Zealand because these nations are in the uttermost parts of the earth from Israel, as Moses predicted:

> "If your outcasts are at the ends of the earth, from there the LORD your God will gather you, and from there He will bring you back" (Deut 30:4)

Once it is realised that ten means all and that Israel being led captive into all the nations followed directly on from the Romans' domination, it becomes obvious that there is no need for any time gap or pausing and restarting of a prophetic clock. As we established in *Dancing in the Dragon's Jaws*, the last two thousand years have been *the times of the Gentiles*.

This also answers two major questions for me. Firstly, why did the statue's feet still include iron instead of being only pottery? Because the Roman Empire consisted of many nations and lasted until the 5th Century in the West and the

---

51　*Jesus and the Victory of God*, Minneapolis; Fortress Press, 1996.

15th in the East; the pottery symbolises all the other nations of the earth. Secondly, why do Nebuchadnezzar's and Daniel's dreams reveal the end of the statue as being in the time of the ten toes? The ten toes still exist and although the stone ultimately grows to become "a great mountain that fills the whole earth" (Dan 2:35), it was a small stone when Jesus came, and it is still growing.

The kingdom of God is not a geographical entity but spiritual – it exists wherever anyone is praying as Jesus did to His Father:

> "Your kingdom come, Your will be done, on earth as it is in heaven" (Matt 6:10)

Jesus perfectly embodied the kingdom of stone in the land of Israel and whenever He made disciples who were willing to live His way, the kingdom of stone grew. On Christmas Day, 1814, it finally reached 'the ends of the earth' (Psa 2:8) from Israel after a Maori chief, Ruatara, had invited English missionaries in Australia to also preach in New Zealand.[52] Today, the stone continues to grow throughout the earth.

However, back in the 1st Century A.D., although the "ten kings" existed and Israel was captive amongst them, they had "not yet received a kingdom" or "authority with the beast". *This is not to happen until* they "have one purpose, and they give their power and authority to the beast" (Rev 17:13), until God has "put it in their hearts to execute His purpose by having a common purpose, and by giving their kingdom to the beast, until the words of God will be fulfilled" (Rev 17:17).

---

52 William Williams, *Christianity Among the New Zealanders*, first published 1867, reprinted in Edinburgh; The Banner of Truth Trust, 1989, p. 13. Also http://www.nzhistory.net.nz/culture/missionaries/samuel-marsdens-first-service, 19 Feb, 2009.

'On His Horns Were Ten Diadems'

The ten horns or ten kings therefore also represent *all the rulers* of all the nations of the earth acting together. Remember, 'all the nations' specifically means all the Gentiles or non-Jews (the Hebrew word, *goim,* means both Gentiles and nations) so, being the seventh head, they will predictably pick up where the previous six heads left off, eventually attacking Israel.

Now consider the times in which we live. Today, for the first time ever in all of human history, it is possible for all the nations to act together. Before the largest war in human history, World War II, obviously named because most of the world was involved, the world was divided over almost any issue. To prevent this happening again, on 24 October 1945, the United Nations was created. Then, horrified by the Holocaust, on 29 November 1947 the United Nations passed Resolution 181, agreeing to restore Jewish sovereignty to half of the land of Israel (the other half was to be for the Arab population while the UN was to keep control of the Jerusalem-Bethlehem area).[53] Thus, on 14 May 1948, after almost two thousand years, the nation of Israel re-emerged from out of 'all the nations'.

The Arab nations then rejected Resolution 181 and in the ensuing war, the Jordanians captured Jerusalem, holding it for almost twenty years until the Six Day War of 1967 when Israel recaptured it. The UN General Assembly's Resolution 242 of 1967 still calls for Israel to withdraw, as does every one of the peace plans being mooted today. Given that the UN's armed forces are increasingly seen as the most legitimate vehicle for world peace-keeping, it is not hard to imagine that any day soon the terrible plight of the Palestinians could thus provoke *all the Gentile nations* to take action against Israel who would be standing alone.

We will return to this later but, in the meantime, consider

---

53 http://daccess-dds-ny.un.org/doc/RESOLUTION/GEN/ NR0/038/88/IMG/NR003888.pdf?OpenElement, 31 Jan, 2012.

  Slouching Towards Bethlehem

this yet to be fulfilled prophecy from about 520 B.C.[54]

> 1. The burden of the word of the LORD concerning Israel. Thus declares the LORD who stretches out the heavens, lays the foundation of the earth, and forms the spirit of man within him,
> 2. "Behold, I am going to make Jerusalem a cup that causes reeling to *all the peoples* around; and when the siege is against Jerusalem, it will also be against Judah.
> 3. "It will come about in that day that I will make Jerusalem a heavy stone for *all the peoples;* all who lift it will be severely injured. And *all the nations* of the earth will be gathered against it…
> 9. "And in that day I will set about to destroy *all the nations* that come against Jerusalem" (Zech 12:1-9 emphasis added)

Notice the 'alls' in this prophecy – "all the peoples" (v. 2), "all the peoples" (v. 3), "all the nations" (v. 3), "all the nations" (v. 4) or Gentiles i.e. every nation on the earth *except Israel.* And they want to remove Jerusalem from Jewish hands.

All the "Alls" in the Divine Overview of History

This is perfect symmetry. God has always loved everyone but His strategy was to choose one willing couple, Abram and Sarai, and make of their family a nation which could demonstrate to every other nation what it is like to serve the living God (Gen 12:3; 22:15-18). As Paul says, the kingdom of God was offered to "the Jew first and also to the Greek [i.e. Gentile]" (Rom 1:16).

Accordingly, after giving them new covenant names of Abraham and Sarah, God placed their descendants in a land at the connecting point of three continents, "in the midst of the earth among the peoples" (Isa 24:13), around a very high-profile city, Jerusalem, "the city of the great King"(Psa 48:2, Matt 5:35).

---

54 Date of Zechariah 1:1, *The Zondervan Pictorial Encyclopedia of the Bible*, edit. Merrill C. Tenney, 1977, Vol 5, p. 1044.

He then became a Man in this land and was crucified outside this city for the sins of all mankind. When all in Israel who would accept Jesus as Messiah had done so, God then judged all in Israel who had rejected Him, sending them "captive into all the nations" (Luke 21:24) and allowing their land and their city to be trampled down by the Gentiles. He then offered His kingdom to "all the nations" (Matt 28:19) for a particular time:

> "And this gospel of the kingdom shall be preached in the whole world for a witness to all the nations, and then the end shall come" (Matt 24:14)

Then as the "times of the Gentiles" come to a close and *all* the Gentiles who will accept Jesus as Messiah are doing so (Rom 11:25), God again turns His attention to the people of Israel:

> For I do not want you, brethren, to be uninformed of this mystery – so that you will not be wise in your own estimation – that a partial hardening has happened to Israel until the fullness of the Gentiles has come in; ***and so all Israel will be saved…*** (Rom 11:25-26 emphasis added)

This fulfils the prophecies of the two comings of Elijah, as we saw in our previous study. He restores them to their land, their city and eventually to the rain of the Spirit:

> Be patient, therefore, brethren, until the coming of the Lord. Behold, the farmer waits for the precious produce of the soil, being patient about it, until it gets the early and the late rains. You too be patient; strengthen your hearts, for the coming of the Lord is at hand (Jas 5:7-8)

As God begins to reap His final harvest of the land of Israel, so that '*all* Israel will be saved' (Rom 11:26), *all* the nations who have rejected His kingdom gather around their land and their city, Jerusalem, where they will face His judgement of them, of us all.

Notice, all of this would have been readily understood in the 1st Century church, without their needing to know any details of our time.

Overall Summary Thus Far

In our study of Chapter 12, *Dancing in the Dragon's Jaws*, we saw:

(i) Satan is portrayed as a great red dragon with seven heads and ten horns, seeking to destroy a woman and her child. The woman is the nation of Israel and the child is Messiah, Jesus of Nazareth. The seven heads have crowns and are the seven successive Gentile empires that Satan has used and will use in his attacks. He began with Egypt nearly four thousand years ago, followed by the Assyrians, the Babylonians, the Medo-Persians, the Greeks and the Romans while the seventh is yet to come and will comprise 'all the nations'.

(ii) During the time of the sixth head, Rome, Satan's apparent success with the death of Jesus of Nazareth is reversed by His resurrection and ascension so Satan rounds on the woman. She is saved by escaping to the wilderness for "a time, times and half a time" i.e. three and a half years. We found that this time period is metaphorical and symbolises "the times of the Gentiles" as well as the 'partial hardening of Israel'. It was foreshadowed by Elijah's drought and so was book-ended by the two metaphorical comings of Elijah, during which time God put aside Israel in order to work with the Gentiles.

(iii) This putting aside and partial hardening is the consequence and penalty for Israel as a nation rejecting Jesus as Messiah. It includes the loss of their land and their city of Jerusalem and ends with the regaining of

Jerusalem, possibly by Israeli forces in 1967 or by their future retaking of the Temple Mount. In other words, it has lasted almost two thousand years.

(iv)   Even during the woman's time in the wilderness, the dragon tries to destroy her and this is seen in the supernatural persistence of antisemitism even after Messiah has come and gone from the earth. Failing to annihilate the Jewish race, the dragon turns his attention to the rest of the woman's children whom we found to be all true followers of Jesus, whether Jew or Gentile.

This laid the basis for Chapter 13 where we now see:

(v)   Satan uses two wild beasts to attack the woman's children. The first beast is a composite being, part lion, bear and leopard. This beast exists in John's time, the time of the Roman Empire, and we established from Daniel 2 that these three animals symbolise the previous Babylonian, Medo-Persian and Greek Empires respectively. John's first beast therefore takes us back through ancient Middle Eastern history. It is a spiritual entity, the 'principality and power' behind these Gentile kingdoms, one of the 'world forces of this darkness'.

(vi)   Like the dragon, the first beast has seven heads and ten horns, showing it exists in the times of the seven successive Gentile kingdoms or empires, six of which have dominated Israel while the seventh is yet to come. The first two were Egypt and Assyria, followed by Daniel's four: Babylonia, Medo-Persia, Greece and Rome. This vision is therefore to reveal more about the beast, the principality and power behind these empires. In contrast to the dragon's seven heads having crowns, this beast has crowns on its ten horns. These crowns are to draw our attention to the ten contemporaneous kings on the seventh and last head who are to rule over Israel after the Romans but who had not yet in John's time become "a kingdom with the beast".

(vii) While ten can be literal, the Scriptures also often use ten as a metaphor meaning numerous and all. One use, Zechariah 8:23, is specific – "ten men" is a metaphor for "all the nations" of the Gentiles.

(viii) Jesus predicted in 30 A.D. that after the Romans crushed Jerusalem, Israel would be "led captive into all the nations" (Luke 21:24) and, in 70 A.D., they were. We see therefore that the ten toes/horns/kings are not literal but metaphorical, being fulfilled by "all the nations".

(ix) "All the nations" were not united or acting together at that time – Israel was scattered amongst all the nations, even to the uttermost parts of the earth. In John's time (c. 100 A.D.), the ten kings had "not yet received a kingdom… [nor] authority as kings with the beast for one hour" (Rev 17:12). This will only happen when they "have one purpose, and they give their power and authority to the beast" (Rev 17:13).

(x) Jesus identified the kingdom He was inaugurating in the 1st Century as the stone of Daniel 2 which has been growing ever since and which will eventually replace all other kingdoms, fill the whole earth, and last forever. When all the nations do have one purpose and gather against Israel and Jerusalem, and "to wage war against the Lamb" (Rev 17:14), it will be the last "one hour" before the Second Coming.

We can therefore chart the history of Israel's captivities and the seven heads and ten horns as follows:

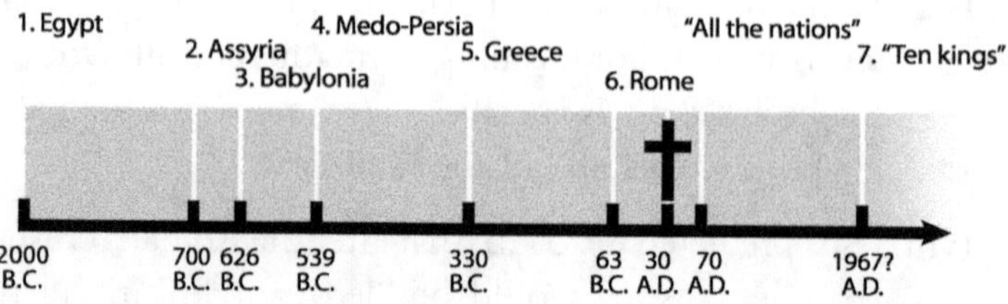

Figure (i) - Timeline of the Seven Heads and Ten Horns

"All the nations" held Israel in exile from 70 A.D. as *separate nations*; in 1948, "all the nations" acting as the *United Nations* restored Israel's sovereignty in the Promised Land; in 1967, Israel regained Jerusalem, seemingly ending the "times of the Gentiles" (i.e. the nations); in response, all the nations acting as the United Nations condemned Israel and demanded that Israel hand back Jerusalem to "all the nations" to be shared with the Palestinians. This seems to be the "one purpose" of the ten horns/kings with John's first beast, and they therefore comprise its seventh head.

4
'His Fatal Wound…'
Miracle or Metaphor?

That was a long explanation of the first two verses! However, we needed to undo a lot of misunderstanding and we can now move much faster. Let us now pick up our text at verse 3:

> 3. And I saw one of his heads as if it had been slain, and his fatal wound was healed. And the whole earth was amazed and followed after the beast;
> 4. and they worshiped the dragon, because he gave his authority to the beast, and they worshiped the beast, saying, "Who is like the beast, and who is able to wage war with him?"
> …
> 14. And he deceives those who dwell on the earth… telling those who dwell on the earth to make an image to the beast who had the wound of the sword and has come to life (Rev 13)

Some today take v. 3 to mean that there will be a popular political leader who will survive an assassination attempt and then turn out to be the Antichrist. Accordingly, they carefully watched Pope John Paul II or President Ronald Reagan, both of whom were popular and survived being shot.

The writers of the futuristic *Left Behind* series, however, take v. 14 literally where John adds that the fatal wound would be inflicted by 'the sword'. In book 6, *Assassins,* they make much of several of their heroes trying to shoot the Antichrist, Nicolae Carpathia, but being strangely, divinely, thwarted. It then emerges in book 7, *The Indwelling*, that Carpathia has actually been surreptitiously stabbed through the head with a 'fifteen- to eighteen-inch' blade before rising from the dead to become leader of their projected Global Community.[55]

---

55   Tim LaHaye & Jerry B. Jenkins, *The Indwelling*, Wheaton, Illinois;

However, these writers do not seem to have read this passage carefully enough – what of the wound being to only 'one of his heads' (v. 3), thus leaving the other six uninjured? Verse 4 adds that it is when everyone sees the seven-headed beast survive this fatal wound that they follow it.

On the other hand, if this first beast is the spiritual principality behind the Gentile kingdoms or empires, how can it be fatally wounded in one of its heads and miraculously recover?

When and What Was the Wound?

One way to find *how* this can happen is to first establish *when* the wound happens. From our earlier study, we have a major key – after the wound was healed, the beast was 'given authority to act for forty two months' (v. 5). Since we know this time period is "the times of the Gentiles" and began in the 1st Century, the fatal blow is not a still future occurrence but must have already been struck, and the beast healed, two thousand years ago.

As for what the wound is, its most obvious feature is that it is a head wound and its most overlooked feature is that it is actually the fulfilment of the oldest prophecy there is regarding spiritual warfare. At the very dawn of time, God told the dragon ('the serpent of old who is called the devil and Satan', Rev 12:9) that he would be wounded in the head by Messiah:

> "And I will put enmity between you [the serpent] and the woman, and between your seed and her seed; He will bruise you on the head, and you shall bruise Him on the heel"
> (Gen 3:15)

Tyndale, 2000, p. 152.

                    Slouching Towards Bethlehem

As we considered briefly in our previous study in Revelation chapter 12, this is an extraordinary metaphor.

Think of a man on foot being attacked by a venomous snake – just as the serpent strikes at his heel, the man crushes the head of the snake so both receive a fatal wound. The interpretation is given there that the dragon who persecutes the woman and her Child is 'the serpent of old who is called the devil and Satan, who deceives the whole world' (v. 9). The woman's Seed i.e. descendant, born without the seed of a man, is Jesus of Nazareth, born of a virgin woman through direct creation by the Holy Spirit (Matt 1:22-25); Satan's seed, Jesus taught, is anyone, everyone, who follows Satan's lead in rejecting Him as Messiah the King (John 8:44).

Satan struck Jesus "on the heel" when he inspired those involved in His crucifixion by the Romans. In Hebrew, the expression to seize by the heel has both a literal and a figurative meaning. The first is to snare or trap, as in Job 18:9, and the second, to usurp or supplant. Jacob's name is literally 'heel-catcher',[56] given him because at birth he grasped his twin brother Esau's heel, an act later recognised by Esau as foreshadowing Jacob's usurping or supplanting Esau's role as the first-born (Gen 25:26 and 27:36). In Satan's case, he snared Jesus to usurp His role as the true ruler of the earth.

Little did he realise that in his greatest triumph, in the very act of crucifying Christ, he won a battle but lost the war of the ages because it was through the cross that Jesus bruised him "on the head". As Paul explains, the crucifixion was:

> God's wisdom in a mystery… which none of the rulers of this age has understood, for if they had understood it, they would not have crucified the Lord of glory (1 Cor 2:7-8)

How exactly did Jesus wound Satan "on the head"? By offering fallen mankind another head or leader and a very different

---

56 *NAS Exhaustive Concordance of the Bible,* Nashville; Holman, 1981, p. 1531 and p. 1577.

kingdom, the kingdom of God (Luke 4:43). Later, He sent Paul to preach:

> ...to open their [Jews' and Gentiles'] eyes so that they may turn from darkness to light and from the dominion of Satan to God (Acts 26:18)

So everyone who believes in Jesus immediately changes kingdoms, 'from the domain of darkness... to the kingdom of His beloved Son' (Col 1:13). We then, as members of the Body of Christ, all have a part in the final outworking of Satan's downfall:

> The God of peace will soon crush Satan under your feet (Rom 16:20)

So why was only one of the beast's seven heads fatally wounded? Because the blow was struck in the time of the sixth head, the Roman Empire, when the Roman soldiers crucified Jesus. The head wound is *the removing of the serpent's and the first beast's ultimate authority from over any and all who commit themselves to Jesus as Messiah.*

John also adds another detail about this wound, describing:

> the beast who had the wound of the sword and has come to life (Rev 13:14)

This is not just any wound nor randomly inflicted – it is 'the wound of the sword'. It is not literal, requiring a literal sword, but a spiritual or metaphorical wound from a spiritual or metaphorical sword. It is struck by 'the sword of the Spirit, which is the word of God' (Eph 6:17) which comes from His mouth (Rev 19:15).

This is perfectly consistent – since the seven-headed beast is spiritual, the principality and power of the Gentiles, it can only be struck with the spiritual sword, the word of God, in His timing.

'His Fatal Wound Was Healed'

How then can the beast's 'fatal wound' be healed? Remember the Genesis prophecy is that both the woman's Seed and the serpent would be 'bruised.' This word comes from an Old English word, *brysan,* which means to crush[57] while the Hebrew, *shuph,* means to bruise or overwhelm.[58] We know that both of these wounds are serious because they are fatal yet both the Seed and the beast live again.

In hindsight, as Christians we can readily understand how Jesus was 'bruised' and how the apparent defeat in His humiliating death instead led to His being highly exalted, with a name above every name (Phil 2:8-9). Jesus explained this as the basis for our making disciples:

> "All authority has been given to Me in heaven and on earth. Go, therefore, and make disciples of all the nations"
> (Matt 28:18-19)

What then of the beast's wound? How can he survive? If Jesus has "all authority in heaven and on earth", does this mean that Satan now has none? No, because in 30 A.D. 'authority to act for forty-two months was given to him' (Rev 13:5) by Jesus.

Satan originally gained authority over the earth when the first man, Adam, submitted to him, but he lost it to Jesus, 'the second man' (1 Cor 15:45-47) when Jesus refused his tempting. As we noted earlier, Jesus' refusal and unswerving commitment to instead do the will of the Father (Luke 4:8) means *He was Himself the beginning of the Kingdom coming to earth.* This is why, as we also saw earlier in Revelation 12:10, when Jesus was resurrected and ascended, 'the loud voice in heaven' announced to all of Creation:

---

57 *Concise Oxford Dictionary,* p. 117.
58 *NAS Exhaustive Concordance of the Bible,* p. 1603.

> "Now the salvation, and the power, and the kingdom of our God
> and of His Christ have come, for the accuser [i.e. Satan] of our
> brethren has been thrown down"

But, and this is a huge but, in the wisdom of God, Satan is allowed to carry on for a time. Even after hearing the heavenly voice, John sees believers being martyred:

> And they overcame him because of the blood of the Lamb and
> because of the word of their testimony and they did not love
> their life even when faced with death.
> For this reason, rejoice, O heavens and you who dwell in them.
> Woe to the earth and the sea, because the devil has come down
> to you, having great wrath, knowing that he has only a short
> time (Rev 12:11-12)

Here now in Revelation 13, the Holy Spirit is showing the 1st Century Christians, and you and me, that He remains sovereign over everything, despite all appearances to the contrary:

> 3. And I saw one of his heads as if it had been slain, and his
> fatal wound was healed. And the whole earth was amazed and
> followed after the beast;
> 4. and they worshiped the dragon, because he gave his
> authority to the beast, and they worshiped the beast, saying,
> "Who is like the beast, and who is able to wage war with him?"
> 5. And there was given to him a mouth speaking arrogant words
> and blasphemies; and authority to act for forty-two months was
> given to him. (Rev 13)

All those not understanding the ways of God and the sacrifice of Christ think the beast (that is, the feral State) is invincible. The beast therefore increases in arrogance and to devastating effect on the people of God:

> 6. And he opened his mouth in blasphemies against God, to
> blaspheme His name and His tabernacle, that is, those who
> dwell in heaven.
> 7. And it was given to him to make war with the saints and to
> overcome them; and authority over every tribe and people and

So, when we ask why, if Jesus really is Messiah with "all authority in heaven and on earth", do Satan and the beast still appear to hold all the reins of power, John's answer is that:

(i)   Like Pontius Pilate, these spiritual powers do not have anything that has not been "given" to them by God the Father (John 19:11, Rev 13:5 & 7).

(ii)   God is allowing these principalities and powers to remain in authority over all the earth and to 'wage war against the saints and to overcome them' (v. 7).

(iii) This is how it will be for 'forty two months' (v. 5).

Those not believing John, and the Spirit of God, i.e. the rest of the whole world, saw only that the sixth head, the Roman Empire, could do anything it liked – rule, control, oppress, persecute, torture, kill – and withstand any assault, seemingly even from Messiah: 'The whole earth was amazed and followed after the beast' (v. 3).

Did the whole earth consciously think of Jesus as assaulting the Roman Empire or striking the sixth head? Of course not – all they saw was the apparent invincibility of the Roman legions. They thought the beast was all-powerful and they began to worship the principality and power of the state, but *in a very particular way*, as we will see when we consider the second beast.

5

'To Make War with the Saints' and To Overcome Them

Of course, 'saints' is in the usual Biblical sense of everyone who trusts in Jesus.[59] John is predicting that even those trusting in Jesus will be 'overcome' by the beast for 'forty two months' i.e. *the last two thousand years.* For all that the 1st Century saints knew of Jesus in their own lives, in the midst of the terrible threats and persecution, John was encouraging them to see the big picture, and they really did need all the encouragement they could get:

> 10. If anyone is destined for captivity, to captivity he goes; if anyone kills with the sword, with the sword he must be killed. Here is the perseverance and the faith of the saints
> (Rev 13)

They were called to accept their lot, to not fight their Roman conquerors but simply to *persevere and trust God in whatever circumstances they would find themselves.* Of course, Jesus Himself had already told them this when He commanded them to "turn the other cheek" when struck and "walk the second mile" when pressed into service by the Roman soldiers (Matt 5:39 & 41). The Roman yoke was simply not going to be broken in the 1st Century.

Paul and Barnabas had likewise prepared the saints everywhere they went:

> And after they had… made many disciples, they returned to Lystra and to Iconium and to Antioch, strengthening the souls of the disciples, encouraging them to continue in the faith, and

---

59   e.g. Acts 9:32, Romans 1:7, Ephesians 1:1, Philippians 1:1, Colossians 1:2.

They knew they were not going to see all of the Kingdom come on earth at that time but only a foretaste in their hearts where He ruled:

There are, of course, many issues raised by this attitude of acceptance and not fighting back against murderous persecution. The Jewish people had adopted it virtually en masse from 135 A.D. until the Holocaust, beginning to fight back in the Warsaw Ghetto uprising in April 1943, so today Israel's battle-cry is, 'Never again!'[60]

Let there be no doubt, however, these warnings were not cowardly or despairing, nor were they pious platitudes. John was writing from his captivity on the Isle of Patmos, having already lost his own brother James (Acts 12:2), and his first listeners would have likewise seen many friends and family members arrested and executed for their faith. Many died unarmed in the Roman arenas with the battle-cry of a wholly other world on their lips, "Maranatha!" – "O Lord, come!" (1 Cor 16:22) while John ends Revelation, "Come, Lord Jesus!" (Rev 22:20). It has often been noted that in the times of the most intense persecution of Christians, the Book of Revelation becomes some of the most relevant and reassuring of the Scriptures.

---

60 www.ushmm.org/outreach/wgupris.htm, downloaded 25 Apr, 2008.

The Saints' Last Two Thousand Years

How accurate has John's prediction been? What has been the actual experience of the saints over the last 2,000 years? Being overcome. Consider a few examples in overview.

(i) Up to Constantine, 312 A.D.

For the first three hundred years and throughout the Roman Empire, until the apparent conversion of the Emperor Constantine in 312 A.D., Christians were frequently officially persecuted or executed for their faith.[61] The Book of Acts ends in about 62 A.D. with Paul awaiting trial and martyrdom before Nero (Acts 28:16 & 30) but Cornelius Tacitus, writing in 115 A.D., records that two years later in 64 A.D. Emperor Nero tried to avoid the blame for the fire that destroyed Rome's ghettos:

> Consequently, to get rid of the report, Nero fastened the guilt and inflicted the most exquisite tortures on a class hated for their abominations, called Christians by the populace. Christus, from whom the name had its origin, suffered the extreme penalty during the reign of Tiberius at the hands of one of our procurators, Pontius Pilatus, and a most mischievous superstition, thus checked for the moment, again broke out not only in Judaea, the first source of the evil, but even in Rome, where all things hideous and shameful from every part of the world find their centre and become popular. Accordingly, an arrest was first made of all who pleaded guilty; then, upon their information, an immense multitude was convicted, not so much of the crime of firing the city, as of hatred against mankind. Mockery of every sort was added to their deaths. Covered with the skins of beasts, they were torn by dogs and perished, or were nailed to crosses,

---

61 In *Introducing Early Christianity*, Laurie Guy corrects the popular misconception of 'a continual bloodbath of myriads upon myriads', instead identifying the persecutions as 'typically local rather than empire-wide' and recognising at least ten 'scattered showers… rather than a general rain' during this time (pp. 50-52).

                              Slouching Towards Bethlehem

or were doomed to the flames and burnt, to serve as a nightly illumination, when daylight had expired. Nero offered his gardens for the spectacle, and was exhibiting a show in the circus, while he mingled with the people in the dress of a charioteer or stood aloft on a car. Hence, even for criminals who deserved extreme and exemplary punishment, there arose a feeling of compassion; for it was not, as it seemed, for the public good, but to glut one man's cruelty, that they were being destroyed.[62]

Although eventually 'there arose a feeling of compassion' for the Christians, Tacitus nevertheless describes them as 'hated for their abominations', holding to 'a most mischievous superstition' and 'hatred against mankind', 'who deserved extreme and exemplary punishment'. We will come back to why he thought this when we consider the significance of emperor-worship.

In 112 A.D. Pliny Secundus, governor of Bithynia (today's northwest Turkey), wrote to the Emperor Trajan:

> I interrogated them whether they were Christians; if they confessed it I repeated the question twice again, adding the threat of capital punishment; if they still persevered, I ordered them to be executed. For, whatever the nature of their creed might be, I could at least feel no doubt that contumacy and inflexible obstinacy deserved chastisement.[63]

What exactly were they doing wrong to deserve capital punishment?

> ... the whole of their guilt or error was that they were in the habit of meeting on a certain fixed day before it was light, when they sang in alternate verses a hymn to Christ, as to a god, and bound themselves by a solemn oath, not

62 *Annals* XV.44, http://www.earlychristianwritings.com/tacitus.html, 26 Apr, 2008.
63 *Epistles*, X.96, http://www.textexcavation.com/plinytestimonium. html, 26 Apr, 2008.

> to any wicked deeds, but never to commit any fraud, theft
> or adultery, never to falsify their word, nor deny a trust
> when they should be called upon to deliver it up; after
> which it was their custom to separate, and then reassemble
> to partake of food, but food of an ordinary and innocent
> kind. Even this practice, however, they had abandoned
> after the publication of my edict, by which, according to
> your orders, I had forbidden political associations.[64]

In other words, the 'whole of their guilt' according to Pliny
was that they met regularly to worship Jesus, lived rightly and
ate together!

Assyrian rhetorician Lucian of Samosata, writing in the
middle of the 2nd Century A.D., adds:

> The poor wretches have convinced themselves, first and
> foremost, that they are going to be immortal and live
> for all time, in consequence of which they despise death
> and even willingly give themselves into custody; most of
> them. Furthermore, their first law-giver persuaded them
> that they were all brothers one of another after they had
> transgressed once and for all by denying the Greek gods
> and by worshipping the crucified sophist himself and
> living under his laws.[65]

In 303 A.D., the Emperor Diocletian issued an edict 'ordering
the razing of the churches to the ground and the destruction
by fire of the Scriptures, and proclaiming that those who
held high positions would lose all civil rights, while those in
households, if they persisted in their profession of Christianity,
would be deprived of their liberty'.[66]

(ii) Up to the Reformation, circa 1500 A.D.

Many today think that with Constantine's conversion in 312

---

64 Ibid.

65 *The Passing Peregruis*, para 13, http://www.tertullian.org/rpearse/
lucian/peregrinus.htm, 26 Apr, 2008.

66 *Cambridge History of the Bible*, Cambridge University Press, 1963.

                                    Slouching Towards Bethlehem

A.D. and his establishing of Christianity as the state religion, Roman persecution ended. However, Constantine's approach created many more problems for the saints:

> [There was] a massive influx of superficial converts from paganism. This resulted in declining moral standards and the adoption of some pagan and idolatrous practices… *the persecuted church of the martyrs became before long the persecuting state church.* Legal coercion was used at first against Christian groups deviating from the mainstream 'Catholic Church' and later against pagan worship.[67]

Not even the fall of the Roman Empire interrupted this persecution of the saints by the state church. For the next twelve hundred years, the Roman Catholic Church became the state church of many of the nations to which it had spread. It unashamedly used the sword against any who disagreed, whether Jews, Muslims or dissenting Christians, as can be seen in the Crusades and the Inquisition. Thomas Aquinas (1225-1274) explains:

> If the heretic still remains pertinacious the church, despairing of his conversion, provides for the salvation of others by separating him from the church by the sentence of excommunication and then leaves him to the secular judge to be exterminated from the world by death.[68]

Sadly, Aquinas was no extremist. In 1879, Pope Leo XIII officially described Aquinas as 'the prince and master of all Scholastic doctors' and designated him 'patron of all Catholic universities, academies, colleges, and schools throughout the world.'[69]

The outworking of this doctrine is graphically illustrated by the Albigensian or Cathar Crusade (1209-1229). The Cathars'

---

67 Tony Lane, *The Lion Concise Book of Christian Thought*, Oxford; Lion Hudson Plc, 1996, p. 11, emphasis added.
68 *Summa Theologiae, IIaIIae* q.11 a.3. http://www.newadvent.org/cathen/14663b.htm, 19 Feb, 2009.
69 www.newadvent.org/cathen/14663b.htm, 19 Feb, 2009.

beliefs were more Gnostic than Christian so Innocent III commanded this attack on southern France in which most of the population was put to death, an estimated one million people, including any Catholics who refused to turn against their neighbours. Tragically, this Crusade then led to the creation of the infamous Inquisition.[70]

The Church also turned on any of its own leaders who questioned its behaviour in the light of the Scriptures. Only in recent years has the wickedness of this persecution been publicly acknowledged, especially by Pope John Paul II who began confessing his church's sins as part of the observances of the Great Jubilee of the Year 2000. One example he gave was the killing of high-profile Czech saint, Jan Hus, who was burned at the stake in 1415 for advocating the supremacy of the Scriptures over the authority of the church.[71] On December 17, 1999, John Paul expressed his "deep regret for the cruel death inflicted on Jan Hus and for the consequent wound of conflict and division which was thus imposed on the minds and hearts of the Bohemian people" and called for an inquiry as to whether Hus might be cleared of heresy.[72]

Another high-profile saint, John Wycliffe of Oxford, dared to publish an English Bible in 1378 so that his countrymen could read or hear it for themselves. He argued for doctrines today considered orthodox but many followers, known as the Lollards, were burnt at the stake for heresy. Wycliff himself escaped this fate only because he died before they could catch him but forty four years later, in 1428, the Pope ordered his 'heretical' bones to be dug up and burned.[73]

---

70 http://xenophongroup.com/montjoie/albigens.htm, 8 Aug, 2008. Also www.cathar.info/1206_crusade.htm.

71 www.czech.cz/en/czech-republic/history/all-about-czech-history/hussitism-and-the-heritage-of-jan-hus/, 26 Apr, 2008.

72 www.encyclopedia.com/doc/1G1-58915588.html, 28 Apr, 2008.

73 www.wycliffe.org/Explore/WhoWeAre/History/JohnWycliffe.aspx, 26 Apr, 2008.

                    Slouching Towards Bethlehem

Rather than give more examples, I recommend the reading of *Foxe's Book of Martyrs,* written by John Foxe in the 16th Century and giving many detailed accounts of the persecution of the saints by the state church.

(iii) From the Reformation to today

Sadly, the saints often fared no better when the Reformers won out as, to rework Lane's phrase above, 'the persecuted church of the martyrs *again* became before long the persecuting state church. Legal coercion was used at first against Christian groups deviating from the mainstream '*Reformed* Church' and later against pagan worship'.[74]

Many Reformers seemed to think nothing of drowning the Anabaptists, mockingly calling this 'the third baptism', as capital punishment for teaching 'believers' baptism' instead of infant baptism.[75] As for their dealing with pagan worship, consider the case of Michael Servetus (1511-1553). Sentenced to be burned alive in 'a slow fire' by the Catholic Inquisition in Lyons, France, for denying the Trinity and infant baptism, Servetus fled to the Reformers' stronghold in Geneva, Switzerland, only to be arrested and condemned again by them. John Calvin argued for him to be more mercifully beheaded for his heresy but the majority of the leaders of the churches of Geneva, Zurich, Berne, Basle, and Schaffhausen ensured he was indeed slowly burned with green wood, adding a garland of sulphur.

As Blaise Pascal rightly observed, 'Men never do evil so completely and cheerfully as when they do it from religious conviction'.

Three hundred and fifty years later this execution was formally renounced on a monument erected on the site:

---

74 Tony Lane, *The Lion Concise Book of Christian Thought,* Oxford; Lion Hudson Plc, 1996, p. 11, emphasis added.
75 www.cob-net.org/anabaptism.htm, 3 May, 2008.

> Dutiful and grateful followers of Calvin our great
> Reformer, yet condemning an error which was that of
> his age, and strongly attached to liberty of conscience,
> according to the true principles of the Reformation and
> of the Gospel, we have erected this expiatory monument.
> October 27th, 1903.[76]

The murderous persecution by these state churches only ceased as they gradually came to accept the 16th Century Anabaptists' (and Biblical) revelation of the necessity of a clear separation of church and state. While there can be no excuse for killing anyone who disagrees with our beliefs, we nevertheless must recognise the demonic inspiration of these actions by even professing and genuine Christians. We need to see that *this was nothing less than their being overcome by the beast.* This happens *wherever the power of the state is used to further the aims of emperors, pagan or Christian, and of church leaders, Catholic or Reformed.*

Lastly, as a recent example, consider the Dutch Reformed Church of South Africa's collusion with their government during the apartheid era.[77] Although not itself murderous, this denomination supported a murderous regime, denounced anti-apartheid churches such as Desmond Tutu's Anglicans and persecuted its own dissenting saints, such as Beyers Naudé. This remarkable theologian was the son of a founding member of the Broederbond as well as its youngest member in 1939 but he repented and befriended Archbishop Tutu and Nelson Mandela.[78] Forced to resign in 1963, his last sermon to his congregation challenged: "We must show greater loyalty to God than to man".[79] He was eventually vindicated and greatly

---

76 www.banneroftruth.org/pages/articles/article_detail.php?457, 3 May, 2008.

77 www.country-studies.com/south-africa/religion-and-apartheid. html, 28 Apr, 2008.

78 www.southafrica.info/what_happening/news/beyers-naude.htm, 3 May, 2008.

79 Adam Bernstein, *C.F. Beyers Naude Dies; Cleric Opposed Apartheid*

honoured after the apartheid regime fell, receiving a state funeral in September 2004 while the Dutch Reformed Church of South Africa formally renounced apartheid in 1986.[80]

We must understand that none of us are immune to this demonic temptation to force our own way on others, especially our own religious way.

The Saints Overcoming

In what sense then are the saints to be 'overcomers'? The Book of Revelation begins with the resurrected Lord Jesus urging the saints of the seven churches to 'overcome' by rejecting false teaching and prophecies (Rev 2:2, 6, 14-15, 20, 24), repenting from sin (Rev 2:5; 16; 3:4-5, 19) and by persevering under extreme trial (Rev 2:13; 3:10). He told the disciples in Smyrna:

> "Do not fear what you are about to suffer… Be faithful until death, and I will give you the crown of life… He who overcomes will not be hurt by the second death" (Rev 2:10-11)

We also saw in Revelation 12:11 that the saints 'overcame' the devil 'because of the blood of the Lamb and because of the word of their testimony, and they did not love their lives even to death'. Unfortunately, the most obvious way anyone can be seen to not love their lives 'even to death' is by being *tested to death*.[81]

Happily, John also sees the souls of the martyrs underneath the heavenly altar (Rev 6:9). This would have been greatly significant to his 1st Century audience because they knew that that was where the blood of godly sacrifices was poured out (e.g. Exodus 29:12). The martyrs had overcome death. They

---

Regime, Washington; *Washington Post*, Sep 8, 2004.

80 http://philtar.ucsm.ac.uk/encyclopedia/christ/cep/drcsa.html, 21 Feb 2009.

81 This can also be said of the metaphorical death of believers daily taking up their cross (Luke 9:23-24) but in this context, John is referring to martyrdom.

---

had been 'slain because of the word of God, and because of the testimony which they had maintained' (Rev 6:9) and yet 'this is the victory that overcomes the world – our faith' (1 John 5:4).

Does this mean that the saints never get miraculously delivered from persecution or death? Clearly not. Although the apostle Peter was eventually martyred, he had earlier been supernaturally rescued from prison and death by an angel who broke off his chains, walked him past two sets of guards and caused the iron gate to open 'by itself' (Acts 12:1-11).

The attitude in the Early Church was like that of Shadrach, Meshach and Abed-nego. Threatened with a fiery death by Nebuchadnezzar if they would not worship his image, they responded:

> "If it be so, our God whom we serve is able to deliver us from the furnace of blazing fire; and He will deliver us out of your hand, O king. But even if He does not, let it be known to you, O king, that we are not going to serve your gods or worship the golden image you have set up" (Dan 3:17-18)

They were full of faith either way – they trusted that God could deliver them and they would still trust Him if He did not. In their case, He did deliver them.

Consider too Paul's astonishing exhortation:

> 35. Who can separate us from the love of Christ? Shall tribulation, or distress, or persecution, or famine, or nakedness, or peril, or sword?
> 36. Just as it is written, "FOR THY SAKE WE ARE BEING PUT TO DEATH ALL DAY LONG; WE WERE CONSIDERED AS SHEEP TO BE SLAUGHTERED".
> 37. But in all these things we overwhelmingly conquer through Him who loved us.
> 38. For I am convinced that neither death, nor life, nor angels, nor principalities, nor things present, nor things to come, nor powers,
> 39. nor height, nor depth, nor any other created thing, shall be able to separate us from the love of God, which is in Christ Jesus our Lord (Rom 8:35-39)

Slouching Towards Bethlehem

Notice that those being slaughtered like sheep for their faith in Jesus 'overwhelmingly conquer', not by surviving but by dying. They cannot be separated from the love of Christ, overcoming even death as well as the 'principalities and powers' (v. 38).

We *must* live in the light of eternity, trusting in the absolute reliability of the word of God. Satan can only kill our mortal bodies which will sooner or later die anyway, as Jesus warns us:

> "Do not fear those who kill the body but are unable to kill the soul; but rather fear Him who is able to destroy both soul and body in hell" (Matt 10:28)

He does not promise us that we will not die or be killed; He promises us eternal life after we die:

> "I am the resurrection and the life; he who believes in Me will live even if he dies, and everyone who lives and believes in Me will never die. Do you believe this?" (John 11:25-26)

Summary of the First Beast's Fatal Wound

The first beast is fatally wounded in one of its seven heads yet it miraculously survives:

(i)   The seven heads are Gentile empires which ruled over Israel and in John's day, 96 A.D., "five have fallen, one is and one is yet to come". The 'fatal wound' (v. 3) was inflicted on the dragon and the first beast in John's day, the time of the sixth head, Rome.

(ii)   This wounding fulfils the Scriptures' first messianic prophecy of Genesis 3:15 where the seed of the woman is to "bruise the head" of 'the serpent of old'. Jesus of Nazareth is the Seed of the woman, being born of a virgin, and Satan's head wound is the loss of his headship over every one of his subjects who repents and enters the kingdom of God.

(iii) While receiving his head wound, Satan is allowed to bruise the Seed's heel by having Jesus crucified. The outcome is to turn around the entire fall of mankind – Messiah's wound is healed by His resurrection and His granting of eternal life to all who trust in His atoning death.

(iv) Satan's wound, his loss of headship, is also for all eternity in those believers who now comprise the new Creation (2 Cor 5:21). Even though he is allowed to kill us, we 'overwhelmingly conquer' because all he can kill are our mortal bodies which will be no loss at all after resurrection and in eternity.

(v) He is therefore allowed to use the first beast to blaspheme against God and His people (v. 6), 'to make war on the saints and to overcome them' (v. 7) for 'a time, times and half a time' (v. 5) i.e. for the last 2,000 years.

(vi) Even a cursory glance at the fate of the saints over this time shows the fulfilment of this with frequent persecution and martyrdom caused by first beast, initially through the Roman empire and then through the state church, whether Roman Catholic or Protestant.

(vii) Those watching on, 'the whole earth', not yet aware of what Jesus has done in the light of eternity (v. 8), conclude, "Who is like the beast, and who is able to wage war with him?" (v. 4) so they submit or worship this beast (v. 8).

6

The Eleventh Horn
Subduing Three

Before we look at the second beast of Revelation 13, we need to consider Daniel's prediction of its coming, made over six hundred years before John, in about 550 B.C. As we saw earlier, Daniel had a vision of four great beasts, the fourth of which had ten horns which are ten kings but they do not have it all their own way:

> While I was contemplating the [ten] horns, behold, another horn, a little one, came up among them, and three of the first horns were pulled out by the roots before it; and behold, in this horn were eyes like the eyes of a man, and a mouth uttering great boasts (Dan 7:8)

The eleventh horn also attacks the people of God:

> I kept looking, and that horn was waging war with the saints and overpowering them until the Ancient of Days came, and judgment was passed in favour of the saints of the Highest One, and the time arrived when the saints took possession of the kingdom (Dan 7:21-22)

Finally, Daniel is given the interpretation:

> "As for the ten horns, out of this kingdom [the fourth beast i.e. Roman Empire] ten kings will arise; and another will arise after them, and he will be different from the previous ones and will subdue three kings.
> And he will speak out against the Most High and wear down the saints of the Highest One, and he will intend to make alterations in times and in law; and they will be given into his hand for a time, times, and half a time..." (Dan 7:24-25)

The eleventh horn will rule on earth until Judgement Day:

> "…But the court will sit for judgment, and his dominion
> will be taken away, annihilated and destroyed forever. Then
> the sovereignty, the dominion and the greatness of all the
> kingdoms under the whole heaven will be given to the people
> of the saints of the Highest One; His kingdom will be an
> everlasting kingdom, and all the dominions will serve and obey
> Him" (Dan 7:26-27)

This eleventh horn significantly differs from the other ten in:

(i)   *Appearance.* The eleventh horn grows, from being "a little one" to "larger than its associates" (v. 20). It alone has "eyes like the eyes of a man, and a mouth" (v. 8) so that it appears to be "like" a man.

(ii) *Longevity.* Whereas the ten only have their unified power for "one hour", the last possible 'hour' before the Second Coming, the eleventh has his dominion for "a time, times, and half a time" (v. 25), which we have established as the "times of the Gentiles" i.e. the last two thousand years. This horn therefore, while it becomes most apparent after the ten have begun to unite, has actually existed from the time of Christ up to the present.

(iii) *Methods.* The ten try to "combine with one another" by alliances and intermarriages but fail to "adhere to one another, even as iron does not combine with pottery" (Dan 2:43). However the eleventh uses coercion, pulling a third of the ten horns "out by the roots" so that "three of them fell" (Dan 7:20) i.e. ceded power to him.

(iv) *Purpose.* The ten rule their own people for their own differing purposes which stops them combining but the eleventh has the purpose of the beast which the ten only accept at the end. He "speaks out against" God and His people, changing "times and laws" (Dan 7:25), and has done for the last two thousand years.

                                    Slouching Towards Bethlehem

(v) *Kind*. He is "different from the others" (v. 24). The ten are "all the nations", i.e. clearly human, but the eleventh is a spiritual being which is why he only appears to be "like" a man and why he can rule for two thousand years.

As a new Christian I was taught, and believed, that the eleventh horn was a human individual. It is not. As will be seen next, it is *the spirit of antichrist.*

What then are the "three horns" that will be "pulled out by the roots before it" (v. 8), i.e. the three kings whom the eleventh will subdue (v. 24)? Ten being a metaphor for all, these three represent a third, a poetic device often seen in the Book of Revelation. For example, 'a third of the earth' and 'a third of the trees' will be burned (Rev 8:7), 'a third of the sea', 'a third of the creatures' and 'a third of the ships' will be destroyed (Rev 8:8-9) and 'a third of mankind' (Rev 9:15). Accordingly, we see that this eleventh horn will come to subdue or dominate a third of the nations of the earth.

Today, the nations of the earth do seem to be uniting. We talk of the 'global village' and global economy. Perhaps epitomised by the dismantling of the Berlin Wall, the whole world does seem to have entered a new and unprecedented phase in history. In 1992, American political scientist, Francis Fukuyama, presumed to label this as 'the end of history', on the dual premise that democracy is the highest possible form of evolved human government and that it is now so widespread as to be unstoppable:

> What we may be witnessing is not just the end of the Cold War, or the passing of a particular period of post-war history, but the end of history as such... That is, the end point of mankind's ideological evolution and the universalisation of Western liberal democracy[82] as the final

---

82 A 'liberal democracy' is a country or state based on the liberty and equal rights of all citizens and governed by elected representatives.

form of human government.[83]

He does have a point in that coercive empires have been largely replaced by voluntary groupings of states or nations such as the U.S.A. or the European Union (EU). In the last ninety years, the fifty-three colonies of the British Empire became the British 'Commonwealth of Nations'; in the last twenty years, the Iron and Bamboo Curtains have fallen and the Marxist bloc has broken up into independent nations which then joined capitalist and military alliances such as the EU or the North Atlantic Treaty Organisation (NATO).

Political or ideological totalitarian regimes seem to have been superseded by common economic interests, based around products like oil (OPEC - Oil Producing and Exporting Countries) or regions (ASEAN - Association of South East Asian Nations, and NAFTA - North American Free Trade Association) or simply status, influence and wealth (G-7, G-20). And, of course, every nation on earth now voluntarily belongs to the United Nations.

However, the eleventh horn which uproots and subdues three of the ten, i.e. a third of all the nations, will not be overcome in this way. The 'end of history' will not come because we have evolved in our ideas and political behaviours, as nice as that would be, but sadly, it will only come because…:

> … the court will sit for judgment, and his [the eleventh horn's] dominion will be taken away, annihilated and destroyed forever. Then the sovereignty, the dominion, and the greatness of all the kingdoms under the whole heaven will be given to the people of the saints of the Highest One; His kingdom will be an everlasting kingdom, and all the dominions will serve and obey Him (Dan 7:27-28)

As we will establish next, Daniel's eleventh horn is the spirit of anti-Christ and *John's second beast.*

---

83 Francis Fukuyama, *The End of History and the Last Man,* New York; Free Press, 1992.

                    Slouching Towards Bethlehem

Summary of the Eleventh Horn

In Daniel chapter 7, Daniel sees that besides the ten horns, i.e. "ten kings" which are "all the nations", there is an eleventh horn:

(i)   Whereas the ten are human, the eleventh is 'different' a spirit (vv. 8 and 24).

(ii)   It subdues "three kings" or one third of all the nations (vv. 8 and 24).

(iii) This spirit is allowed to attack the people of God for "a time, times and half a time" (v. 25), this time period being "the times of the Gentiles" i.e. the last two thousand years.

(iv)   It meets its end when "the court will sit for judgement", i.e. Judgement Day, and only then "the sovereignty, the dominion and the greatness of all the kingdoms under the whole heaven will be given to the people" of God (vv. 26-27).

7

The Second Beast
'Out of the Earth'

As we will see, John's second beast is also a spiritual being, creates false prophets, is contemporaneous with the first beast which was given authority for 'forty two months' (v. 5) i.e. "a time, times and half a time" and the "times of the Gentiles", and only comes to an end on Judgement Day (Rev 19:20). We will also see that today, in its latest, present form, it is already ruling over one third of the nations of the earth.

Returning then to Revelation 13:

> 11. And I saw another beast coming up out of the earth; and he had two horns like a lamb, and he spoke as a dragon.
> 12. And he exercises all the authority of the first beast in his presence. And he makes the earth and those who dwell in it to worship the first beast, whose fatal wound was healed.
> 13. And he performs great signs, so that he even makes fire come down out of heaven to the earth in the presence of men.

Later, John refers to this beast as 'the false prophet':

> And the [first] beast was seized, and with him **the false prophet** who performed the signs in his presence, by which he deceived those who had received the mark of the beast and those who worshiped his image… (Rev 19:20, emphasis added)

There has been much speculation about the identity of this second beast, ranging from 1st Century provincial governors[84], to the Popes[85], to an apostate Protestant church leader as the

---

84 L. Michael White, *The Antichrist: A Historical Puzzle*, www.pbs.org/wgbh/pages/frontline/shows/apocalypse/antichrist/white.html, 23 Sep, 2011.

85 Thomas Foster, *Amazing Book of Revelation Explained*, Blackburn, Vic., Australia; Acacia Press, 1983, p. 71; Walter J. Veith, http://

---

last great Antichrist; from all of modern Western civilisation to the United States of America in particular.[86] Some look for a less material interpretation, identifying it as an 'ideology – whether religious, philosophical or political' [87] or as 'false religion and false philosophy in whichever form these appear'.[88]

I would go a step further than a human being, entity or ideology – the second beast is the *spirit* of antichrist.[89] Consider its six identifying features:

(i) It has 'two horns like a lamb' but speaks 'as a dragon' (v. 11)

John's warning that this beast only looks '*like* a lamb' is from Jesus' earlier teaching:

> "Beware of the false prophets, who come to you in sheep's clothing, but inwardly are ravenous wolves. You will know them by their fruits…" (Matt 7:15)

We are to ignore the outward appearance, harmless as it may appear, of anyone offering to lead us. Instead, we are to focus on their words and the "fruits" i.e. outcome of their words. Here John leaves us in no doubt that the words of this 'lamb' are demonic: 'he spoke as a dragon' and John has just told us that 'the great dragon' symbolises 'the devil and Satan' (Rev 12:9).

Remember too how Jesus describes the *inward nature or spirit* of false prophets: they are "ravenous wolves", wild beasts

amazingdiscoveries.org/S-deception_beasts_earth_Revelation_power.html, 23 Sep, 2011.

86 Larry A. Wright, http://wrightworld.net/secondbeastofrevelation13.htm, 23 Sep, 2011.

87 Michael Wilcock, *The Message of Revelation*, Leicester, England; Inter-Varsity Press, 1975, p. 127.

88 William Hendriksen, *More Than Conquerors,* Grand Rapids; Baker Book House, 1986, p. 148.

89 Laurie Guy likewise notes its explicit counterfeiting of the Holy Spirit in *Making Sense of the Book of Revelation*, Oxford; Regent's Park College, 2009, pp. 121-122.

that devour. That is what is under this lamb's appearance –
John's second beast is not a man or an entity or an ideology
but a spirit.

In Revelation, John uses the Greek word *arnion*, 'little
lamb', some 29 times, 28 referring to Jesus but on this one
occasion, to the beast that looks like a lamb. Why? Because it
is seeking to usurp the place of "the Lamb of God who takes
away the sins of the world", not to do His work but to steal
the honour due Him.

(ii) It is specifically called 'the false prophet' (Rev 19:20.
Also in Rev 16:13)

In Revelation 19:20, it has deceived the people. In Revelation
16:13-16, John sees it sending out other 'unclean spirits' which
are 'spirits of demons' to deceive 'the kings of the whole world'
into gathering for the battle of Har-Magedon. Its fruits are
horrendous.

**(iii) It has miraculous powers, even making 'fire come down
out of heaven'** (v. 13)

This fire is the second beast's most distinctive feature so we
will examine that closely soon.

(iv) It has great authority and longevity (v. 12)

It uses 'all the authority of the first beast' which has been
'given authority to act for forty two months' (v. 5) i.e. three
and a half years, "a time, times and half a time" and therefore
the last two thousand years. This means that the second beast
cannot be a single individual but it literally 'inspires' many
individuals, as we will see.

(v) It makes everyone 'worship the first beast' (v. 12)

Here we see the second beast's whole reason for being, its
primary purpose – to divert the worship that should be given

                               Slouching Towards Bethlehem

to God the Father and Jesus as His image (John 5:23) instead to *the state and its image.*

(vi) Its origin is 'out of the earth' rather than 'the sea' of the first beast (v. 11)

James the Lord's brother contrasts 'the wisdom from above' (Jas 3:17) with the 'bitter jealousy and selfish ambition' which causes us to 'be arrogant and lie against the truth' (Jas 3:14). He concludes:

> This wisdom is not that which comes down from above, but is earthly, natural, demonic. (Jas 3:15)

Note this natural wisdom from the earth is also 'demonic'. Given that this beast is trying to usurp the Lamb, it is clearly bitterly jealous and selfishly ambitious.

We have also seen that sometimes 'the sea' represents all the Gentile nations (e.g. Rev 17:15). In those instances, 'the earth' then represents Israel. Since the revelation of the Christ was most specifically given to and preserved by Israel's prophets, it follows that the counterfeit or Antichrist as a mirror-image also originates in Israel. Some assume from this that the Antichrist will be Jewish, but Gentiles can just as surely lead heresies that have split away from the twin Jewish revelations of monotheism and Messiah, as we will see. John wrote:

> Beloved, do not believe every spirit, but test the spirits to see whether they are from God, because many false prophets have gone out into the world… This is *the spirit of the antichrist*, of which you have heard that it is coming, and now it is already in the world (1 John 4:1-3, emphasis added)

Let us be clear that we really know what this means.

The Spirit of Antichrist

We can easily misunderstand or underestimate this term because, in today's parlance, 'anti' means 'opposed to or against', as in anti-aircraft guns, anticlimax, antisemitic, antivivisection etc. The *Concise Oxford Dictionary* therefore defines 'antichrist' as:

> *n.* enemy of Christ; great personal opponent of Christ expected by early Church to appear before the end of world.[90]

However, this is only partially true. The Greek word, *anti*, also means 'in place of', to denote a replacement, an equivalent or a similarity. For example, it is used in Mark 10:45 of Jesus coming to "give His life a ransom *for* many", i.e. on behalf of many.[91] 'The spirit of the antichrist', then, is not just one opposed to Christ but a demonic spirit which specifically seeks to replace or usurp Christ.

John therefore gives us several descriptions in his first two letters of how this spirit works: it causes 'many antichrists' to appear (1 John 2:18), denies Jesus is the Christ and equal with the Father (1 John 2:22), denies Jesus came as God in human form (1 John 4:2, 2 John 1:7) and tries to ignore Jesus altogether (1 John 4:3). This is why in Revelation 13, we see the spirit of antichrist perverting the whole earth's worship:

> 12. ...And he makes the earth and those who dwell in it to worship the first beast, whose fatal wound was healed.
> 13. And he performs great signs, so that he even makes fire come down out of heaven to the earth in the presence of men (Rev 13)

Prophets often have 'signs and wonders' attesting to their supernatural ministry. The beast has too. This is because God allows false prophets to arise even with true signs and wonders to teach us to look beyond appearances, to listen and be faithful to Him only. Consider Moses' warning to Israel:

> 1. "If a prophet or a dreamer of dreams arises among you and

---

90 *Concise Oxford Dictionary,* 1985, p. 37.
91 Kittel's *Theological Dictionary of the New Testament,* pp. 61-62.

gives you a sign or a wonder
2. and the sign or the wonder comes true, concerning which
he spoke to you, saying, 'Let us go after other gods (whom you
have not known) and let us serve them',
3. you shall not listen to the words of that prophet or that
dreamer of dreams; for the LORD your God is testing you to find
out if you love the LORD your God with all your heart and with all
your soul.
4. You shall follow the LORD your God and fear Him; and you
shall keep His commandments, listen to His voice, serve Him,
and cling to Him" (Deut 13:1-4)

This was the ultimate test of Israel's love for God. A sham miracle they could easily reject but a true wonder attributed to another god? Would they continue to choose the God of Abraham, Isaac and Jacob, to love Him with all their heart and soul? Would they look past the appearance even of supernatural signs and wonders to discern what was actually being *said and proposed for worship?*

Why did He set this test? Even a newly married couple just beginning to know each other intimately can validly expect the other to not go off with someone else. Look again at the false prophet's words:

> "Let us go after other gods (whom you have not known) and let
> us serve them" (Deut 13:2)

Moses' comment, "whom you have not known", was the key to Israel's passing this test. Having come to know God, they were not to go off with another. Instead, like survivors from a sinking ship holding on to floating wreckage, they were to "cling to Him".

God has not changed. As in Moses' day, He has always tested His people's love of Him. Will *we* love Him enough to be discerning? Will *we* look beyond even the most spectacular supernatural effects to discern what is being said to us, to consider if it is God or the dragon, Christ or antichrist, speaking to us? And what exactly are these 'great signs' (v. 13)?

'… Makes Fire Come Down Out of Heaven'

There is a particular sign the second beast offers as his credentials:

> 13. And he performs great signs, so that he even makes fire come down out of heaven to the earth in the presence of men (Rev 13)

Some today, reading about this fire in the light of 21st Century technology, speculate about laser beams from satellites orbiting the earth. Others, in the light of the Scriptures, interpret this as lightning bolts (Job 1:16).

However, there is a supernatural fire from heaven which has a long Biblical history. Remember, Elijah called down supernatural fire to prove the LORD and not Baal was the true God, even pouring three lots of water over the wood of his burnt offering to prove it was not natural fire (1 Kin 18:21-39). Elijah also called down fire to judge his mockers (2 Kin 1:9-16) and we know that John and the 1st Century church knew of this fire because he and James wanted to follow Elijah's example, until reproved by Jesus (Luke 9:51-56).

This heavenly fire was also seen in Moses' time on four occasions: when he and Aaron offered the first offerings of the Law's sacrificial system (Lev 9:23-24); when God judged Nadab and Abihu for offering 'strange fire' (Lev 10:1-2), and others for complaining (Num 11:1-3, 16:35). Gideon saw it (Jud 6:21) as did David (1 Chron 21:26) and all the Israelis in Solomon's time, when they dedicated the Temple in Jerusalem (2 Chron 7:1-3).

Daniel saw it in his famous vision of the Ancient of Days: "a river of fire… flowing and coming out from before Him" (Dan 7:10). Daniel goes on: "And behold, with the clouds of heaven, One like a Son of Man was coming" (Dan 7:13). This connection of the Ancient of Days, the Son of Man and the river of fire is echoed in Revelation 22:1 where John sees 'a river of the water of life… flowing from the throne of God and of the Lamb'. Since Jesus had identified Himself as the Son of Man (Matt 26:63-64) and the living water as symbolising the Holy Spirit (John 7:37-39), these two visions are obviously of the Father, Son and Holy Spirit.

We see then that all these visible occurrences of heavenly fire prefigure the Holy Spirit, flowing from the throne of God and of Messiah. As for the fulfillment, John the Baptist identifies this as the work of Jesus of Nazareth:

> "I baptise you with water; but One is coming who is mightier than I… He will baptise you with the Holy Spirit and fire"
> (Matt 3:11. Also Luke 3:16)

This first occasion was, of course, on the Day of Pentecost in 30 A.D., when Jesus immersed the entire early church in the Spirit and fire:

> And there appeared to them tongues as of fire distributing themselves, and they rested on each one of them. And they were all filled with the Holy Spirit and began to speak with other tongues, as the Spirit was giving them utterance (Acts 2:3-4)

This ability of the Son of Man, or the Christ, to baptise others in the Holy Spirit and fire is the primary evidence of His identity. It is implicit in the titles Christ and Messiah. Anglicised from the Greek *christos* and Hebrew *meschiach*, both mean 'the anointed one' or literally 'the one who has had olive oil poured on his head'. The olive oil symbolises the Holy Spirit and the pouring of oil upon the head of Israel's high priests,[92] kings,[93] and prophets[94] was to symbolise their being empowered by the Holy Spirit for their work.

The nation therefore recognised three anointed roles: priests, kings and prophets. However, they were also promised an ultimate Messiah, one who would be God in human form

---

92 Leviticus 8:12, Psalm 133:2.
93 1 Samuel 10:1, 16:13, 2 Kings 9:3.
94 1 Kings 19:16.

(Isa 9:6-7) and would hold all three roles as prophet, high priest and king (Deut 18:15, Zech 6:13). The Christ or Messiah therefore means 'the One with the Holy Spirit'.

There was also to be a twist – He would come so humbly that He would not be outwardly recognisable (Isa 53:1-3, Zechariah 9:9). Remember John the Baptist's testimony after he had baptised Jesus, a carpenter of Nazareth:

> "I did not recognise Him, but… I have beheld the Spirit descending as a dove out of heaven, and He remained on Him. And I did not recognise Him, but He who sent me to baptise in water said to me, 'He upon whom you see the Spirit descending and remaining upon Him, this is the One who baptises in the Holy Spirit'.
> And I have seen, and have borne witness that this is the Son of God" (John 1:31-34)

John must have known something of Jesus because their mothers were relatives (Luke 1:36) and Mary stayed with Elizabeth for the three months before John's birth (Luke 1:56) when Elizabeth prophesied about Jesus (Luke 1:43). However, this was not enough for John to recognise Him as Messiah – he was promised he would see a manifestation of the Holy Spirit on Messiah, fulfilled by "a dove out of heaven", and this was to be greater than on all other spiritual leaders of Israel – they had only ever received visitations of the Spirit (e.g. Judges 14:6, 19, 15:14 and 16:20) but Messiah has the Holy Spirit "remaining upon Him".

Not only does Messiah have the Holy Spirit but He can give the Holy Spirit to others. So 'fire from heaven' was a manifestation of the Holy Spirit being given to others by the Christ; the second beast therefore offers a counterfeit experience of the Holy Spirit to lure the unwary to worship the image of the first beast.

External and Internal Testimonies

There are, of course, two kinds of evidence we each need to believe that Jesus is the Messiah: external, factual evidence and internal, personal experience. Some refer to these as objective and subjective. According to the Scriptures, the external evidence to any human being in every generation, anywhere on the earth, of Jesus being Messiah is that He died on the cross and was resurrected (e.g. Luke 24:25-27). Like any knowledge of the past, this can only be received by faith i.e. by trusting in the testimony of the Old Testament and the testimony of the apostles and other eyewitnesses of the 1st Century. We can also hear testimonies of people encountering Him in our day.

However, the internal evidence to anyone in every generation anywhere of Jesus being Messiah is that He can still do it, i.e. still immerse every one of us in the Holy Spirit. As Peter explained on the Day of Pentecost:

> "This Jesus God raised up again, to which we are all witnesses. Therefore having been exalted to the right hand of God, and having received from the Father the promise of the Holy Spirit, He has poured forth this which you both see and hear…
> Therefore let all the house of Israel know for certain that God has made Him both Lord and Christ…" (Acts 2:32-36)

So there is a way to know for certain — the ultimate proof to anyone, that Jesus is who He says He is, comes when we pray to Him. When He answers by "pouring forth" the Holy Spirit, and we "see and hear" the manifestations (as described in more detail in 1 Cor 12), we know that He had to have been raised from the dead or else He would not be answering us.

This 'inner witness' also provides clear evidence that when we 'receive Him' as Messiah, we 'become children of God' (John 1:10-12). As Paul writes:

> The Spirit Himself testifies with our spirit that we are children of God (Rom 8:16)

John also explains:

> If we receive the testimony of men, the testimony of God is greater; for the testimony of God is this, that He has testified concerning His Son. The one who believes in the Son of God has the testimony *in himself* (1 John 5:9-10, emphasis added)

Since Jesus offers this supernatural attesting experience to all who call upon Him (John 7:37-41), the dragon and the beast offer a counterfeit spiritual experience and have done for the last two thousand years.

'Led Astray'

Paul describes this counterfeit experience to the Corinthians, using the analogy of a bride being led astray from her bridegroom:

> I betrothed you to one husband, that to Christ I might present you as a pure virgin. But I am afraid, lest as the serpent deceived Eve by his craftiness, your minds should be led astray from the simplicity and purity of devotion to Christ.
> For if one comes and preaches another Jesus whom we have not preached, or you receive a different spirit which you have not received… you bear this beautifully (2 Cor 11:2-4)

Notice the Corinthians were not being threatened by 21st Century laser beams or Biblical lightning bolts but simply tempted to 'receive a different spirit' from a clever speaker. What is a 'different spirit'? Any supernatural spirit or anointing other than the Holy Spirit. These men misleading the Corinthians were preaching an erroneous message *with a demonic anointing* which can create an impressive subjective experience. This is why, for example, followers of Joseph Smith (also known as Mormons or Latter Day Saints) can readily testify to their own 'inner witness'. This is despite Smith's teaching that God has evolved [95] rather than has always been

---

95   http://lds.org/ldsorg/v/index.jsp?vgnextoid=2354fccf2b7dbo1oVgnV

God, 'from everlasting to everlasting' (Psa 90:2).

Paul's reproof of the church for accepting false preachers could seem to limit this deception to church-goers, but not so. The Greek word to preach, *kerusso*, means:

> to herald… The herald had a high place in Greek antiquity, belonging to the court. He carried a sceptre, was renowned for his cleverness and wisdom and was required to have a strong and resonant voice.[96]

Far from only frequenting churches, the one who preaches with a different spirit can also be wholly *secular and political.*

Counterfeit Fire

Consider Adolf Hitler's personal testimony, speaking in Wurzberg on 27 June 1937:

> "As weak as the individual may ultimately be in his character and actions as a whole, when compared to Almighty Providence and its will, he becomes just as infinitely strong the instant he acts in accordance with this Providence. Then there will rain down upon him the power that has distinguished all great phenomena in this world.
> And when I look back on the five years behind us, I cannot help but say: this has not been the work of man alone. Had Providence not guided us, I surely would often have been unable to follow these dizzying paths. That is something our critics should above all know.
> At the bottom of our hearts, we National Socialists are devout! We have no choice: no one can make national or world history if his deeds and abilities are not blessed by Providence." [97]

CM1000004d82620aRCRD&locale=0&sourceId=8b9a945bd384b010V
gnVCM1000004d82620a____&hideNav, 26 Nov, 2010.
96 Kittel, p. 430.
97 Hitler, *Speeches And Proclamations 2*, Domarus (ed), p. 908, quoted by Michael Burleigh, *Sacred Causes: Religion and Politics from the*

Notice Hitler's description of this "power from on high" – all he had to do was "act in accordance" with it and it "rained down upon him". He assumed all such power was provided by Almighty Providence and made no allowance for any demonic counterfeit.

We may even know when Hitler received his demonic call and anointing. He was just sixteen and a half when in November 1905, he and his friend August Kubizek went to see a performance of Richard Wagner's opera *Rienzi, the Last of the Tribunes* at the Linz Memorial Theatre. The opera is Wagner's longest, lasting five hours, and is an extravagant, passionate story of a medieval Roman leader. Afterwards, Kubizek says, Adolf was struck speechless. Although it was well after midnight, he silently led Kubizek through the misty streets of Linz to the summit of Freinberg Hill where they stood under a dazzling array of stars:

> Adolf stood in front of me; and now he gripped both my hands and held them tight. He had never made such a gesture before. I felt from the grasp of his hands how deeply moved he was. His eyes were feverish with excitement. The words did not come smoothly from his mouth as they usually did, but rather erupted, hoarse and raucous. From his voice I could tell even more how much this experience had shaken him.
> Gradually his speech loosened, and the words flowed more freely. Never before and never again have I heard Adolf Hitler speak as he did in that hour, as we stood there alone under the stars, as though we were the only creatures in the world.
> I cannot repeat every word that my friend uttered. I was struck by something strange, which I had never noticed before, even when he had talked to me in moments of the greatest excitement. It was as if another being spoke out of his body, and moved him as much as it did me. It

European Dictators to al-Qaeda, London; HarperCollins, 2006, pp. 102-103.

     Slouching Towards Bethlehem

wasn't at all a case of a speaker being carried away by his own words. On the contrary; I rather felt as though he himself listened with astonishment and emotion to what burst forth from him with elementary force. I will not attempt to interpret this phenomenon, but it was a state of complete ecstasy and rapture, in which he transferred the character of Rienzi, without even mentioning him as a model or example, with visionary power to the plane of his own ambitions. But it was more than a cheap adaptation. Indeed, the impact of the opera was rather a sheer external impulse which compelled him to speak. Like flood waters breaking their dykes, his words burst forth from him. He conjured up in grandiose, inspiring pictures his own future and that of his people.[98]

While Kubizek would not attempt to interpret this phenomenon, he could see 'it was a state of complete ecstasy and rapture', and this surely was a spiritual experience. As Hitler himself 'listened with astonishment and emotion to what burst forth from him with elementary force', it transformed his belief in his ultimate destiny, as Kubizek continues:

> Hitherto I had been convinced that my friend wanted to become an artist, a painter, or perhaps an architect. Now this was no longer the case. Now he aspired to something higher, which I could not yet fully grasp. It rather surprised me, as I thought that the vocation of the artist was for him the highest, most desirable goal. But now he was talking of a mandate which, one day, he would receive from the people, to lead them out of servitude to the heights of freedom.
> It was an unknown youth who spoke to me in that strange hour. He spoke of a special mission which one day would be entrusted to him, and I, his only listener, could hardly understand what he meant. Many years had to pass before

---

98 August Kubizek, *The Young Hitler I Knew,* London; Greenhill Books, 2006, pp. 117-119.

I realized the significance of this enraptured hour for my
friend.
His words were followed by silence.
We descended into the town. The clock struck three. We
parted in front of my house. Adolf shook hands with
me, and I was astonished to see that he did not go in
the direction of his home, but turned again towards the
mountains.
"Where are you going now?" I asked him, surprised. He
replied briefly, "I want to be alone".[99]

Hitler heard a call, 'a mandate which, one day, he would receive
from the people, to lead them out of servitude to the heights
of freedom', and like the apostle Paul after his encounter on
the road to Damascus, he did not 'immediately consult with
flesh and blood' (Gal 1:16-17):

In the following weeks and months he never again
mentioned this hour on the Freinberg. At first it struck
me as odd and I could find no explanation for his strange
behavior, for I could not believe that he had forgotten it
altogether. Indeed he never did forget it, as I discovered
thirty-three years later. But he kept silent about it because
he wanted to keep that hour entirely to himself. That I
could understand, and I respected his silence. After all, it
was his hour, not mine. I had played only the modest role
of a sympathetic friend.
In 1939, shortly before war broke out, when I, for the first
time visited Bayreuth as the guest of the Reich Chancellor,
I thought I would please my host by reminding him of
that nocturnal hour on the Freinberg, so I told Adolf
Hitler what I remembered of it, assuming that the
enormous multitude of impressions and events which
had filled these past decades would have pushed into the

---

99   Ibid., Otto Wagener also wrote in his *Hitler: Memoirs of a
Confidant* that ideas 'bubbled out of him, so that I hardly felt he was
speaking on the basis of thought; rather the words seemed to come
from him by themselves.' Edited by Henry Ashby Turner Jr., Yale
University Press, Newhaven, 1985, p. 319.

                                    Slouching Towards Bethlehem

background the experience of a seventeen year old youth. But after a few words I sensed that he vividly recalled that hour and had retained all its details in his memory. He was visibly pleased that my account confirmed his own recollections.

I was also present when Adolf Hitler retold this sequel to the performance of *Rienzi* in Linz to Frau Wagner, at whose home we were both guests. Thus my own memory was doubly confirmed. The words with which Hitler concluded his story to Frau Wagner are also unforgettable for me. He said solemnly, "In that hour it began".[100]

What in this opera appealed so much to this teenager? *Rienzi, the Last of the Tribunes* is based on the life of Cola di Rienzi (1313-1354), a heroic Italian revolutionary who dreamed of restoring Rome from the degradation and wretchedness of his time to its former glory and grandeur. He roused the populace and in 1347, with the help of Pope Clement VI, he overthrew the corrupt nobles who were oppressing them. Initially magnanimous, he assumed the title of *tribune* i.e. defender of the people, hence the opera's title. However, he ended up offending both the Pope and the people who turned against him and set fire to the Capitol in which he and a few followers were hiding. As he sought to escape, they stabbed him to death before dragging his body through the streets.

Somehow in Wagner's operatic telling of this story, Hitler heard a voice calling him to restore a glorious empire which he later proclaimed as *Das Dritte Reich* or the Third Reich.[101] He boasted it began with his becoming Chancellor on January 30, 1933, and would last for one thousand years,[102] perhaps

---

100 Ibid.
101 The First Reich was the Holy Roman Empire which lasted a thousand years, from the crowning of Charlemagne in 800 A.D. to the abdication of Francis II in 1806. The Second Reich was Otto von Bismarck's German Empire of 1871-1918.
102 Nuremberg Rally, 5th September, 1934, William L. Shirer, *The Rise and Fall of the Third Reich*, p. 5.

to match the First Reich or even the Biblical millennium of Revelation 20, but it only lasted twelve years and four months.

It seems that *Rienzi* not only precipitated Hitler's demonic calling but also, in a Faustian bargain, predicted his downfall.

Recognising Counterfeits

How can we recognise counterfeit spirituality? Many years ago I read how FBI agents were trained to identify and deal with counterfeit money. Before examining phoney bills, they were sent first to observe how paper money is created at the Federal Mint. They became thoroughly familiar with genuine bills, not just the appearance but the feel and characteristics of the paper, the tones and smells of the inks. I did not initially understand their strategy but it was explained – if they only studied counterfeit notes, even memorised all the mistakes ever made, they could still be deceived by any new forgeries with new mistakes. However, by putting all their energies into recognising real money, they only had to see any deviations from the genuine and that covered every possibility.

Is this not exactly Moses' strategy? Remember, he warned Israel that false prophets would perform true signs and wonders but then they would urge:

> "Let us go after other gods (whom you have not known) and let us serve them" (Deut 13:2)

Israel's sole defence would be their first-hand knowledge of the only true God. Jesus confirmed this for His disciples and us too when He prayed at the Last Supper:

> "This is eternal life, that they may know You, the only true God, and Jesus Christ whom You have sent" (John 17:3)

Paul likewise warns, as we just saw, that we must not let ourselves 'be led astray from the simplicity and purity of devotion to Christ' (2 Cor 11:3). Having come to know Jesus, we are to remain devoted to Him as this devotion has a 'simplicity and purity' which we can actually sense.

This is not hard – a child can do it – but the temptation of the spectacular can be very strong. Many years ago I had a very enthusiastic Christian friend who became overly mystical. His choice of books encouraged him until he began having supernatural experiences similar to the writers. As he told me of walking along a beach in showers of golden rain, I felt increasingly uneasy but also unwilling to judge the source of his delight due to my own very limited knowledge of God. However, as I kept listening, I began to see these experiences were increasingly unrelated to Jesus. When he started receiving revelations that smoking marijuana is fine with God, I knew my inner reserve was reliable and I could reject the source of his experiences. The Lord had already shown me that marijuana is not fine with Him, confirming it from the Scripture, 'do not get intoxicated because that is dissipation' (Eph 5:18).

The spirit of antichrist, however, has a particular focus.

8

'To Worship the First Beast'
What is Worship?

Returning to Revelation chapter 13:

> 12. …And he makes the earth and those who dwell in it to worship the first beast, whose fatal wound was healed…

The second beast's whole reason for being is to provoke worship of the first beast. The signs and wonders he performs are all for that purpose, but he has a particular way of getting everyone to do it:

> 14. And he deceives those who dwell on the earth because of the signs which it was given him to perform in the presence of the beast, telling those who dwell in the earth to make an image to the beast who had the wound of the sword and has come to life.

His way is to deceive mankind into making 'an image to the beast', or as the NIV translates it, 'to set up an image in honor of the beast'. The second beast then performs what seems to be an extraordinary feat:

> 15. And there was given to him to give breath to the image of the beast, that the image of the beast might even speak and cause as many as do not worship the image of the beast to be killed.

The living image then begins to speak but, casting aside persuasion and subtlety, it adds deadly force to coerce all who dwell on the earth to worship it.

At this point imagination and speculation can run riot as we remember Dr. Frankenstein's monster or consider that our technology today is on the brink of adding artificial intelligence to inanimate robots. However, as we will see next, 'the image of the (first) beast' is far more than a carefully stitched and electrified conglomeration of dead human body-parts or even than an extremely clever robot. And it is not a talking statue, as in the *Left Behind* series [103], or an amplified metal mask, as in *The Wizard of Oz.*[104]

The first beast is the 'principality and power' of the Gentiles i.e. the feral state; its 'image' is a flesh-and-blood, real, live man.

'Worship the Image of the Beast'

Jesus the Christ or Messiah walked on earth as a real, live man who is 'the image of the invisible God' (Col 1:15), 'the exact representation of His nature' (Heb 1:3). It should therefore be no surprise that the counterfeits are also real, live men.

One of the least understood but most common phenomena of mankind's political history is that, regardless of ideology but especially in atheistic movements, we ultimately end up like the 1st Century Romans in emperor worship, making gods or deifying our leaders.

Consider, for example, Marxism's explicitly atheistic regimes in the Soviet Union, Albania, China and Cambodia where Karl Marx's dictum 'religion is the opiate of the people' was, ironically, most demonstrated. Tragically, his disciples did not understand that their atheistic faith is one of the strongest opiates, inducing delusions of altruistic leaders and unselfish human society, while those most intoxicated by it lose all sense of good and evil beyond self-indulgence or self-preservation.

Astonishingly, some theologians have claimed that deification was the originating motive for the writing of the

---

103 Tim LaHaye & Jerry B. Jenkins, *The Indwelling: the Beast Takes Possession,* Tyndale House, 2000, p. 349.
104 Starring Judy Garland, this much-loved musical fantasy of 1939 was based on a novel by L. Frank Baum.

New Testament manuscripts. Believing these were fabricated many years after Jesus by a church unacquainted with His reality, they assume the church was simply following the world by proclaiming His divinity. The outcome has been bizarre attempts to demythologise Jesus and His teachings. It does not seem to have occurred to these theologians that the exact opposite is equally possible – that the world has mythologised their leaders as counterfeits of what God had always promised He would provide in reality in Messiah. This dilemma can only be resolved by trusting in the Scriptures and the Holy Spirit as 'the truth' (John 17:17 and 1 John 5:6b).

The truth is, God has 'set eternity in our hearts' (Eccl 3:11), even our pagan hearts, and He promised from the beginning of time to give us a Son born only of a woman (Gen 3:15), who would be God incarnate, i.e. in human form (Isa 9:6). *If we refuse to accept His Messiah, we will simply seek a god-king somewhere else.*

Remember John's exact words in Revelation 13:

> 12. …And he [the second beast, the spirit of antichrist] makes the earth and those who dwell in it to worship the first beast [the principality and power of the state or empire]

As they worship the power of their own empire, the second beast then focusses their worship on 'an image' of it:

> 14. And he deceives those who dwell on the earth…, telling those who dwell in the earth to make an image to the beast…

That image is its emperor.

Deification

Of course, this was neither unique nor new to Roman times. The ancient Egyptians' gods were initially personifications of the powers of nature (e.g. the sun, moon and stars, rivers) or embodiments of concepts (e.g. love, fertility, war, wisdom, death). Then, as their empire grew, and with it their monarch's affluence and influence, the pharaohs adopted titles such as Son of Ra, Aten or Osiris; Ra and Aten were names of the Egyptian sun-god, and Osiris was their god of the netherworld and afterlife. The Pharaoh then became the gods' representative on earth.[105]

The emperor in ancient China, from the third millennium B.C., was called the Son of Heaven. Interestingly, in the light of our previous study, *Dancing in the Dragon's Jaws*, he was symbolised by a golden dragon with five claws on each foot. Nearly everything associated with him was preceded by the epithet 'dragon' – the imperial throne was called the Dragon Throne, he slept in a 'dragon bed', rode in a 'dragon boat' and dressed ceremonially in silk 'dragon robes'.[106]

The Babylonian emperor Nebuchadnezzar set up in the 7th Century B.C. a golden image of himself to be worshipped; we will consider this more closely in Book 3.

The Greek leader Antiochus IV, inheritor of a fourth of Alexander's vast empire, made his beliefs evident in the 2nd Century B.C. when he assumed the name *Theo Epiphanes* (the manifest God) and called for worship of himself as the human form of Zeus. The Ptolemies, inheritors of another quarter which included Egypt, happily perpetuated the concept. Cleopatra apparently persuaded her lover Julius of his divinity as Caesar of the burgeoning empire of the Romans.

As for the Roman populace, their empire began with a well-founded fear of kings as tyrants and for several centuries, it functioned as a republic but always under threat. 1st Century historian Plutarch observed that they therefore appointed Julius (100-44 B.C.), their first Caesar, as dictator for life...:

… in the hope that the government of a single person

---

105   *The Zondervan Pictorial Encyclopedia of the Bible*, Vol 2, pp. 251-254.
106   http://arts.cultural-china.com/en/84Arts8067.html, 6 Mar, 2012.

would give them time to breathe after so many civil wars and calamities... This was indeed a tyranny avowed, since his power was not only absolute, but perpetual too.[107]

Seeing this drove Brutus and his co-conspirators to assassinate Julius, believing their task to be, in William Shakespeare's memorable phrase, 'a piece of work that will make sick men whole'.[108] They were to find the phenomenon is not so easily dealt with:

> The people called Caesar "god" and honored him as such in his lifetime. A statue was dedicated to him in the temple of Quirinus in 45 B.C. with the words "To the invincible god". Before his death he had his own temple under the name *Jupiter Julius* – this was the first step in establishing the cult, by honoring a living hero as the Greeks did. The second step in the cult of Caesar was taken with his official apotheosis [or deification] after his death. As a dead hero he was transferred to the number of the gods. The senate and people declared him a god and during the celebration in honor of the *divus Julius* the appearance of a comet was taken as proof that his soul had been received into the number of the immortals.[109]

The Roman Catholic Church still perpetuates the idea today in their canonisation of 'saints', where 'the presence of an individual in heaven... [is proved by] the performance of miracles through the intercession of that person.'[110] The Scriptures, however, forbid us praying to anyone other than the Lord Himself (1 Tim 2:5) and routinely refer to all believers in Jesus as saints (e.g. Acts 9:13 & 32, Rom 1:7).

Brutus's 'carnal weapons' could not pull down the stronghold in the minds of the Roman people (2 Cor 10:4)

---

107 *Lives of Noble Greeks and Romans*, Plutarch (50-120 A.D.). http://ebooks.adelaide.edu.au/p/plutarch/lives/chapter48.html, 10 Mar, 2012.
108 William Shakespeare, *Julius Caesar*, Act II, Scene 1.
109 Scott David Foutz, http://www.theologywebsite.com/history/rulercult.shtml, 3 Jun, 2008.
110 www.catholicapologetics.org/ap070400.htm, 13 Feb, 2012.

     Slouching Towards Bethlehem

and as long as their empire existed, there was always another Caesar. The next was Julius' grand-nephew Augustus who reigned from 27 B.C. to 14 A.D.

> To many, Augustus, for his achievements, was a god on earth; only a supra-human being could have brought stability out of chaos. Not surprisingly, therefore, Augustus found himself the object of acclamations of divinity. However, …he certainly did not wish to be seen as a god on earth… [because this] would have undermined his carefully worked relationship of *princeps* with the nobility. Yet it would have been cavalier to have snuffed out the political enthusiasm expressed through the medium of religion.
>
> The desire to worship the living emperor was tempered therefore; the so-called "imperial cult" came to be the worship of *Roma*, and only incidentally of Augustus, who protected her. This subsidiary role was present also in the notion of the *genius Augusti*, the guardian-spirit which was held to attend the head of the national family as it attended the head of the domestic family.[111]

Augustus set clear limits in Rome and in the West:

> He allowed altars, not temples, to be set up to his "genius", associated with the worship of *Dea Roma*, the deified spirit of Rome.[112]

However, in the East where these things were more easily accepted,[113] Augustus allowed them to build a temple to worship *Dea Roma et Augustus* i.e. Rome and himself. Notice

---

111   David Colin Arthur Shotter, *Augustus Caesar*, New York; Routledge, 2nd edition, 2005, pp. 72-73.

112   E.M. Blaiklock, Emeritus Professor of Classics at Auckland University; article on emperor worship, *Zondervan Pictorial Encyclopedia of the Bible,* Vol 2, p. 303.

113   William Barclay wrote, 'Such was the reverence of Smyrna for Rome that as far back as 195 B.C. it was the first city in the world to erect a temple to the goddess Roma'. *Letters to the Seven Churches,* London; SCM Press, 1957, p. 29.

how perfectly this fulfils Revelation's description – the second beast (the spirit of antichrist) would cause people to worship both the first beast (at that time, Rome) and the image of that beast (the emperor).

"Satan's Throne... Where Satan Dwells"

This temple of *Dea Roma et Augustus* was in the city of Pergamum[114] so when the Lord spoke to the church there, He described Pergamum in very strong terms:

> "I know where you dwell, where Satan's throne is; and you hold fast My name, and did not deny My faith, even in the days of Antipas, My witness, My faithful one, who was killed among you, where Satan dwells" (Rev 2:13)

Pergamum was famous for its great library, second only to Alexandria in the ancient world, and for inventing parchment to replace papyrus, the English name deriving directly from the city's.

However, as explained by E.M. Blaiklock, it was even more famous for its religious achievements, and the city's paganism lay in three strata. The bottom stratum dated from the 5th Century B.C. Anatolian period, when they celebrated both Dionysus, the god of vegetation, and Aesclepius, the god of healing whose temples literally crawled with non-poisonous snakes thought to be his embodiment.

> Snakes, and the handling of reptiles, were associated, as
> a drama of Euripides shows, with the cult of Dionysus.
> Snakes were the symbol of Aesclepius. A Pergamenian coin
> shows the emperor Caracalla standing spear in hand before
> a great serpent twined around a bending sapling. He raises
> his right hand in the salute which Hitler's Nazis brought
> back to another pagan world... Christians who associated
> the serpent with Satan must have found the cult of the
> god of healing, and his serpent-infested temple, peculiarly

---

114 Also known as Pergamon

revolting and diabolical.[115]

Aesclepius's symbol of a snake wrapped around his staff is still used today as a medical symbol, as on medic-alert bracelets.[116]

The second stratum in Pergamum was Greek, from early in the 2nd Century B.C., and can also be still seen today in their Altar of Zeus the Saviour. Built to celebrate a victorious battle, it was rediscovered in 1871, dismantled and reassembled by German archaeologists for the Museum of Pergamon in Berlin. Some have thought the u-shaped altar could be imagined as a large throne and is therefore "Satan's throne". However, as we saw earlier from Pliny Secundus, it was specifically the Christians' refusal to worship Caesar that led to their martyrdom and this was in the time of the third and topmost Roman stratum. E.M. Blaiklock again:

> When Attalus III [the King of Pergamum who was childless] bequeathed the kingdom to Rome in 133 B.C., the legacy was no doubt approved by his people, who saw little future for liberty and independence in the growing chaos of the Middle East... [The Romans] accepted the royal bequest and... for two and a half centuries, Pergamum remained Rome's official centre in Asia...[117]

---

115 E.M. Blaiklock, *Cities of the New Testament*, London; Pickering & Inglis, 1965, pp. 104-105.

116 This symbol is often confused with the *caduceus*, a staff entwined by two serpents and topped by a pair of wings, carried by Hermes, the messenger of the gods. For example, in 1902 the US Army medical corps adopted the caduceus as their insignia. As for Aesclepius's staff with its single snake, it counterfeits Moses's staff with the bronze snake which brought healing to ancient Israel (Num 21:8-9), but in exactly the opposite way to pagan understanding. Whereas the Anatolians, Greeks and Romans looked to the snakes for healing, in Jewish thinking the bronze snake signified that God had judged their sin (Num 21:5-7), which is why Jesus said it prefigured His crucifixion (John 3:14-15). We see then that Aesclepius was also an antichrist figure, usurping Jesus's role as the Healer. And this was only the first stratum faced by the Christians in Pergamum.

117 *Cities of the New Testament*, p. 103.

The imperial cult, the worship of the spirit of Rome and of
the emperor, with its loyalty test of formal incense burnt
at the foot of Caesar's statue, found a centre, appropriately
enough in Pergamum, and coloured the city's life. The first
temple of the cult was located there in 29 B.C... At the
end of the 1st Century [A.D.], a second temple was built
in honour of Trajan and a third for Servetus a century
later. Only the first temple functioned when John wrote
his letter from Patmos, but its presence and its ritual was
enough to make Rome's authority oppressively apparent in
the city.[118]

With astonishing subtlety, Pergamum had mingled and
synthetised the deities of three races, of three successive
periods... [culminating in] the worship of the emperor
in the centre of his cult, where that worship was thought
to conflict with no other, and to be withal a test of true
loyalty.[119]

John's prophecy therefore has extraordinary significance for all
of us: *worship of the emperor created a place for Satan to dwell
and reign.* The effect in those days was intense persecution of
the people of God so we must learn what to look for in our day.

Why Worship The Emperor?

Why would anyone want to do this? Of course, there were
natural reasons because, as Plutarch wrote, their emperors
offered peace after 'so many civil wars and calamities'.
However, there was also an overtly spiritual reason. Commonly
titled Saviour, they were held to be divinely inspired:

There was no way to explain a power so great without
appeal to a divine ("demonic" in the Greek sense) nature
residing in the soul of Augustus. According to the customs
of the time, the feelings of his subjects had to find

118   Ibid., p. 104.
119   Ibid., p. 106.

                                Slouching Towards Bethlehem

expression in divine honors.[120]

Amongst the Greeks a *daemon*, or demon, was a divine influence or power which determined their lot or fortune in life (cf. *theos* which denoted a god in person). Accordingly, while the Romans worshipped the emperor's 'genius', the Hellenists worshipped his 'demon', which is chilling when we consider the Biblical meaning of the word.

The emperor was only one of many gods that the Romans believed protected their empire but the *pax deorum*, i.e. 'peace of the gods', would only be maintained as long as they practised appropriate ceremonies:

> Many Roman histories relate stories of kings dethroned and cities destroyed for not sacrificing correctly… and of people and cities, even Rome, saved for sacrificing and worshipping correctly. (Both) Roman commoners and the nobility believed this peace was essential to the continued security of Roman power. It was, therefore, especially offensive to them when Christians refused to sacrifice to those gods… Believing this denial of the gods to be an attack on Rome, many Romans despised Christians.[121]

In an extraordinary irony, the Christians' 'denial of the gods' led to them being called 'atheists'.

Lastly, the emperor-worshippers were also worshipping the empire *of which they were part.* To the degree they honoured and worshipped their leader, they were also honouring and worshipping their own significance. As Samuel Johnson observed in another context, sometimes 'patriotism is the last refuge of a scoundrel'.

---

120   Scott David Foutz, www.theologywebsite.com/history/rulercult. shtml, 3 Jun, 2008.
121   Neil Manzullo, *The Roman Persecution of Christians,* 2000.

Summary of the Second Beast

We see that John's second beast is a spiritual being which:

(i) Looks like a lamb but speaks from the dragon. It is the spirit of antichrist and inspires a particular kind of false prophet.

(ii) Calls down fire from heaven, enabling the antichrists to counterfeit Jesus baptising us in the Holy Spirit.

(iii) Is contemporaneous with the first beast which is given authority for 'forty two months' (v. 5) i.e. "a time, times and half a time" and the "times of the Gentiles" i.e. the last two thousand years. It will only come to an end on Judgement Day (Rev 19:20).

(iv) Causes people to worship the first beast and then to make a living image of it to worship. This first beast is the principality and power of the State or Empire and its living image is its primary leader or emperor.

This phenomenon was not confined to the Romans – many ancient peoples including the Egyptians, Chinese, Babylonians and Greeks likewise worshipped their leaders. However, John is revealing why:

(v) In his day, the Romans were worshipping Rome and the Caesars.

(vi) Pergamum, the city of the temple of *Dea Roma et Augustus*, was the place where Satan was dwelling and enthroned (Rev 2:13) – the inhabitants had given such honour to this manifestation of the spirit of antichrist.

9

20th Century Emperor Worship
Repeating History

We have all been impacted by emperor-worship far more recently and far more widely than we may have realised. For example, for those of us who live in South East Asia, Australia and New Zealand, it led directly to many of our nations being invaded or attacked by Japan in World War II.

From at least as far back as the 7th Century A.D., the Tenno, or emperor, of Japan was considered to be divine. The great Japanese chronicles of that time, the *Kojiki* and the *Nihongi*, recorded the imperial line's descent from the most powerful of their deities, *Amaterasu Omikami*, the Sun Goddess, which is why their 20th Century battle flag was the Rising Sun. Their national religion of State Shintoism, a synthesis of early Shintoism, Buddhism and Confucianism, taught the Japanese people that their divine emperor was destined to rule over all the earth. With an 'ethic of absolute loyalty and unhesitating sacrifice', the military's battle cry of "*Banzai!*" (lit. ten thousand years) was wishing "Long life to the Emperor!" [122]

Japan's last officially worshipped emperor, Hirohito, died as recently as January 7th, 1989. Emperor from 1926, he did not renounce his imperial divinity until compelled to by the victorious Allied Forces on 1 January, 1946. Before that day, Rudolph Rummel, Professor Emeritus of Political Science at the University of Hawaii, estimates that from 1937 over thirteen and a quarter million Chinese had died resisting his empire, of whom 10,489,000 were civilians and prisoners of

---

122   Meirion and Susie Harries, *Soldiers of the Sun - The Rise and Fall of the Japanese Army*, New York, Random House, 1991.

---

war,[123] as well as 2,015,000 of other nationalities.[124]

Two million Japanese also died in the process of extending Hirohito's empire, so his renunciation of deity brought great relief even to Japan.

Meanwhile, in Nazi Germany in the 1930s, Albert Speer wrote of the power of this phenomenon:

> I sat as usual in the jump seat close behind Hitler and shall never forget that surge of rejoicing, the ecstasy reflected in so many faces. Wherever Hitler went during those first years of his rule, wherever his car stopped for a short time, such scenes were repeated. The mass exultation was not called forth by rhetoric or suggestion, but solely by the effect of Hitler's presence. Whereas individuals in the crowd were subject to this influence only for a few seconds at a time, Hitler himself was eternally exposed to the worship of the masses. At the time I admired him for nonetheless retaining his informal habits in private. Perhaps it is understandable that I was carried along by these tempests of homage. But it was even more overwhelming for me to speak with the idol of a nation a few minutes or a few hours later, to discuss building plans with him, sit beside him in the theater, or eat ravioli with him in the Osteria. It was this contrast that overwhelmed me.
>
> Only a few months before I had been carried away by the prospect of drafting and executing buildings. Now I was completely under Hitler's spell, unreservedly and unthinkingly held by him. I was ready to follow him anywhere. Yet his ostensible interest in me was to launch me on a glorious career as an architect. Years later, in Spandau, I read Ernst Cassirer's comment on men who of their own accord threw away man's highest privilege: to be an autonomous person. Now I was one of them.[125]

---

123   www.hawaii.edu/powerkills/CHINA.TAB6.2.GIF and www.hawaii.edu/powerkills/CHINA.TAB6.1.GIF, 28 Jul, 2011.
124   www.hawaii.edu/powerkills/NOTE2.HTM, 31 May, 2009.
125   Albert Speer, *Inside The Third Reich*, New York and Toronto:

                                 Slouching Towards Bethlehem

Ernst Cassirer had written:

> But here are men, men of education and intelligence, honest and upright men who suddenly give up the highest human privilege. They have ceased to be free and personal agents.[126]

These German leaders had not only 'ceased to be free and personal agents' – they had begun to worship the State as embodied in Hitler.

Is It Really Worship?

Reading Speer's description of 'the worship of the masses', 'tempests of homage', 'the idol of the nation', it can seem to be simply hyperbole. However, Biblically, it was literally worship because our god or gods are whoever or whatever we ultimately obey or serve.

Remember when Satan offered Jesus all the kingdoms of the world and their glory: "if You fall down and *worship* me". Jesus responded:

> "Go away, Satan! For it is written, 'YOU SHALL WORSHIP THE LORD YOUR GOD, AND SERVE HIM ONLY' " (Matt 4:9-10)

In paraphrasing Moses (Deut 6:13 & 10:20), Jesus shows that worship and serving in this sense are synonymous. Our English word 'worship' comes from 'worth-ship', meaning to accord worth, to consider worthy or valuable.[127] Therefore, whatever we give the place of ultimate worth or value in our lives by serving or obeying is the true object of our worship.

The worship of mammon (Matt 6:24), the idol of riches, is not us literally bowing down before piles of gold or dollar bills but rather whenever we accord more value to the demands of

---

Macmillan, 1970, p. 85.

126 Ernst Cassirer, *The Myth of the State,* New Haven; Yale University Press, 1946, p. 286.

127 *Concise Oxford Dictionary,* p. 1243.

---

money than to those of God in our everyday lives. It is often not flushed out of hiding until we have to make decisions requiring honesty, such as in filing an untrue tax return to pay less – God commands us to be truthful but if we value the money over the truth, we are worshipping and serving mammon rather than worshipping and serving God.

In the same way, if we disobey God in order to obey any human leader we have accorded more worth or respect to them than to Him. Peter and John willingly submitted to the government of their day (1 Pet 2:13-17), but were unequivocal about the limits of their obedience when commanded "not to speak or teach at all in the name of Jesus", saying:

> "Whether it is right in the sight of God to give heed to you rather than to God, you be the judge; for we cannot stop speaking what we have seen and heard" (Acts 4:18-20)

Soon after, Stephen's obeying God rather the government cost him his life (Acts 6:8-8:1). Likewise James, Peter and Paul.

To those of us living today in the West, this stark choice of life or death at the hands of our government seems far from our personal experience but it happens under every totalitarian or religious-political regime.

It can also begin apparently harmlessly in free societies. When Queen Victoria died in 1901, she was held in such high regard throughout the whole British Empire that statues of her were mass produced as souvenirs of her reign. *The Evening Post* in New Zealand reported that she was 'the embodiment of the Empire' and 'embodied all that was solid and virtuous about the British Empire'.[128] A Canadian journalist wrote that she was perceived…:

> …by the world at large to have represented such an influence to hold the world in peace as perhaps never

---

128 'Curious Object', *Evening Post*, Wellington, 19 Oct, 2011. (My thanks to Olivia Ladyman for this reference.)

                    Slouching Towards Bethlehem

before was embodied in any human being.[129]

Notice the extraordinary agreement of this 20th Century Canadian with the Roman view of their emperors in the 1st Century. English clergyman, the Reverend A. Carman, openly considered the temptation:

> Were we in the habit of deifying monarchs, we would not, in Queen Victoria, have the worst example of history for such exaltation.[130]

He was quick to add, however, that Queen Victoria as a Christian would herself have fought such exaltation.

Let us be clear regarding the image of the beast that is worshipped – it is any political leader who shapes him or herself and his or her nation to live out Louis XIV's dictum, "L'état, c'est moi!" ("The state? That's me!"). This leader is not necessarily worshipped because he or she is a good individual (there is often much evidence to the contrary) but simply because he or she becomes the personification or embodiment of the State.

And remember – wherever Satan is able to create an image of the beast to be worshipped, he will dwell and be enthroned (Rev 2:13) and the results are inevitably horrific. As will be established soon, in the last one hundred years this has meant the death of at least 269 million men, women and children.

Forewarned Is Forearmed

> And the whole earth was amazed and followed after the beast; they worshiped the dragon because he gave his authority to the beast; and they worshiped the beast, saying, "Who is like the

---

129 'The Queen', *Messenger and Visitor*, 23 Jan, 1901, p. 4. Quoted by Gordon L. Heath, *A War with a Silver Lining: Canadian Protestant Churches and the South African War* (1899-1902), Montreal; McGill-Queen's University Press, 2009, pp. 105-106.
130 Quoted by Heath from 'The Empire's Noble Queen', *Christian Guardian*, 30 Jan, 1901, p. 72.

---

beast, and who is able to wage war with him?"
(Rev 13:3-4)

We must never underestimate the impact of these leaders – 'the whole earth was amazed', marvelling at their apparently unique qualities, abilities and charisma:

> "For false Christs and false prophets will arise and will show great signs and wonders, so as to mislead, if possible, even the elect. Behold, I have told you in advance" (Matt 24:24-25)

"The elect" here means Christians. Paul therefore warns us of the wiles of a man who is yet to come:

> …that is, the one whose coming is in accord with the activity of Satan, with all power and signs and false wonders, and with all the deception of wickedness for those who perish, because they did not receive the love of the truth so as to be saved.
> (2 Thess 2:9-10)

'All the deception of wickedness' especially includes flattery. Three thousand years ago, Solomon observed:

> A man who flatters his neighbor is spreading a net for his steps
> (Prov 29:5)

Hitler was democratically elected to power in 1933. While his brown-shirted stormtroopers initially bullied all opposition, he turned instead to deceiving every section of society. He 'beguiled the working masses with the cry that the National Socialists were truly 'socialists' and against the money barons' while simultaneously having secret meetings with 'the influential industrial magnates', assuring them 'he was an enemy of state economy'. He lionised the military, promising them they would be the liberators of 'the enslaved German nation we have today. Germany is bound hand and foot by the peace treaties',[131] and exalted the millions of small farmers as

---

131 William Shirer, *The Rise and Fall of the Third Reich*, New York; Simon & Schuster, 1960, pp. 142-143.

'the fount of biological health and future national greatness'.[132] He had the Christian hope, *Gott Mit Uns* (God With Us), on every soldier's belt buckle while actually planning to eradicate all trace of Christianity from Germany:

> In Hitler's eyes Christianity was a religion fit only for slaves, a rebellion against the natural law of selection by struggle and the survival of the fittest. He declared, "Taken to its logical extreme, Christianity would mean the systematic cultivation of human failure... The evil that is gnawing at our vitals is our priests, of both creeds [Catholic and Protestant]. I can't at present give them the answer they've been asking for but... it's all written down in my big book. The time will come when I'll settle my account with them... They'll hear from me all right. I shan't let myself be hampered by judicial samples".[133]

Paul therefore warns us to watch leaders who claim, like Hitler, to be Christian by examining how they speak and what they want in return:

> For such men are slaves, not of our Lord Christ but of their own appetites; and by their smooth and flattering speech they deceive the hearts of the unsuspecting (Rom 16:18)

Paul scrupulously avoided behaving like this himself:

> For we never came with flattering speech, as you know, nor with a pretext for greed – God is witness (1 Thess 2:5)

Our best defence, however, is not our self-controlled vigilance because that will always lapse. Our best defence against any lie will always be the truth. We all need to receive and to maintain, in Paul's memorable phrase, 'the love of the truth so as to be saved' (2 Thess 2:10). God will give us this love if we will but ask Him for it.

---

132 Michael Burleigh, *The Third Reich: A New History*, London; Pan Mcmillan Ltd, 2001, p. 108.
133 Alan Bullock, *Hitler: A Study in Tyranny*, Harmondsworth, U.K.; Penguin Books, 1962, p. 389.

The Truth We Need to Love

In this situation, there are four issues of truth that are essential for us all to identify and acknowledge regarding:

(i) our own spiritual state (1 John 1:8)

(ii) God's antidote in the person of Jesus (John 14:6)

(iii) His message (John 17:17) and

(iv) the Holy Spirit (1 John 5:6).

Any political or religious leader, therefore, who actively promotes alternatives to any of these four, should never be followed. Let us examine each more closely.

(i) Our own spiritual state or condition

In the introduction to his autobiography which was subtitled, *The Story of My Experiments with Truth*, the remarkable Mahatma Gandhi wrote:

> In judging myself, I shall try to be as harsh as truth... For it is an unbroken torture to me that I am still so far from Him Who, as I fully know, governs every breath of my life, and Whose offspring I am. I know that it is the evil passions within that keep me so far from Him, and yet I cannot get away from them.[134]

Each of us likewise needs to acknowledge our state, as the Scriptures teach, 'that sin dwells in me, ...that evil is present in me, the one who wants to do good' (Rom 7:20-21). John gives us strong warning but, unlike Gandhi, he also reveals the way out:

> 8. If we say we have no sin, we are deceiving ourselves, and the truth is not in us.
> 9. If we confess our sins, He is faithful and righteous to forgive us our sins and to cleanse us from all unrighteousness.

---

134 M.K. Gandhi, *An Autobiography (or The Story of My Experiments with Truth)*, Harmondsworth, U.K.; Penguin Books, 1983, p. 17.

10. If we say we have not sinned, we make Him a liar, and His
word is not in us (1 John 1:8-10)

This is where we are most vulnerable. If we flatter ourselves by denying our own sinfulness, we will not understand the message of Christ and the antichrist messages will then appeal to us.

Paul summarised what these would be:

3. But I am afraid, lest as the serpent deceived Eve by his craftiness, your minds should be led astray from the simplicity and purity of devotion to Christ.
4. For if one comes and preaches *another Jesus* whom we have not preached, or you receive *a different spirit* which you have not received, or *a different gospel* which you have not accepted, you bear this beautifully (2 Cor 11:3-4, emphasis added)

So Jesus Himself, the Holy Spirit and the gospel are always being counterfeited or supplanted by 'another Jesus', 'a different spirit' and 'a different gospel'. Do we recognise and understand the differences?

(ii) 'Another Jesus'

Muhammad, for example, presents his followers with a Jesus who is a great prophet but explicitly not divine:

No son did Allah beget, nor is there any god along with Him (Surah 23:91)

Say not: "Three [trinity]!" Cease! [It is] better for you for Allah is [the only] One God; glory be to Him [far exalted is He] above having a son. (Surah 4:171) [135]

Hitler also presented his followers with another Jesus, an antisemitic failure of a war-lord. To his audience in Munich on April 12, 1922, he explained:

"My feeling as a Christian points me to my Lord and

---

135 Mark A. Gabriel, *Jesus and Muhammad*, Lake Mary, Florida; Charisma House, 2004, p. 101.

Savior as a fighter. It points me to the man who once in loneliness, surrounded only by a few followers, recognized these Jews for what they were and summoned men to fight against them and who – God's truth! – was greatest not as a sufferer but as a fighter. In boundless love as a Christian and as a man I read through the passage which tells us how the Lord at last rose in His might and seized the scourge to drive out of the Temple the brood of vipers and adders. How terrific was his fight against the Jewish poison. Today, after two thousand years, with deepest emotion I recognize more profoundly than ever before the fact that it was for this that He had to shed his blood upon the Cross..." [136]

Today, even within the church, some 'progressive', 'radical' theologians are trying to separate the 'historical Jesus' from the 'Biblical Jesus', denying His deity. American Bishop John Shelby Spong, for example, wants to liberate 'my Christ' from 'a killing literalism',[137] arguing that Jesus was not born of a virgin, did not do miracles, was actually marrying Mary Magdalene at the wedding in Cana and did not rise from the dead. Similarly, New Zealand's Emeritus Professor of Religious Studies, Sir Lloyd Geering O.N.Z., Australia's Barbara Thiery, the Jesus Seminar [138] and the Sea of Faith Network.[139] They seem quite happy to ignore John's warning:

> 8. Watch yourselves, that you do not lose what we have accomplished, but that you may receive a full reward.
> 9. Anyone who goes too far and does not abide in the teaching of Christ, does not have God; the one who abides in the teaching, he has both the Father and the Son (2 John 1:8-9)

---

136 Norman H. Baynes, ed., *The Speeches of Adolf Hitler: April 1922-August 1939*, Vol. 1, New York; Oxford University Press, 1942, pp. 19-20. See also www.hitler.org/speeches/04-12-22.html, 14 Dec, 2009.
137 *Born of a Woman: A Bishop Rethinks the Birth of Jesus*, San Francisco; Harper, 1992, p. 12.
138 http://virtualreligion.net/forum/ 9 Nov, 2011.
139 www.sofn.org.uk, 9 Nov, 2011.

Going 'too far' in this issue means leaving behind God Himself. For any wanting a thorough examination and debunking of these theologians on their own grounds from a scholarly, historical perspective, see N.T. Wright's books.[140]

Despite any theologian's claims to superior education or understanding, the only Jesus worth knowing is described in detail in the New Testament and confirmed in our own hearts by the Holy Spirit. In Paul's words, what we all need is:

> ...a true knowledge of God's mystery, that is Christ Himself, in whom are hidden all the treasures of wisdom and knowledge...
> I say this so that no one will delude you with persuasive argument...
> For in Him all the fulness of Deity dwells in bodily form...
> (Col 2:2-4, 9)

(iii) 'A different spirit'

Jesus said:

> When He, the Spirit of truth, comes, He will guide you into all the truth...
> He will glorify Me; for He will take of Mine, and shall disclose it to you (John 16:13-14)

Therefore, any spirit or any spiritual experience that does not guide us into the truth and glorify Jesus is to be rejected. The only spirit to whom we are allowed to submit is the Holy Spirit and, here is the essential issue, *we can only receive the Holy Spirit by calling on the risen Jesus Christ.* As Peter explained to the thousands of Jewish spectators on the Day of Pentecost:

> 32. "This Jesus God raised up again, to which we are all witnesses.
> 33. "Therefore having been exalted to the right hand of God, and having received from the Father the promise of the Holy

---

140 *Who Was Jesus?* London; BPC Paperbacks Ltd, 1992. Also, with Marcus Borg, *The Meaning of Jesus (Two Visions)*, New York; Harper Collins, 1999.

Spirit, He has poured forth this which you both see and hear"
(Acts 2:32-33)

This is also why Paul says we must trust that God has raised Him from the dead (Rom 10:9), not to fulfill a religious creed but so that we can personally receive the promised Holy Spirit from Him. As Solomon wryly noted:

A sated man loathes honey,
But to a famished man any bitter thing is sweet. (Prov 27:7)

If we are truly satisfied with the Holy Spirit, we will readily avoid the beast's counterfeit fire.

(iv) 'A different gospel'

It is easy today to overlook the original meaning of the word 'gospel' or 'good news' but, in the light of this study, it had a chilling secular beginning. The 'good news', as inscribed in 9 B.C. in Priene, a city in the kingdom of Pergamum, was announcing 'the birthday of the god Augustus' as 'the beginning of the good tidings for the world through him'[141]:

> The Greek noun (*euangelion*, neuter singular) is rarely found in the sense of "good tidings" outside of early Christian literature… In the plural, it means a sacrifice for good tidings… In the sense of "good news", the singular appears for the first time outside of Christian literature in a papyrus letter from an Egyptian official of the 3rd Century A.D. in connection with the ascension of the emperor Julius Verus Maximus. The plural is found in this sense, however, in the Priene calendar inscription of about 9 B.C. which speaks of the birth of the emperor Augustus as "the beginning of good tidings" for the world.[142]

The inscription goes on:

---

141   http://craigaevans.com/Priene%20art.pdf, 13 Feb, 2012.
142   Millar Burrow, *The Origin of the Term "Gospel"*, Yale University; *Journal of Biblical Literature*, Vol. 44, No. 1/2 (1925), pp. 21-33. www.jstor.org/pss/3260047, 13 Feb, 2012.

> Since providence, which has ordered all things and is
> deeply interested in our life, has set in most perfect order
> by giving us Augustus, whom she filled with virtue that he
> might benefit humankind, sending him as a savior, both
> for us and for our descendants, that he might end war and
> arrange all things…[143]

The Romans had a gospel – their good news was that their emperors were gods to be worshipped, sent by 'providence' to save the empire's citizens from wars and chaos.

The opening verse of the Gospel of Mark was therefore a radical and open challenge to emperor-worship, being first published in Rome:[144]

> The beginning of the gospel of Jesus Christ, the Son of God
> (Mark 1:1)

Mark recorded that Jesus' had a very different gospel. The good news is that He came to save us from our sins (Matt 1:21); that every one of us can know God our Creator, if only we will turn to and trust Him (Mark 1:15, Luke 16:16); that He will Himself help us to turn away from evil and chaos (Acts 3:26). Paul spelled out this gospel in detail:

> 1. Now I make known to you, brethren, the gospel which I
> preached to you, which also you received, in which also you
> stand,
> 2. by which also you are saved, if you hold fast the word which I
> preached to you, unless you believed in vain.
> 3. For I delivered to you as of first importance what I also
> received, that Christ died for our sins according to the Scriptures,
> 4. and that He was buried, and that He was raised on the third
> day according to the Scriptures (1 Cor 15:1-4)

Writing to the Romans, he explained further:

> For I am not ashamed of the gospel, for it is the power of God for

---

143   www.textexcavation.com/augustus.html, 13 Feb, 2012.
144   F.F. Bruce, *The New Testament Documents: Are They Reliable*, 6th edition, Downers Grove, Illinois; IVP Academic, 2003, p. 42.

> salvation to everyone who believes, to the Jew first and also to
> the Greek...
> We are preaching that if you confess with your mouth Jesus as
> Lord, and believe in your heart that God raised Him from the
> dead, you will be saved (Rom 1:16 and 10:8-9)

The choice facing every Roman citizen was therefore which gospel would they accept – that of the emperor-worshippers or that of the Jesus-worshippers?

Finally, of course, the Roman Empire and its emperors came to an end. Tragically, their gospel did not. As we will see next, in the last one hundred years this same message was accepted by most of the citizens of Germany, Italy, the USSR, Italy, Japan, China, the Middle East and South East Asia.

Lastly, within our churches, we see a variety of different gospels. Bishop John Shelby Spong claims in his book, *Liberating the Gospels*, that he is also 'freeing Jesus from 2,000 years of misunderstanding'.[145] He writes passionately of his 'ultimate commitment to Jesus the Christ as my Lord'[146] but in *Why Christianity Must Change or Die*, he spells out what that means for the Gospels of Matthew, Mark, Luke and John:

> But let it be clearly stated, the Gospels are not in any
> literal sense holy, they are not accurate, and they are not to
> be confused with reality...[147]
>
> So it needs to be said clearly that the God presence of
> this Jesus will lead us ultimately beyond every religious
> definition. Indeed, it will lead us beyond Jesus himself.
> That becomes essential to human development whenever
> our idolatrous convictions identify the Messenger of

---

145 *Liberating the Gospels: Reading the Bible with Jewish Eyes*, San Francisco; HarperCollins, 1996, front cover. He also wrote *Rescuing the Bible from Fundamentalism (A Bishop Rethinks the Meaning of Scripture)*, San Francisco, Harper, 1992.

146 Ibid., Preface, pp. xii-xiii.

147 John Spong, *Why Christianity Must Change or Die: A Bishop Speaks to Believers in Exile*, New York; HarperOne, 1999, p. 108.

                    Slouching Towards Bethlehem

God with God. So the Ground of Being will finally be worshipped apart from any system of religious thought.[148]

So Bishop Spong's liberating of the gospels is to simply deny their holiness, accuracy and reality. He urges us to leave Jesus behind and to follow him instead, because he is freeing, rescuing and liberating Jesus, the Bible, the Gospels, Christianity and us all.

This is obviously the spirit of antichrist speaking through him, with 'another gospel' to the Scriptures' simple message: only God in Christ can help us with our issues with sin, personally forgive us and change our hearts.

In summary, we must always hold fast to the truth about our personal spiritual state, Jesus as Messiah, His message as preserved in the Scriptures, and our need of Him and everything He does by the Holy Spirit.

Prepared Beforehand

The worship of Hitler in Germany was no sudden aberration – the people had been prepared by their culture for centuries. As we saw in our study of Revelation 12, *Dancing in the Dragon's Jaws*, William L. Shirer concluded that the behaviour of most German Protestants in the first Nazi years was the natural outworking of Martin Luther's passionate antisemitism and his advocacy of absolute obedience to political authority. Shirer, himself a Protestant, further writes:

> There is not space in this book to recount adequately
> the immense influence that Martin Luther, the Saxon
> peasant who became an Augustinian monk and launched
> the German Reformation, had on the Germans and their
> subsequent history. But it may be said, in passing, that
> this towering but erratic genius, this savage anti-Semite
> and hater of Rome, who combined in his tempestuous
> character… the coarseness, the boisterousness, the

---

148   Ibid., p. 224.

fanaticism, the intolerance, the violence, but also the
honesty, the simplicity, the self-scrutiny, the passion
for learning and for music and for poetry and for
righteousness in the eyes of God – left a mark on the life
of the Germans, for both good and bad, more indelible,
more fateful, than was wrought by any other single
individual before or since.

Through his sermons and his magnificent translation of
the Bible, Luther created the modern German language,
aroused in the people not only a new Protestant vision of
Christianity but a fervent German nationalism and taught
them, at least in religion, the supremacy of the individual
conscience. But tragically for them, Luther's siding with
the princes in the peasants' uprisings, which he had largely
inspired, and his passion for political autocracy ensured a
mindless and provincial political absolutism... [149]

In July 1525, in his infamous *Open Letter Concerning the Hard
Book Against the Peasants*, Luther had written against what he
called the 'mad dogs':

Let everyone who can smite, slay and stab secretly or
openly, remembering that nothing can be more poisonous,
hurtful or devilish than a rebel... A rebel is not worth
answering with arguments for he does not accept them.
The answer for such a mouth is a fist that brings blood
from the nose... their ears must be unbuttoned with
bullets until their heads jump off their shoulders...
He who will not hear God's word when it is spoken in
kindness must listen to the headsman when he comes with
the axe. [150]

Shirer comments:

Here, as in his utterances about the Jews, Luther employed
a coarseness and brutality of language unequalled in

---

149   *The Rise and Fall of The Third Reich*, p. 91.
150   Martin Luther, *Works* IV, p. 261.

          Slouching Towards Bethlehem

German history until the Nazi time.[151]

Although for a brief time after this the German peasants recovered some liberties, by 1648 the princes were confirmed again as absolute rulers of their numerous domains and serfdom was reimposed. Shirer summarises:

> Germany never recovered from this setback. Acceptance of autocracy, of blind obedience to the petty tyrants who ruled as princes, became ingrained in the German mind…[152]

He directly attributes to Luther's influence…:

> …the ease with which German Protestantism became the instrument of royal and princely absolutism from the sixteenth century until the kings and princes were overthrown in 1918. The hereditary monarchs and petty rulers became the supreme bishops of the Protestant Church in their lands… In no country with the exception of Czarist Russia did the clergy become by tradition so completely servile to the political authority of the State.[153]

'For The Good of the People'

In 1990, BBC documentary-maker Laurence Rees asked a former member of the Nazi party, Wilfred von Oven, for his overall impression of the Third Reich. Rees expected that, with the benefit of fifty years' hindsight…:

> …this intelligent and charming man [would refer] to the horrible crimes of the regime – crimes he freely admitted had occurred – and the damage Nazism had wreaked upon the world. "Well", he finally said, "if I was asked to sum up my experience of the Third Reich in one word, that word would be – Paradise".
> "Paradise"? That didn't coincide with anything I had read

---

151 *The Rise and Fall of The Third Reich*, p. 236.
152 Ibid., p. 92.
153 Ibid., p. 236.

in my history books. Nor did it square with the elegant, sophisticated man who sat in front of me, who did not, come to that, look or talk as I had imagined a former Nazi should. But "Paradise"? How was it possible he could say such a thing? How could any intelligent person think of the Third Reich and its atrocities in such a way?[154]

When Hitler gained control in 1933, he was not only welcomed for unifying the nation but also for the order he brought, like the Roman emperors' Pax Romana, to a Germany chaotic and demoralised after World War I. He stopped the ruinous rampant inflation of the mark while his famous autobahns so impressed Dwight D. Eisenhower that Eisenhower introduced this Government-funded interstate highway concept to the USA, thus hugely impacting much of today's Western culture.[155]

It was not only the Germans who saw a clear benefit in concentrating power in the hands of an individual. Earlier, Fascist leader Benito Mussolini had become famous for making Italy's trains run on time, even though he actually did not.[156] During World War II, as in any grave crisis, even the most democratic of nations passed laws granting extraordinary temporary powers to their leaders. It is at these times that any nation becomes especially vulnerable to John's second beast, as it entices people of every race, nationality, locality and era to seek out and worship a personification or embodiment of their particular kingdom or empire to save or deliver them:

> 14. And he [the second beast] deceives those who dwell on the earth…, telling those who dwell in the earth to make an image

---

154 *Auschwitz: The Nazis and the Final Solution*, London; BBC Books, 2005, p. 7.

155 Eric Schlosser's book *Fast Food Nation: The Dark Side of The All-American Meal* describes the astonishing flow-on effect from highways to food that could be eaten while driving, to today's obesity epidemic. Published by Houghton Mifflin Harcourt in Boston, 2001.

156 www.snopes.com/history/govern/trains.asp, 30 Mar, 2010.

                                    Slouching Towards Bethlehem

> to the [first] beast…
> 15. And there was given to him to give breath to the image of
> the beast, that the image of the beast might even speak and
> cause as many as do not worship the image of the beast to be
> killed (Rev 13)

Notice in v. 15, if enticement fails, the living image will also use deadly coercion to enforce the worship.

In the 1st Century A.D., Pliny Secundus wrote that he was making Christians bow down to the statue of Trajan and to 'curse Christ, which a genuine Christian cannot be induced to do'.[157] Those who would not, he executed but, as we saw earlier, these were in such large numbers, women and children included, that he wanted further clarification of his orders.

Looking back, we may today want to attribute Pliny's behaviour to a dim-witted, superstitious age. However, the second beast's deception is such that there has been more emperor-worship in our times than at any other time in history. And consequent fatalities. In 1972 it was estimated that over 110 million people had been wrongly put to death in the 20th Century.[158] However, in 2008 and following new disclosures from changing regimes in Russia and China, this figure was recalculated by Rudolph Rummel, Professor Emeritus of Political Science, University of Hawaii, to a truly horrifying 262,000,000.[159] Rummel has coined the term 'democide' to describe this phenomenon of 'death by government' and to help us gain perspective, he points out that 'democide murdered six times more people than died in combat in all the foreign and internal wars of the century' (which he estimates at 38,500,000).[160]

---

157 *Epistles* X.96.
158 Gil Elliot, *Twentieth Century Book of the Dead*, London; Allen Lane Penguin Press, 1972.
159 *Statistics of Democide: Genocide and Mass Murder Since 1900*, www.hawaii.edu/powerkills/NOTE5.HTM, 5 Jun, 2008.
160 www.hawaii.edu/powerkills/20TH.HTM, 6 Jun, 2008.

From Russia, With Love…

Or more precisely, from Georgia, when Joseph Stalin died, four million attended his funeral in Red Square.[161] In 2008, he was voted Russia's third most popular historical figure in a nationwide poll.[162]

Despite numerous official attempts since 1956 to discredit him, on 21st December, 2010, the 131st anniversary of Stalin's birth, Gennady Zyuganov, First Secretary of the Communist Party and presidential candidate, called for the 're-Stalinisation' of Russian society:

> Stalin's era was the most productive, victorious and unique in the history of our state.[163]

So, let us consider his era.

In the aftermath of the Russian Revolution of 1917, when a popular uprising overthrew the Tsar, the Bolsheviks usurped it and by 1929, Josef Stalin had become the new tyrant of the USSR. He was so determinedly in sole charge that on the slightest suspicion he killed not only rivals among his enemies but also among his closest allies and friends. During the period known as the Great Terror (1937-1939), Stalin's whims were life or death to everyone around him. Embracing the state religion of atheism, he was antisemitic and anti-Christian as well as increasingly paranoid. As Alexander Solzhenitsyn noted, 'Mistrust was his world-view'.

To punish Ukraine for resisting his collectivisation plans, Stalin exported so much grain from this former 'breadbasket of Europe' between 1932 and 1933 that an estimated 7,000,000 Ukrainians died of starvation. In doing so, *he was 'causing as*

---

161   http://azeri.org/Azeri/az_latin/latin_articles/latin_text/latin_73/eng_73/73_stalin_cult.html, 11 Feb, 2011.

162   http://www.news.com.au/breaking-news/communists-lay-carnations-for-stalin/story-e6frfkuo-1225974765203, 11 Feb, 2011.

163   http://www.msnbc.msn.com/id/40766930/ns/world_news-europe/, 11 Feb, 2011.

many as do not worship the image of the beast to be killed'. He deported another 10,000,000 to exile in Siberia or to become 'citizens' of the infamous Gulag Archipelago[164] where it is estimated some 39,000,000 of many nationalities died due to 'lethal forced labour or in transit'.[165] Overall, it has now been estimated that of the 61,911,000 people killed by the USSR between 1917 and 1987, some 43,000,000 were due to Stalin alone.[166] He was planning to annihilate or deport between two and four million Jews, some of whom he had accused of 'medical assassinations' in the so-called Doctor's Plot, when he died in 1953.[167]

He is most revered for defeating Hitler's invasion after Hitler broke their peace treaty, a deal which Stalin had happily described as "cemented with [Poland's] blood", despite his losing 25 million civilians and soldiers,[168] many of whom, like Solzhenitsyn, he had neglected to even arm. At war's end, when 2,500,000 Russian prisoners of war were repatriated, Stalin charged them with 'high treason' for surrendering. Some 300,000 were executed by the NKVD[169] and the rest were sent to the gulags for between ten and twenty five years so that few survived.[170]

---

164   The name was coined by Solzhenitsyn from GULag, the Russian acronym for the prison camps which he described as a vast chain of islands with their own language and culture.
165   www.historyplace.com/worldhistory/genocide/stalin.htm, 5 Jun, 2008.
166   Rummel, *Lethal Politics: Soviet Genocide And Mass Murder Since 1917*, published on www.hawaii.edu/powerkills/NOTE4.HTM, 5 Jun, 2008.
167   Alexander Rashin, *Why Didn't Stalin Kill All the Jews?* New York; Liberty Publishing House, 2003.
168   www.bbc.co.uk/history/worldwars/wwtwo/hitler_russia_invasion_01.shtml, 11 Feb, 2011.
169   *Narodnyy Komissariat Vnutrennikh Del,* i.e. The People's Commissariat for Internal Affairs.
170   Mark Elliott, *Pawns of Yalta: Soviet Refugees and America's Role in Their Repatriation,* University of Illinois Press, 1982, quoted on www.vho.org/GB/Journals/JHR/5/1/Lutton84-94.html, 11 Feb, 2011.

In his defence, German Jewish writer, Lion Feuchtwanger, wrote in his *Moscow 1937 (Report on a Journey for my Friends)*:

> It is manifestly irksome to Stalin to be worshipped as he is, and from time to time he makes fun of it. Of all the men I know who have power, Stalin is the most unpretentious. I spoke frankly to him about the vulgar and excessive cult made of him, and he replied with equal candour. He thinks it is possible even that 'wreckers' [171] may be behind it in an attempt to discredit him.[172]

Joseph Stalin may have mocked his worshippers but he never allowed them to disobey or not serve him.

Let us also be clear that no-one believed he was God Almighty, the Creator of all. His daughter, Svetlana Alliluyeva, described the grief of the servants at the dacha where he died:

> Men, women, everyone, started crying all over again… No one was making a show of loyalty or grief. All of them had known one another for years… No one in this room looked on him as a god or a superman, a genius or a demon. They loved and respected him for the most ordinary human qualities, those qualities of which servants are the best judges of all.[173]

He was worshipped as the Roman emperors were before him, as the living image of the first beast, with predictable, inevitable results.

Aleksandr Yakovlev puts the figure at 1.8 million, as reported by Interfax News Agency, Moscow; BBC Monitoring Service, U.K., 5 Mar, 2003.

171 Stalin's catch-phrase for saboteurs and spies.

172 L. Feuchtwanger, Moscow 1937, quoted http://harikumar. brinkster.net/paper/march2003/cultindividual.html, 27 Oct, 2008.

173 Ibid., *20 Letters to a Friend*, 27 Oct, 2008.

10

The Bitter Fruit
The Beasts' Killing Fields

We could examine the appalling consequences of emperor-worship throughout the last two thousand years. For example, in 8th Century China, after the An Lushan rebellion against the Tang Empire, some 36 million people disappeared from census figures between 753 and 764 A.D.[174] In the 12th and 13th Centuries, 30 million 'Persian, Arab, Hindu, Russian, Chinese and European' men, women and children were put to death for resisting the Mongol Khans whose empire was larger than Alexander's.[175] In the 14th Century, Tamerlane (Timur the Lame) killed between 15 and 20 million in Central Asia and northern India[176] while in China, the Ming overthrow of the Yuan Dynasty led to 30 million perishing.[177] In 17th Century China, the Manchu emperors killed 25 million or 17% of China's population.[178] Two centuries later, they put down the Taiping Rebellion at a cost of another 20-30 million deaths.[179] All of these emperors fulfilled Revelation 13:15.

The problem is that we might think these were historical aberrations, somehow 'over there' and irrelevant to us today. Let us therefore consider the last one hundred years and put

---

174 http://necrometrics.com/pre1700a.htm#AnLushan, 10 Nov, 2011. 'Atrocitologist' Matthew White notes that this may be partially due to undercounting in 764 A.D.

175 Rummel, www.hawaii.edu/powerkills/DBG.CHAP3.HTM, 4 Jul, 2011.

176 http://necrometrics.com/pre1700a.htm#India1366, 4 Jul, 2011.

177 *The Cambridge History of China: Alien Regimes and Border States*, 907-1368, 1994, p. 622. Quoted by Matthew White, http://necrometrics.com/pre1700a.htm#Yuan, 10 Nov, 2011.

178 http://necrometrics.com/pre1700a.htm#India1366, 4 Jul, 2011.

179 http://public.wsu.edu/~dee/CHING/TAIPING.HTM, 4 Jul, 2011.

20th Century emperors Hirohito, Hitler, and Stalin in context.

As mentioned earlier, Hirohito died as recently as January 7th, 1989 – but not before 13,283,000 Chinese, 2,015,000 of other nationalities and some 2,000,000 Japanese had died for his empire.[180] There was little relief for the Chinese, however, where the phenomenon only gained ground, not now centred in Hirohito but in the victorious Mao Zedong. As the Communist Party handed over more and more control to their 'Great Helmsman', between 1958 and 1962, 43,000,000 died of starvation from the famine caused by Mao's exporting grain to fund his nuclear ambitions. Another 2 or 3 million were summarily executed for disobedience.[181]

In 1966, fearful of his revolution being tainted by Stalin's, Mao launched his Cultural Revolution in which another three million were killed by his youthful Red Guards as they sought to purge the nation of counter-revolutionaries who were often guilty only of being older or educated. In China alone, one fifth of the earth's population at that time submitted even their thought lives to Mao. Instead of 'the mind of Christ' (1 Cor 2:16), his 'little red book', *The Thoughts of Chairman Mao*, became the Chinese standard of all righteous thought. Until he died in 1976, Mao was China's god incarnate, 'causing as many as do not worship the image of the beast to be killed' and jealously guarding his claim to be the only image to be worshipped.

Between 1949 and 1987, Rummel concluded in 2008, the Communist Chinese regime brought about a staggering 76,702,000 deaths and *all in peacetime*.[182] Appallingly, the

---

180 Rummel, www.hawaii.edu/powerkills/DBG.TAB6.2.GIF, 31 May, 2009.

181 Frank Dikötter, *Mao's Great Famine: The History of China's Most Devastating Catastrophe, 1958-1962*, New York; Bloomsbury and Walker Press, 2010. Also Jung Chang and Jon Halliday, *Mao: The Unknown Story*, London; Jonathan Cape, 2005, pp. 456-457.

182 Rummel, www.hawaii.edu/powerkills/NOTE5.HTM, 22 Dec, 2010.

                                    Slouching Towards Bethlehem

latest research published by Frank Dikötter in 2010 indicates this may rise by another seven million.[183]

During the same period, North Korea's 'Great Leader' Kim Il Sung also created a political personality cult, likewise killing his opponents while his agricultural policies also led to mass starvation and an estimated death toll of 1.6 million.[184] His 'new and unique system of revolutionary thought, theory, and methodology that reflects the needs arising from an era of self-reliance' he called *Juche* (or 'Kimism'). It was based on his revelation that 'Man is the master of all things, and must decide everything for himself' but, of course, only under the 'proper guidance of a revolutionary commandant'.[185] When he died in 1994, the cult continued around his son Kim Jong-il, the 'Dear Leader', whose regime admitted to 250,000 dying over the next four years due to a famine caused by centralised planning. However, Kim Jong-il's mentor, Hwang Jang-Yop, who defected in 1997, estimated the real death toll at 2.5 million.[186] When Kim Jong-il died in December 2011, his son Kim Jong-un pledged to continue these policies, so we need to pray for an end to North Korea's misery.

Cambodia fared no better. Between 1975 and 1979, 'Brother Number One' Pol Pot led his nation to the notorious 'killing fields'. The Cambodian Genocide Program at Yale University observes that:

> The Cambodian genocide, in which at least 1.7 million people (21% of the entire population) lost their lives, stands as one of the worst human tragedies of the modern era. In Cambodia, as in Nazi Germany, East Timor,

---

183   Rummel established 38 million dead between 1958-1962; Dikötter documents 45 million.

184   Rummel, www.hawaii.edu/powerkills/SOD.CHAP10.HTM, 28 Dec, 2011.

185   http://world.kbs.co.kr/english/event/nkorea_nuclear/general_04b.htm, 17 Dec, 2007.

186   David Lee, www.nkmissions.com/10part_report/Thesis/famine.shtml, 28 Dec, 2011.

Guatemala, Yugoslavia, and Rwanda, extremist politics conspired with a diabolic disregard for human life to produce repression, misery, and murder on a massive scale. The Cambodian genocide is unique in that for many years, the crimes of the Khmer Rouge remained largely undocumented.[187]

Note that this proudly secular institution acknowledges this 'disregard for human life' to be 'diabolic' or demonic. While not intending us to take this description literally, they grope for words to describe the complete absence of human compassion.

This horrendous episode of mass murder only ended because the Vietnamese army invaded in 1979. Pol Pot was never brought to justice and he died on 15th April, 1998. Famous survivor, Dith Pran, whose story *The Killing Fields* became the Academy Award-winning movie of 1984, describes the historical connection: 'everyone had to pledge total allegiance to Angka, the Khmer Rouge government'.[188] The movement's name alludes to the former glory of the Khmer empire. The emperors of Angkor had ruled over much of the Southeast Asian mainland until the early 15th Century, having been founded by Jayavarman II (reigned 802-850 A.D.) around the cult of the god-king. Pol Pot was simply the new Khmer god-king.

Consider Albania under 'Supreme Comrade' Enver Hoxha's rule (1943-85). Proclaiming the first completely atheistic nation on earth, Hoxha achieved this distinction by executing all Muslim and Christian leaders. Or consider Romania, where from 1971 to 1989 Nicolae (self-proclaimed 'Genius of the Carpathians') and Elena ('Mother of the Nation') Ceausescu developed their personality cult while the people starved.

---

187   www.yale.edu/cgp, 30 Apr, 2007.
188   www.dithpran.org/killingfields.htm, 30 Apr, 2007.

How They Saw It

In Italy, Benito Mussolini discarded his original republican ideals to form a fascist totalitarian state in 1926. Proclaiming himself *Il Duce*, the Leader, Mussolini initially impressed even Germany's Adolf Hitler but was executed by Italian partisans in 1945. A devout atheist and admirer of Nietzsche's philosophy, he began by redefining the state as the ultimate worth, writing:

> The foundation of Fascism is the conception of the State, its character, its duty and its aim. Fascism conceives of the State as an absolute, in comparison with which all individuals or groups are relative, only to be conceived of in their relation to the State.[189]

Having deified the State, John's first beast, Mussolini even saw it as a living being:

> The conception of the Liberal State [i.e. democracy] is not that of a directing force, guiding the play and development, both material and spiritual, of a collective body, but merely a force limited to the function of recording results [i.e. elections]: on the other hand, the Fascist State is itself conscious and has itself a will and a personality – thus it may be called the "ethic" State… For Fascism, the growth of empire, that is to say the expansion of the nation, is an essential manifestation of vitality.[190]

Dismissing democracy as merely 'recording results', he embraced 'a directing force, guiding the play and development, both material and spiritual' which is 'conscious and has itself a will and a personality'. Mussolini's credo, as quoted in the Foreword, summarises John's second beast's raison d'etre:

> Tutto nello Stato, niente al di fuori dello Stato, nulla contro lo Stato (Everything in the State, nothing outside the State, nothing against the State)

---

189 *The Italian Encyclopedia*, 1932; www.fordham.edu/halsall/mod/mussolini-fascism.html, 4 Feb, 2010.
190 Ibid.

And he was setting up himself as the visible image of the invisible State.

Meanwhile, Adolf Hitler quickly outgrew his admiration of *Il Duce*, having received revelations of his own. Democratically elected in 1933, he rose up in a time of national foment and economic disaster in Germany by appealing to baser instincts, fears and insecurities. In just five years, he had welded the German people, discouraged and disillusioned by the loss and reparations of World War I, into a psychological and technological unit that could readily again challenge the whole of Europe to war. By December, 1938, at the opening of his magnificent Chancellery, he clearly saw himself as the *embodiment of their empire*:

> I stand here as representative of the German people. And whenever I receive anyone in the Chancellery, it is not the private individual Adolf Hitler who receives him, but the Fuehrer [Leader] of the German nation – and therefore it is not I who receive him, but *Germany through me*.[191]

Joseph Stalin had thought similarly in December 1929 when he thanked the Russian people for some birthday congratulations in plainly Biblical terms, seeing himself as the image of their ideology:

> I regard your greetings as addressed to the great Party of the working class which bore me and reared in its own *image and likeness*.[192]

This apparent denial of receiving personal glory is easily mistaken for humility.[193] Adolf Hitler also actively sought to

---

191 *Inside the Third Reich*, p. 165, emphasis added.

192 *J. V. Stalin: Works*, Volume 12, cited in http://harikumar.brinkster. net/paper/march2003/cultindividual.html, 27 Oct, 2008. Emphasis added.

193 For example, Bill Bland's *The Cult of the Individual (1934-1952)* argues that Stalin was genuinely humble and accuses his enemies of creating the personality cult around him. Quoted on http://harikumar. brinkster.net/paper/march2003/cultindividual.html, 27 Oct, 2008.

                    Slouching Towards Bethlehem

perpetuate this public illusion. Choosing resplendent uniforms for his entourage, he told Speer of his private reasons:

> He loved such pomp; that his own dress was modest was a matter of careful strategy: "My surroundings must look magnificent. Then my simplicity makes a striking effect".[194]

However, in 1944, after suffering three military catastrophes, Hitler discarded public modesty in his speeches:

> I often feel that we will have to undergo all the trials the devil and hell can devise before we achieve Final Victory… I may be no pious churchgoer, but deep within me I am nevertheless a devout man. That is to say, I believe that he who fights valiantly obeying the laws which a god has established and who never capitulates but instead gathers his forces time after time and always pushes forward – such a man will not be abandoned by the Lawgiver. Rather, he will ultimately receive the blessing of Providence. And that blessing has been imparted to *all great spirits in history.*[195]

Speer's conclusion:

> In a sense he was worshipping himself. He was forever holding up to himself a mirror in which he saw not only himself but also the confirmation of his mission by divine Providence. His religion was based on the "lucky break" which must necessarily come his way…If there was any fundamental insanity in Hitler, it was this unshakable belief in his lucky star. *He was by nature a religious man, but his capacity for belief had been perverted into belief in himself.*[196]

In terms of 'causing as many as do not worship the image of the beast to be killed', Hitler seems almost to have been in a perverse competition with Stalin to be the worst genocidal

---

194 *Inside the Third Reich*, p.159.
195 Ibid., p. 693, emphasis added.
196 Ibid., p. 459, emphasis added.

dictator of all time. Besides his most obvious victims of the Holocaust's six million Jews, the Soviet Union lost twenty and a half million and the other nations' seven million in resisting Hitler. Seven million German soldiers and citizens also died trying to extend his empire. Appallingly, Stalin and Hitler were later eclipsed by Mao.

Useful Idiots

Understanding this demonic seduction to emperor-worship helps explain the phenomenon of what Lenin and Stalin were said to have called their 'useful idiots':[197] prominent aristocrats, writers, intellectuals, philosophers and artists who would willingly justify the regime's murderous activities. In a BBC radio documentary of this name broadcast in July 2010,[198] Doris Lessing, winner of the Nobel Prize for Literature in 2007, admitted her role as such, along with George Bernard Shaw, H.G. Wells, Jean-Paul Sartre, André Malraux, famed black singer Paul Robeson, and Pulitzer Prize winning journalist, Walter Duranty. Duranty was the Moscow correspondent for *The New York Times* from 1922 to 1936 and publicly denounced fellow correspondents Gareth Jones and Malcolm Muggeridge of the *Manchester Guardian* for daring to write of the Soviet government's causing the Ukrainian famine. Muggeridge had become disillusioned as a socialist during his time in Russia and, as incredible as this may seem, he became an outcast among English intellectuals and journalists for his dispatches and books about what he had seen.[199]

Bertrand Russell also stood apart:

Stalin condemned millions of peasants to death by

---

197   Athough they used similar terms, the earliest known usage of this term is in a 1948 *New York Times* article on Italian politics.
198   www.bbc.co.uk/worldservice/documentaries/2010/07/100624_doc_useful_idiots_lenin.shtml, 10 Mar, 2012.
199   *Winter in Moscow*, London; Eyre and Spottiswoode, 1934.

---

starvation and millions of others to enforced labour in concentration camps … I am completely at a loss to understand how it came about that some people who are both humane and intelligent could find something to admire in the vast slave camp produced by Stalin.[200]

In regard to Hitler, in the 1930s many English aristocrats including King Edward VIII were notoriously sympathetic towards him. Raymond Aron comments:

> The myth of the Revolution serves as a refuge for utopian intellectuals; it becomes the mysterious, unpredictable intercessor between the real and the ideal.[201]

Rejecting Jesus as the only reliable 'intercessor between the real and the ideal' and ruling out any possible supernatural or spiritual explanation, they settle for myths and ignore John's revelation and careful warning. In their case, Paul's chilling prophecy about antichrists is fulfilled:

> 9. …whose coming is in accord with the activity of Satan, with all power and signs and false wonders,
> 10. and with all the deception of wickedness for those who perish, because they did not receive the love of the truth so as to be saved.
> 11. For this reason God will send upon them a deluding influence so that they will believe what is false,
> 12. in order that they all may be judged who did not believe the truth, but took pleasure in wickedness (2 Thess 2:9-12)

Malcolm Muggeridge, however, having loved and believed the truth, avoided this deception and 'deluding influence', famously abandoning his pleasure in wickedness to come at last to faith in Jesus.[202]

200　*Why I am Not a Communist*, essay published in *Portraits from Memory and Other Essays*, New York: Simon & Schuster, 1956, p. 230.
201　Raymond Aron, *The Opium of the Intellectuals*, Piscataway, New Jersey; Transaction Publishers, 2001, p. 65.
202　*Conversion: The Spiritual Journey of a 20th Century Pilgrim*, Eugene, Oregon; Wipf & Stock Publishers, 2005.

Competing Antichrists – *Captain Corelli's Mandolin* and *Charlie Wilson's War*

Each antichrist regime is lethal — even worse is the carnage when they collide. China suffered because of Japanese Hirohito-worship from 1935, followed by their own Mao-worship from 1948, but it became even worse for them in 1958 when Mao sought to catch up with Stalin's obtaining of nuclear weapons and again in 1968 when Mao tried to purge any possible Stalinist tainting of 'his' revolution.

This phenomenon is poignantly illustrated by the popular novel and subsequent movie, *Captain Corelli's Mandolin*[203] which brought to public attention one of the darkest incidents of World War II on the Greek island of Cephalonia. In September 1943, the Italians who had been occupying Greece surrendered to the Allies, causing such bitterness in Hitler that he ordered German troops to attack the 'traitors'. Some 4,750 Italian prisoners were executed and 3,000 drowned in ships sunk by mines while en route to Germany as forced labourers, with the final death toll being 9,646 men and 390 officers.[204] The Greeks, meanwhile, had their own resistance against both Italian and German invaders ruptured by Greek Communists who not only plundered Greek supplies but also killed each other as followers of bitter rivals Trotsky and Stalin.[205]

Thus the Greeks in this time suffered under three competing antichrist regimes: Mussolini's Italians, Hitler's Germans and Stalin's Greeks.

Similarly in Afghanistan, it has been estimated that one million were killed when Afghanistan was invaded by the

203 Louis de Bernières, *Captain Corelli's Mandolin*, London; Secker & Warburg, 1994.

204 http://members.iinet.net.au/~gduncan/massacres.html, 2 Mar, 2009.

205 www.marxists.org/subject/greek-civil-war/revolutionary-history/stinas/memoirs.htm, 2 Mar, 2009.

                                    Slouching Towards Bethlehem

faltering Russian empire in 1979.[206] After ten years, the invaders were finally evicted by the guerrilla warfare of the mujahideen, with huge help from the CIA's supply of Stinger anti-aircraft missiles. This story was popularised by journalist George Crile's book, *Charlie Wilson's War: The Extraordinary Story of How the Wildest Man in Congress and a Rogue CIA Agent Changed the History of Our Times*[207] and the Tom Hanks/Mike Nichols film.[208] Tragically, the Americans severely underestimated the new but mushrooming threat of Islamic fundamentalism while they focussed on fighting communism, and by 1996 the Taliban regime had taken charge. In 2001, the USA and Great Britain tried to topple the Taliban in Operation Enduring Freedom, but twenty years later, the Taliban are still enduring.

---

206 www.guidetorussia.com/russia-afghanistan.asp, 30 Aug, 2010.
207 Grave Press, New York, 2003.
208 *Charlie Wilson's War*, Universal Studios, Dec, 2007.

11

Religious Empires
Non-Christian and Christian

We have so far focussed on major political movements often seen as secular or non-religious. As can be seen from John's revelation, there is simply no such thing – beneath the veneer, they are always spiritually motivated. Now let us focus on the explicitly religious empires, starting with Japan.

It is hard for us today, watching the television replays of September 11, 2001, to comprehend the suicidal motivation of the 19 men who crashed the four airliners into the World Trade Centre, the Pentagon and a Pennsylvanian field, killing 2,975. Imagine, then, how our parents' generation struggled in 1945 to understand the 1,604 Japanese *kamikaze* (lit. divine wind) or *tokkotai* (special attack force) pilots of the Pacific war. These fliers formed waves of massed suicidal attacks called *kikusui* (floating chrysanthemums), sinking 400 ships and killing 9,724 seamen.[209]

Vice Admiral Charles R. Brown, USN, wrote:

> There was a hypnotic fascination to a sight so alien to our Western philosophy. We watched each plunging Kamikaze with the detached horror of one witnessing a terrible spectacle rather than as the intended victim. We forgot self for a moment as we groped hopelessly for the thoughts of that other man up there. And dominating it all was a strange admixture of respect and pity.[210]

---

209 William Manchester, *Goodbye, Darkness: A Memoir of the Pacific War*, London; Michael Joseph, 1981, p. 356.
210 Capt. Rikihei Inoguchi, Cmdr. Tadashi Nakajima & Roger Pineau *The Divine Wind: Japan's Kamikaze Force in World War II*, Annapolis; Bluejacket Books, 1994, Foreword.

                          Slouching Towards Bethlehem

Today, few realise this was only the beginning of *Ten Go* (lit. Heavenly Operation), Japan's planned suicidal defence as its vast empire shrank. By August, 1945, as well as their conventional forces of 790,000 troops facing the attacking force of 550,000 American troops[211], the Japanese had thousands more *kamikaze* planes. They had also developed the rocket-propelled *Okka* bomb, similar to the German V-1 but carrying a suicide pilot with rudimentary controls to guide it to its target. These were supplemented by:

> …nearly 300 Kairyu suicide submarines, two man craft with 600kg of explosive in the nose, which were to be used for close-in ramming attacks. The remaining 40 conventional submarines, plus 115 Koryu five-man suicide submarines, were also to be used to attack the (American) fleet… a further 496 Koryu and 207 Kairyu submarines were under construction. Then there were the Kaitens, the human torpedoes, each some 20m long, carrying a war-head of 1600kg of explosive and capable of sinking the largest American vessel. The Japanese had 120 shore-based Kaitens… in early August 1945 and they were among the most feared weapons because of the difficulty in detecting them. Finally, in the sea-borne attack fleet were almost 4000 Shinyo motor-boats filled with high explosive and ideal for night attacks against troop transports… and thousands of Fukaryu divers, both male and female, armed with lunge mines capable of sinking a landing craft of up to 950 tons.[212]

A year and half earlier, in February 1944, Prime Minister Tojo Hideki, had made an emergency declaration. Author and translator Hiroaki Sato writes of its demand for…:

> …ichioku gyokusai, "100 million gyokusai." It was a demand that the entire Japanese population be prepared to die. Japan's mainland population at the time was 70

---

211 *Wartime Memories*, ed. Peter McQuaid, Auckland; Dolphin Publications Ltd, 1995, pp. 7-9.
212 Ibid.,

million, so he was also ordering Taiwanese and Koreans to meet the same fate.[213]

Gyokusai (lit. shattered jewel) comes from an ancient Chinese proverb: "a great man should die as a shattered jewel rather than live as an intact tile". The Prime Minister was calling for one hundred million honourable deaths rather than surrender. In response, some 28 million civilians joined the National Volunteer Combat Force.[214]

The military had been using the term since May 30, 1943:

> The annihilations termed gyokusai after that saw the number of "shattered" soldiers increase: the Battle of Tarawa (November 21-23, 1943), 4,600 (17 surviving); the Battle of Kwajalein (January 30 to February 5, 1944), 7,900 (105 surviving); the Battle of Biak (May 27 to June 20, 1944), more than 10,000 (520 surviving); the Battle of Saipan (June 15 to July 9, 1944), 29,000 (921 surviving), and so on.[215]

In the Battle of the Philippines (late 1944 to August 1945), Sato records and explains, the Japanese troops abandoned there were ordered:

> "Carry out resistance in perpetuity to provide assistance to the never-ending Imperial Fortune by turning yourselves into human pillars, unperturbed, for the Imperial Nation." The "human pillar" or hitobashira is the idea dating from mythological times of sacrificing a human being to placate whatever it is that is creating havoc. The result: more than 450,000 Japanese soldiers died.
> When Vice Adm. Ito Seiichi showed reluctance to lead Japan's last sizable naval sortie, without air cover, to Okinawa on a similar suicidal mission, he was told, "You are requested to die gallantly in advance of the 100-million

---

213 Hiroaki Sato, www.japanfocus.org/-Hiroaki-SATO/2662, 12 Feb, 2011.
214 *Wartime Memories*, p. 9
215 Sato, Ibid.,

   Slouching Towards Bethlehem

gyokusai." The result: six of the ten warships that made up the fleet were sunk, including the flagship Yamato, with 3,700 men lost.[216]

Perhaps the most shocking instance occurred among civilians on the island of Saipan in July, 1944. Earlier, on 26 June, 1944, in one 'banzai charge', 4,311 Japanese troops had been mown down by American defenders. In despair at their defeat, hundreds of men, women and children, some women with babies, threw themselves off what would become known as Banzai Cliff and Suicide Cliff, shouting *"Tenno Haika! Banzai!"* ("Long live the Emperor! Ten thousand years/ages!").[217]

What could inspire obedience to such a dreadful command? The spirit causing them to worship their Shintoist divine emperor and his empire.

As dreadful as it was to drop the atomic bombs on the civilian populations of Nagasaki and Hiroshima to force Hirohito to surrender, it seemed the only other alternative was for the Allies' flesh and blood to face this *harakiri* (suicide) spirit.

Falling Cherry Blossoms

One Japanese prisoner of war, Michiharu Shinya, became a Christian while incarcerated in Featherston, New Zealand, and wrote:

> It is essential to understand the Japanese concept of "spirit". It was a major reason why the war in the South Pacific became essentially a war of annihilation… (and) included the belief that the human will could surmount physical circumstance. Japanese officers taught their men, and believed themselves, that they could do things no other army could, simply because Japanese troops would not be denied… Death in battle was portrayed as an

216 Sato, Ibid.,
217 Manchester, pp. 270-271.

honour to the family and a transcendent act on the part of
the individual. Every soldier carried a copy of the Emperor
Meiji's Imperial Rescript of 1882. It contains a striking
image. The cherry blossom, beloved of the Japanese,
falls to earth in perfect form. The Rescript counsels, "If
someone should enquire of you concerning the spirit of
the Japanese, point to the wild cherry blossom shining in
the sun". Thus the Japanese honoured the sanctity of death
of the young in battle.[218]

Consider the following, written by Isao Matsuo of Nagasaki,
aged twenty-three, who died in the earlier stage of the
kamikaze attacks in the Philippines:

> Dear Parents. Please congratulate me. I have been given
> a splendid opportunity to die. This is my last day. The
> destiny of our homeland hinges on the decisive battle in
> the seas to the south where I shall fall like a blossom from
> a radiant cherry tree. I shall be a shield for His Majesty
> and die cleanly along with my squadron leader and other
> friends. I wish that I could be born seven times, each time
> to smite the enemy. How I appreciate this chance to die
> like a man! I am grateful from the depths of my heart
> to the parents who have reared me with their constant
> prayers and tender love… Written at Manila on the eve of
> our sortie. Soaring into the sky of the southern seas, it is
> our glorious mission to die as the shields of His Majesty.
> Cherry blossoms glisten as they open and fall.[219]

---

218 Michiharu Shinya, *Beyond Death And Dishonour*, Auckland; Castle
Publishing, 2001, p. 32. The Wellington newspaper *The Dominion*
reported on 29 December, 1945, that 'many of the 800 who returned
home to Japan… had become Christians during their imprisonment in
Featherston… and had declared they would take their Christian faith
back to their people – they came as enemies, but many will go away as
friends'. Quoted in *Wartime Memories*, p. 135.
219 www.ocf.berkeley.edu/~liminal/papers/matsuo/kamikaze.html, 1
Sep, 2007. Also quoted by Lewis M. Andrews Jr. in *Tempest, Fire and
Foe: Destroyer Escorts in World War II and the Men Who Manned Them*,
Victoria, Canada; Trafford Publishing, 2004, p. 383.

                                        Slouching Towards Bethlehem

Of course, not all were willing suicides. Many were coerced or peer-pressured into 'volunteering'. Of the 4,000 *tokkatai* (special attack force) pilots, 3,000 were new conscripts, of whom 1,000 were 'student soldiers' – graduates in philosophy and classical music, English and German literature, lovers of Socrates, Kant, Tolstoy, Goethe, Nietzsche, Schweitzer. Some were Marxists and, astonishingly, there were even a few devout Christians who sang hymns on their last night and carried their Bibles on their final mission.[220] One Christian, Hayashi Ichizo, found solace in Kierkegaard's *The Sickness unto Death* which enabled him to die for his country but not the empire or emperor.[221]

Christian Empires

The Japanese example is an obvious fulfilment of Revelation chapter 13's identification of political religious cults. However, Christendom has also provided many examples, as you would expect, given John's description:

> They went out from us, but they were not really of us
> (1 John 2:18)

We have already considered the terrible historical consequences of professing Christian churches, both Catholic and Reformed, setting up their religious leaders as political leaders. Although it took almost a thousand years, in 1965 Pope Paul VI, leader of Christendom's largest denomination of approximately one billion adherents, officially removed his *triregnum*, i.e. triple-tiered crown, symbol of the pope as 'king of heaven and of earth and of the lower regions'.[222]

---

220 Emiko Ohnuki-Tierney, *Kamikaze Diaries (Relections of Japanese Student Soldiers)*, London; University of Chicago Press, 2007, pp. 20-21.
221 Ibid., pp. 180-183.
222 *Quoadea quoeconcernunt papae dignitatem, auctoritatem, seu potestatem, et infallibilitatem, #13*. In English: Concerning the extent of Papal dignity, authority, or dominion and infallibility, #13.

His four successors – John Paul I, John Paul II, Benedict XVI, and Francis I – have similarly avoided it.

Most Protestants, like the founders of modern America who insisted on the division of Church and State, see the inherent heresy and/or dangers involved. After all, the Pilgrims had travelled to the New World to be free of the Old World's state churches' persecutions. Christian politicians today therefore usually confine themselves to being 'Christian democrats', seeking instead to be "salt and light" in the democratic process.

However, we still need to understand how professing Christian empires and emperors of the 15th, 16th and 17th Centuries also ignored John's dire warning and duly fulfilled it. They were not always deliberately murderous towards those who would not bow the knee to them. When the Portugese and Spanish extended their borders across the Pacific to the Americas, most of the millions who died were killed by epidemics.

Jared Diamond is Professor of Geography and Physiology at UCLA. In his 1998 Pulitzer Prize-winning *Guns, Germs and Steel*, he identifies:

> …one of the key factors in world history: diseases transmitted to peoples lacking immunity by invading peoples with considerable immunity. Smallpox, measles, influenza, typhus, bubonic plague, and other infectious diseases endemic in Europe played a decisive role in European conquests, by decimating many peoples on other continents. For example, a smallpox epidemic devastated the Aztecs after the failure of the first Spanish attack in 1520 and killed Cuitláhuac, the Aztec emperor who briefly succeeded Montezuma. Throughout the Americas, diseases introduced with Europeans spread from tribe to tribe far in advance of the Europeans themselves, killing an estimated 95% of the pre-Columbian Native American population.[223]

---

223 *Guns, Germs and Steel (the Fate of Human Societies)*, New York;

However, this does not excuse what these empires *did* do deliberately as, for example, in Peru.

Pizarro's Conquistadors

When Spanish commander Francisco Pizarro arrived in Peru, he came from the Holy Roman Emperor, Charles V. His brothers, Hernando and Pedro, and four other conquistadors recorded the capture of the Incan emperor Atahallpa on 16 November, 1532. Pizarro cheerfully informed him:

> "Do not take it as an insult that you have been defeated and taken prisoner, for with the Christians who come with me, though so few in number, I have conquered greater kingdoms than yours, and defeated other more powerful lords than you, imposing upon them the dominion of the Emperor, whose vassal I am, and who is King of Spain and of the universal world. We come to conquer this land by his command, that all may come to a knowledge of God and of His Holy Catholic Faith..." [224]

Notice, despite his apparent faith, he was acting in the name of the empire and the emperor, the first beast of Revelation 13, and its living image as promoted by the second beast, the spirit of antichrist. What Pizarro had just done, and was about to do next, is appalling.

The Incans had never before seen armour, swords, guns or horses so these few Christians (62 mounted troopers, 106 foot soldiers and a priest) had concealed them around the town square of Cajamarca. Pizarro had then invited Atahallpa to meet there, promising him friendship and safe passage. When Atahallpa responded with a vast retinue, many crowned with gold, silver and emeralds and borne on ceremonial litters, the Spaniards instead took him captive. As they reported to the Emperor, they had given him fair

W.W. Norton & Co, 1999, pp. 77-78.
224   Ibid., pp. 73-74.

opportunity to become a Christian:

> Pizarro now sent Friar Vicente de Valverde to go speak to
> Atahallpa, and to require Atahallpa in the name of God
> and of the King of Spain that Atahallpa subject himself to
> the law of our Lord Jesus Christ and to the service of His
> Majesty the King of Spain. Advancing with a cross in one
> hand and a Bible in the other …the Friar thus addressed
> him: "I am a Priest of God, and I teach Christians the
> things of God, and in like manner I come to teach you.
> What I teach is that which God says to us in this Book.
> Therefore, on the part of God and of the Christians, I
> beseech you to be their friend, for such is God's will, and
> it will be for your good."
> Atahallpa asked for the Book, that he might look at it, and
> the Friar gave it to him closed..Atahallpa did not know
> how to open the Book, and the Friar was extending his
> arm to do so, when Atahallpa, in great anger, gave him a
> blow on the arm, not wishing that it should be opened.
> Then he opened it himself, and without any astonishment
> at the letters and paper he threw it away from him five or
> six paces, his face a deep crimson.
> The Friar returned to Pizarro, shouting, "Come out! Come
> out, Christians! Come at these enemy dogs who reject the
> things of God. That tyrant has thrown my book of holy
> law to the ground! Did you not see what happened? Why
> remain polite and servile toward this over-proud dog when
> the plains are full of Indians? March out against him, for I
> absolve you!"[225]

At Atahallpa's stubborn refusal to convert, and being assured
that they would not be sinning, Pizarro then gave the signal
to fire the artillery:

> At the same time, the trumpets were sounded, and the
> armoured Spanish troops, both cavalry and infantry,
> sallied forth out of their hiding places straight into
> the mass of the unarmed Indians crowding the square,

---

225 Ibid., pp. 71-72.

                              Slouching Towards Bethlehem

giving the Spanish battle cry "Santiago!" …[This] threw the Indians into panicked confusion. The Spaniards fell upon them and began to cut them to pieces…Since they were unarmed, they were attacked without danger to any Christian. The cavalry rode them down, killing and wounding and following in pursuit… All of the Indian soldiers whom Atahallpa had brought were a mile from Cajamarca ready for battle, but not one made a move, and during all this not one Indian raised a weapon against a Spaniard… If night had not come on, few out of the 40,000 Indian troops would have been left alive. Six or seven thousand Indians lay dead and many more had their arms cut off and other wounds.[226]

The Incas continued to obey every command of the captive Atahallpa, whom they saw as an incarnation of the sun-god, and over the next eight months, they assembled 'history's largest ransom – enough gold to fill a room 22 feet long by 17 feet wide to a height of over 8 feet'.[227] Pizarro then reneged on his promise to free Atahallpa and instead had him executed.

As a god-king, Atahallpa himself had blood on his hands, having just slain hundreds of men, women and children, the family of his half-brother Huascar, to secure his throne. Ironically, Pizarro offered him a choice of being burnt as a pagan or strangled as a Christian. He chose the latter, was baptized as Juan de Atahualpa in honor of John the Baptist, and was duly strangled.

With this foothold secured and the arrival of reinforcements, the Spanish went on to destroy the Incan Empire.

At the same time, further north, in Mexico, Cortés and his conquistadors captured Montezuma, destroying and plundering the Aztec Empire.

To put these events in historical perspective, back in Europe, the Inquisition had just finished torturing, forcibly

---

226 Ibid., p. 73.
227 Ibid., p. 68.

converting or expelling every Jew from Spain and was now aiming at the Protestants. The emperor, Charles V, had presided over Martin Luther's trial at the Imperial Diet of Worms (1521) and the Netherlands and most of northern Europe were about to break away.

Joseph Conrad's *Heart of Darkness*

Tragically, the other European powers became envious of the wealth gathered by the Spanish and Portugese and during the 17th, 18th and 19th Centuries, England, France, the Netherlands and Germany followed in their footsteps.

The most murderous emperor of these empires stepped forward towards the end of the 19th Century: King Leopold II of Belgium. In 1885, at the Berlin Conference on the colonial future of Africa, he manoeuvred himself into having free reign over what he liked to call the Congo Free State, an area of 800,000 square miles or seventy-six times that of Belgium.[228] He ran it as a private hunting estate, plundering it for ivory and rubber in a manner so brutal that in 1919, it was estimated by a Belgian government commission that half of the population had died. Given that the first official census in 1924 showed a surviving population of 10 million, the death toll would be conservatively about 10 million.[229]

Leopold's regime there only came to an end in 1908 because the Belgian government was forced to act against him by an international campaign. Now thought to be 'the first mass human rights movement',[230] it was led by two Britons, diplomat Roger Casement and journalist Edmund Morel, with the help of American missionaries William Sheppard

228 www.guardian.co.uk/world/2002/jul/13/humanities. artsandhumanities/print, 3 Mar, 2012.
229 Adam Hochschild, *King Leopold's Ghost: A Story of Greed, Terror and Heroism in Colonial Africa*, Boston & New York; Mariner Books, 1999.
230 http://famousbelgians.net/leopold2.htm, 3 Mar, 2012.

                              Slouching Towards Bethlehem

and William Morrison,[231] British missionary A.E. Scrivener and the public outrage generated by the writings of Joseph Conrad and Mark Twain.

Conrad's acclaimed *Heart of Darkness*,[232] published in 1903, was based on his experiences as captain of a Belgian riverboat, *Roi des Belges* (French for 'King of the Belgians'), in the Congo in 1889. Perfectly illustrating our point, Conrad's novella tells of an ivory trader named Kurtz who begins as a multitalented idealist but ends up demanding worship from his native workers. Conrad puts all of his despair into Kurtz's infamous last words, "The horror! The horror!" Almost eighty years later, Francis Ford Coppola reworked the story in his multi-award winning movie, *Apocalypse Now*, which is a remarkably accurate title.

As for Mark Twain, he published in 1905 a scathing satire, *King Leopold's Soliloquy*, in which the King argues that at least he 'sends the gospel to the survivors'.[233]

Tragically for the Congo, it has never recovered. After gaining independence from Belgium in 1960, it fell first into the military dictatorship of Joseph-Désiré Mobutu until he was deposed in 1997. Since then, the United Nations report, the armies of Burundi, Rwanda and Uganda and corrupt Zimbabwean and Congolese officials have systematically plundered its vast natural resources and mineral deposits.[234] It was estimated in 2010 that between 3 and 6 million have died because of fighting, disease or malnutrition.[235]

It is possible that some of the perpetrators of these atrocities done in the name of Jesus were actually Christians but there

---

231 www.notablebiographies.com/supp/Supplement-Mi-So/Sheppard-William.html, 5 Mar, 2012.
232 Republished by Oxford World's Classics, Oxford University Press, 2002.
233 www.aaargh.codoh.info/fran/livres10/Soliloquy.pdf, p. 49, 3 Mar, 2012.
234 www.un.org/News/dh/latest/drcongo.htm, 12 Mar, 2012.
235 http://news.bbc.co.uk/2/hi/africa/8471147.stm, 12 Mar, 2012.

is no doubt which spirit inspired their actions – John's second beast, the one that looks like a lamb but speaks as a dragon (Rev 13:11), the spirit of antichrist.

A Small Light in the Darkness

One example, dear to my own heart, of how the Spirit of Christ worked in a nominally Christian empire. When the British Empire reached the shores of New Zealand at the beginning of the 19th Century, there was a vastly better outcome for the indigenous Maori:

> During the early period of contact, 1800-40, Maori society underwent some changes and convulsions… Some European tools and techniques were adopted in commerce and agriculture, but production was still organised and distributed for Maori ends in a Maori way. Various Christian missions had been established since 1814, and after 1830 many Maoris adopted at least the outward forms of Christianity, and were taught to write in their own language… The Europeans brought new infectious diseases, and these increased Maori mortality. But epidemics of some of the most lethal diseases did not occur; the Maoris may have begun to develop immunities by 1840…[236]

In other words, the 'guns, germs and steel' of the immigrants did not have the same one-sided result as elsewhere. The Maori, however, did take up the guns to use against each other:

> The Musket Wars… began when the Ngapuhi… became the first tribe to acquire significant numbers of muskets, and used them to pay off old scores and increase their wealth and prestige. Other tribes who acquired muskets early did likewise. The wars ended [about 1833] when all the tribes had muskets. There were no more easy victories, and the balance was restored. All in all, Maori society bent

---

236 James Belich, *The New Zealand Wars (and the Victorian Interpretation of Racial Conflict)*, Auckland; Penguin, 1988, p. 20.

    Slouching Towards Bethlehem

but did not break under the impact of early European contact.[237]

Then came a dramatic improvement:

> By the 1830's, …the Maori people were more willing to listen to the missionaries. Many Maori leaders were tired of fighting and began turning to the missionaries as peacemakers, healers and teachers. Christian ideas and practices spread rapidly, often carried by Maori teachers and by the new skill of literacy; in the 1830's the missionaries translated and printed thousands of copies of religious texts and sections of the Bible.[238]

The crowning achievement of the time, however, was the making of a covenant between the British and the Maori in 1840, the Treaty of Waitangi.

Britain was undergoing a major reformation, thanks to the extraordinary work of the early Methodists, led by brothers John and Charles Wesley and George Whitefield, and the Clapham Saints led by William Wilberforce and John Newton. In 1807, the Slave Trade Act banned the trade throughout the empire and in 1833, the Slavery Abolition Act led to the total emancipation of British slaves. No longer were 'savages' to be killed, conquered or enslaved but recognised as created in the image and likeness of God, and New Zealand received the benefit:

> Lord Normanby, the Secretary of State for the Colonies, told [New Zealand's first governor, William Hobson] to get the "free and intelligent consent" of chiefs to the treaty, and to deal with them "openly"… to control the thousands of expected emigrants and to protect the rights of the Maori people.[239]

---

237 Ibid.
238 Claudia Orange, *An Illustrated History of the Treaty of Waitangi*, Wellington; Allen & Unwin, 1990, p. 2.
239 Ibid., p. 11.

Normanby was only too conscious of Christendom's previous failings, writing to Hobson:

> …uncivilised Tribes have almost invariably disappeared as often as they have been brought into the immediate vicinity of Emigrants from the Nations of Christendom. To mitigate, and, if possible, to avert these disasters, and to rescue the Emigrants themselves from a lawless state of Society… is the principal object of your mission… Her Majesty's Government authorise you to treat with the Aborigines of New Zealand for the recognition of Her Majesty's Sovereign authority over the whole or any parts of those Islands which they may be willing to place under Her Majesty's Dominion.[240]

Sadly, successive settler governments all too often ignored the Treaty's righteous standards. However, in 1975, the New Zealand government set up the Waitangi Tribunal, a commission of inquiry to address all these issues; it is still at work today.[241]

Other Religious Empires

So far we have examined the political religious empires because they are coercive, often using armed forces. For the sake of completeness, let us briefly consider *non-political* religious movements or what could be called multinational empires of the mind.

Perhaps the two most widely known are Hinduism and Buddhism. Hinduism has had a plethora of god-kings in India and, until quite recently, in Nepal. It also offers a wide variety of gurus who often freely acknowledge Jesus but like to add

---

240 *Instructions from the Secretary of State for War and Colonies, Lord Normanby, to Captain Hobson, recently appointed H.M. Consul at New Zealand, concerning his duty as Lieutenant Governor of New Zealand…, dated 14 August 1839.* www.nz.com/new-zealand/guide-book/history/colonial.aspx, 5 Mar, 2012.
241 www.waitangi-tribunal.govt.nz

                    Slouching Towards Bethlehem

their own revelations as superseding His. Buddhism's most famous god-king is the Dalai Lama, Tenzin Gyatso, who ruled Tibet as the fourteenth reincarnation of the Buddha. Deposed in 1959 by Communist China, he lives in exile in Dharmshala, India, and frequently visits the West seeking support for the restoration of Tibetan sovereignty.

Since both Buddhism and Hinduism accept polytheism, they are usually tolerant of those not accepting their god-kings.

Two lesser known but strongly messianic movements are from the Middle East – the Druze and the Baha'is. The Druze believe that al-Hakim, an Islamic caliph who mysteriously disappeared in Cairo in 1021, is an incarnation of God who will return to usher in a golden age for them. The Baha'is, who branched off from Islam in the mid 1800s, believe their Persian founder, Hoseyn Ali Nuri and also known as Baha'u'llah, is the latest in a series of incarnations of God which includes Zoroaster, Gautama Buddha, Jesus and Muhammad.

In the West, the most common empires of the mind that we encounter today are knocking on our doors – the Church of Jesus Christ of Latter Day Saints (or Mormons) and the Watchtower Society (or Jehovah's Witnesses). The former was founded by Joseph Smith in the 1820s and their claim to be the only true church of God stands or falls entirely on his claims to be, like Muhammad, the only truly reliable prophet. Likewise for all of his successors to this day.

The Watchtower Society also claims to be the only reliable voice of God, offering themselves as the answer to Jesus' question ending the parable of Matthew 24, "Who then is the faithful and sensible slave whom his master put in charge of his household to give them their food at the proper time?" As the rest of that passage makes clear, Jesus is not giving a coded message for an organisation that has only been around since the 1880s. He is calling on all of us who teach His message in every age to remain faithful and humble because He will hold us accountable when He returns. Since the Watchtower Society explicitly denies the deity of Christ,[242] they are not faithful teachers of His message but have instead usurped His place as the only Mediator between God and man (1 Tim 2:5).

The Unification Church's Rev. Sun Myung Moon hints that he is Jesus returned and, of course, the New Age movement has provided many more prophets and messiahs.

While all of these qualify according to John's definition as examples of 'antichrists', and therefore do a huge amount of spiritual damage to all who believe them, none of them are murderous. Tragically, the same could not be said of the doomsday cults of Jim Jones's Peoples' Temple (914 dead in 1978), David Koresh's Branch Davidians (86 dead in 1993), Luc Jouret and Joseph di Mambro's Solar Temple (74 dead in 1994), Rev. Asahara Shokou's *Aum Shinrikyo* who launched the 1995 Sarin gas attacks on Tokyo's subway in which 12 died and 5,500 were injured, Marshall Applewhite's Heaven's Gate (39 dead in 1997) and the Ugandan Movement for the Restoration of the Ten Commandments of God led by self-styled prophet Joseph Kibwetere (721 dead in 2000).

None of us can afford to ignore John's warning:

> Beloved, do not believe every spirit, but test the spirits to see whether they are from God;
> because many false prophets have gone out into the world
> (1 John 4:1)

This brings us now to a religious political empire that needs very careful consideration – Islam.

---

242   www.watchtower.org/e/ti/article_06.htm, 18 Feb, 2012.

12

Muhammad as Emperor
Ruling from Beyond the Grave

Birthed fourteen hundred years ago, the Islamic empire today has 1.6 billion citizens or one quarter of the earth's population.[243] In the light of Daniel 7's eleventh horn, it is interesting to note that the Organisation of the Islamic Conference comprises fifty seven nations[244] or *one-third* of the United Nations' one hundred and ninety three nations.

Although it has no emperor, or Caliph, at the moment, its long-dead leader continues to exercise an influence that is undoubtedly due to John's second beast, as we will see next. The empire itself, being entirely founded on that leader's teachings, has thereby gone feral and is thus another example of John's first beast.

Of course, much needs to be understood about this empire but for the purposes of this study, we will look only at its 6th Century founder, Muhammad (570-632 A.D.),[245] and how his revelations are understood and practised today.

Let it also be clear that we should always respond as suggested in 1142 A.D. by Peter the Venerable, Abbot of Cluny, after the First Crusade and just before the Second, when he called for Islam to be approached not 'as our people often do, by arms, but by words; not by force, but by reason; not in

---

243 Pew Forum, http://pewforum.org/news/display.
php?NewsID=18850, 12 Oct, 2009.
244 www.oic-oci.org/member_states.asp, 19 Mar, 2009.
245 There are many variations in spelling his name, such as Mohammad, Mahomet or Mohamed, and for Islam's holy book, such as Quran, Koran or Qur'an, and for adherents, Mohammedans, Moslem or Muslim. I use what appear to be the most popularly correct – Muhammad, Qur'an and Muslim.

---

hatred, but in love'.[246]

Muhammad saw himself as both prophet and statesman, the lawgiver whose words 'abrogated' or over-wrote those of Moses and every other nation's lawgiver. He was therefore unashamedly political. The Islamic assumption is that the territory occupied by Islam, *dar al-Islam* (house of submission), will eventually overcome and absorb *dar al-harb* (house of war) i.e. all territories still outside the control of Islam. This was explained by renowned Arab historian, sociologist and philosopher Ibn Khaldun (1332-1406):

> In the Muslim community, the holy war is a religious duty, because of the universalism of the (Muslim) mission and (the obligation to) convert everybody to Islam either by persuasion or by force. Therefore caliphate and royal authority are united so that the person in charge can devote the available strength to both of them (religion and politics) at the same time.
>
> The other religious groups did not have a universal mission, and the holy war was not a religious duty to them, save only for purposes of defence… they are not under obligation to gain power over other nations, as is the case with Islam. They are merely required to establish their religion among their own people…
>
> We do not think we should blacken the pages of this book with discussion of their dogmas of unbelief. In general they are well-known. All of them are unbelief. This is clearly stated in the noble Qur'an. To discuss or argue these things with them is not up to us. It is (for them to choose between) conversion to Islam, payment of the poll-tax, or death.[247]

The 'divine imperative' of Islam is to bring the whole earth

---

246 Bruce B. Lawrence, *The Qur'an: A Biography*, Sydney, Allen & Unwin, 2006, p. 100. Tragically, Peter's love was not extended to the Jews as well for he was fiercely antisemitic.
247 *The Muqaddimah: An Introduction to History*, New Jersey; Princeton University Press, 1969, pp. 183-188.

                              Slouching Towards Bethlehem

into submission to Allah which requires the introduction of the Sharia, or law of Islam, into every nation.

Muhammad as Prophet

Muhammad saw himself firstly as *the* prophet whose words 'abrogated' or replaced those of all others. The Qur'an quotes Allah as telling Muhammad:

> Nothing of our revelation (even a single verse) do We abrogate or cause be forgotten, but We bring (in place) one better or the like thereof. Knowest thou not that Allah is able to do all things? (Sura 2:106)[248]

Through this doctrine of *naskh*, nullification or abrogation, Muhammad replaces anything which contradicts him. He obviously met with some scepticism when he first promoted it:

> And when We put a revelation in place of (another) revelation – and Allah knowest best what He revealeth – they say: "Lo! Thou art but inventing". Most of them know not. (Sura 16:101)[249]

Undaunted, he went on to proclaim himself the summation of prophethood, the 'Seal of All Prophets', so that Muslims today believe he is the last or final prophet and there will be none after him.[250]

Sir Hamilton Gibb was Professor of Arabic at the Universities of London and Oxford and also Director of the Center for Middle Eastern Studies at Harvard University. In his classic study on Islam, he wrote:

> Of the two articles of the basic profession of the Muslim faith, "There is but one God and Mohammed is His

---

248 Pickthal, www.cmje.org/religious-texts/quran/verses/002-qmt.php, 17 Sep, 2011.
249 Pickthal, www.cmje.org/religious-texts/quran/verses/016-qmt.php, 17 Sep, 2011.
250 www.answering-christianity.com/sami_zaatri/muhammad_is_last_prophet.htm, 9 Mar, 2009.

Apostle", the first may be assented to by many besides Muslims, whereas it is the second which distinguishes Islam from all other faiths. For its implication is not that Mohammed was *an* Apostle, one amongst many, but that in Mohammed the series of Apostles reached its culmination and that the Koran revealed through him is the final and unchangeable revelation of the Divine Will, abrogating all previous records of revelation.[251]

It is this second article in Islam's basic profession that precisely identifies Muhammad as one more 'image of the beast'. Obviously unaware of Revelation 13, Sir Hamilton began his introduction:

> Probably no well-informed person now shares the belief of our medieval forefathers that the "Turks and infidels" worshipped "Mahomet" in the form of an idol – a double error, since any image or visual symbol in religious worship is anathema to Muslims.[252]

This is literally true as demonstrated in 2001 when Afghanistan's Taliban destroyed the ancient Buddhist statues at Bamiyan despite international outrage and protest. However, little did they realise that in enforcing Muhammad's claim of unique and supreme authority, as God told Ezekiel, "These men have set up their idols in their hearts" (Ezek 14:3). This is perhaps the supreme irony in Islam.

After Muhammad's death in 632 A.D., his empire divided over who should be his successor (Arabic, *khalif*). Many believed Muhammad did not appoint one so they chose Abu-Bakr as Caliph and began to rely on the *sunnah* i.e. Muhammad's practices and traditions. They became known as Sunnis and today make up 80%–85% of Muslims. The other 15-20%, the Shi'ites, accept the *sunnah* but also believe that Muhammad appointed his cousin Ali and his descendants

---

251 *Islam - A Historical Survey*, Oxford; Oxford University Press, 2nd edition, 1968, p. 2, emphasis in original.
252 Ibid., p. 1.

forever to be the *imam*, their highest rank of spiritual teacher. Shi'ites are in the majority in Iran, Iraq, Azerbaijan and Bahrain.[253]

Praying to Muhammad

Visitors to Bahrain today are routinely given material describing an essential difference between Christianity and Islam as simply timing – Jesus called on His disciples in the 1st Century to believe in Him as 'the current Messenger of God' and Muhammad calls on us today to believe in him as today's 'current Messenger':

> A Muslim has to believe in the Messenger of God and follow his teachings, because he is the *only* way to God.[254]

In his acclaimed autobiography *The Islamist*, Mahomed M. Husain tells 'why I joined radical Islam in Britain, what I saw inside and why I left'. He grew up in London's Brick Lane mosque in a form of 'spiritual Islam', following Sheikh Abd al-Latif, master of five Muslim mystical orders and founder of over 400 religious seminaries in India and Bangladesh. He says 'the entire gathering would stand and sing greetings to the Prophet, hoping to invoke his spiritual presence… There was always an ambience that made most of us feel as one, united in purpose, standing and singing praises to the Prophet'.[255] Note, these Muslims were not just thinking about or remembering, but directly addressing, Muhammad in their prayer.

As a teenager, however, Husain became radicalised and politicised, working for the Young Muslim Organisation (YMO UK) and then *Hizb ut-Tahrir* to create a Muslim state

---

253 http://pewforum.org/Muslim/Mapping-the-Global-Muslim-Population%286%29.aspx, 28 Nov, 2011.
254 *Islam and Christianity (as seen in the Bible)*, Discover Islam Centre, Manama, Kingdom of Bahrain, pp. 9-11, emphasis added.
255 Mahomed M. Husain, *The Islamist*, London; Penguin Books, 2007, p. 12.

---

in Britain and ultimately the world. After some ten years, he
became disillusioned, especially by the events of September
11, 2001, and converted back to 'spiritual Islam' via Sufism:

> In my Islamist days… I really had no conception of
> who [Muhammad] was, other than a political leader…
> In the company of Sufis I discovered who the most
> misunderstood man in history really was. I continued
> to meet people who internalised every single one of the
> Prophet's traits: happiness, compassion, fairness, gentility,
> and an aura of inner contentment. The Prophet was alive
> in their hearts, and found expression in their conduct.[256]

However, while living and working in Saudi Arabia, he saw
this contacting of Muhammad being strictly forbidden:

> Medina never disappointed; the presence of the Prophet
> could be felt… [But] Wahhabi religious police, zealous
> and harsh, patrolled the Prophet's mosque to ensure
> nobody worshipped him there. Arrogant guards looked
> down with contempt at the visitors – to them we are
> *mushrikeen*, polytheists, like the "misguided Christians"
> who deify Jesus. The Wahhabis cannot comprehend the
> difference between love and worship. Never in the history
> of Islam has the Prophet been worshipped or deified.
> Islamic theology is sufficiently sound to prevent Islam
> from St Paul's type of Christology…
>
> They broke up gatherings of Shia Muslims and forcefully
> moved on spiritual Muslims… On many instances I found
> myself standing in the intense heat outside the mosque
> beside lovers of the Prophet from central Asia, Turkey
> and Pakistan. They wept out of yearning for him and I
> wondered why they had been expelled…[257]

Notice, Mr Husain condemns the worship of Jesus but sees
nothing wrong in praying to and singing praises to the Prophet
of Islam. On the other hand, the fundamentalist Wahhabis

---

256 *ibid*, pp. 196-197.
257 *ibid*, p. 267.

                                    Slouching Towards Bethlehem

of Saudi Arabia forbid overt worship of Muhammad while nonetheless setting him up in their hearts as the perfect image of Islam. Both views fulfill the prophecy of John's second beast.

And what are the consequences of denying Muhammad's unique role? Wherever the Sharia, or Islamic law, is in force, charges of blasphemy. Muhammad and the spirit that inspired him, fourteen hundred years ago, continue to 'cause as many as do not worship the image of the beast to be killed' (Rev 13:15).

The Spread of Islam

Before his death in 632 A.D., Muhammad had conquered the Arabian Peninsula; within ten years his followers had extended the Islamic empire into Egypt, Libya and Iran; within a hundred years, they ruled from North Africa in the west to Spain and southern Italy in Europe to Central Asia and northern India in the east. This empire was larger than Alexander the Great's and Rome's and not all of this territory was taken with the sword – some was by persuasion, treaties and marriages. However, Indian historian, K.S. Lal estimates that in India between 1000-1500 A.D., 60-80 million Hindus were killed by the Muslim invaders.[258] Although the invasion began in 732 A.D., Professor Lal's work is based on population numbers, starting from the conquest of Afghanistan in 1000 A.D. which culminated in the annihilation or enslavement of its entire Hindu population. To this day, the region is called *Hindu Kush*, or Hindu killer, because so many slaves perished as they were being led away through the mountains.[259]

It is ironic that Muslims today cite the Crusades (1095-1291 A.D.) as a prime reason for their 20th Century angst. At the time, they barely noticed. Thomas F. Madden is Professor of

---

258 *Growth of Muslim Population in Medieval India*, Delhi; Research Publications in Social Sciences, 1973.
259 http://koenraadelst.blogspot.com/2010/10/meaning-of-hindu-kush.html, 29 Oct, 2011.

Medieval History and director of the Center for Medieval and Renaissance Studies at St. Louis University, Missouri. Considered a leading authority on those times, he writes:

> The crusades are today one of the most misunderstood events in western history… (They) are first and foremost an aspect of European history. At the time, few Muslims in the Middle East understood the crusades at all. For western Europeans, the crusades were epic struggles… For Muslims, the crusades were hardly worthy of attention. As late as the 17th Century, the crusades remained virtually unknown in the Muslim world. From the grand perspective of Muslim history, they were simply tiny and futile attempts to halt the inevitable expansion of Islam.[260]

The Crusades' death toll is often quoted as 1 million, 3 million or even up to 9 million.[261] However, with better access to historical records, scholars such as Professor Madden today estimate the figure to be as low as 150,000 Muslims, Christians, Jews, and others:

> The highest death tolls were in conquered cities. Approximately 3,000 died when the Crusaders captured Jerusalem, about 15,000 when the Muslims conquered Antioch. The deadliest battles – Field of Blood and Hattin [Muslim victories in 1119 and 1187 resp.] – killed approximately 10,000 each. As a rough estimate, I would think the total killed in all Crusades between 1095 and 1291 to be around 150,000.[262]

This included most of the Crusaders themselves. For example, in the First Crusade, which is considered the most successful

---

260 Thomas F. Madden, preface to *The New Concise History of the Crusades*, Lanham; Rowman & Littlefield Publishers, Inc., 2006. Also, pp. 217-218. Professor Madden is the editor of *Crusades: The Illustrated History*. See also www.firstthings.com/article/2007/01/crusaders-and-historians-42, 18 Jul, 2011.
261 For example, http://en.wikipedia.org/wiki/Death_toll and http://necrometrics.com/pre1700a.htm, 29 Jul, 2011.
262 E-mail to the author on 18 Jul, 2011.

                              Slouching Towards Bethlehem

because they captured Jerusalem, the first wave was the People's Crusade, led by Peter the Hermit on a donkey. Mostly unarmed, untrained and including women and children, tens of thousands set out. Unfortunately, while Peter was away in Constantinople, the Turks killed or enslaved them all, so that Peter was virtually the sole survivor.[263] The second wave, led by the infamous antisemitic Count Emicho of Leiningen, never made it to the east, attacking instead the Jews of Europe.[264] Peter the Hermit then joined the more organised third wave, or Princes' Crusade, which finally reached and captured Jerusalem in 1099.[265] However, some ninety years later, in 1187, Saladin recaptured it for Islam, and in 1291, the last bastion of the Crusaders, the city of Acre, fell.

We see then that from the 8th Century, for four hundred years, the Islamic empire invaded eastern and southern Europe and North Africa. Over the next two hundred years, the Europeans mounted eight (some count nine) belated and benighted counter-attacks, the Crusades, in which the Muslims indeed suffered tens of thousands of deaths. During those two hundred years, on the eastern front, the Muslims were killing tens of *millions* of Hindus in India and Afghanistan alone.

This slaughter of the Hindus was not complete annihilation. Belgian historian Koenraad Elst explains why:

> Against these rebellious Pagans the Muslim rulers
> preferred to avoid total confrontation, and to accept the
> compromise which the (in India dominant) Hanifite
> school of Islamic law made possible. Alone among the
> four Islamic law schools, the school of Hanifa gave
> Muslim rulers the right not to offer the Pagans the sole
> choice between death and conversion, but to allow them

263　Madden, *The New Concise History of the Crusades,* pp. 15-19.
264　www.crusades-encyclopedia.com/jewishpersecution.html, 5 Sep, 2011.
265　Madden, p. 34.

toleration as zimmis (protected ones) living under 20
humiliating conditions, and to collect the jizya (toleration
tax) from them. Normally the zimmi status was only open
to Jews and Christians (and even that concession was
condemned by jurists of the Hanbalite school like Ibn
Taymiya), which explains why these communities have
survived in Muslim countries while most other religions
have not.[266]

Will Durant, the American historian, concluded: 'The Islamic
conquest of India is probably the bloodiest story in history'.[267]

The Last One Hundred Years

Bringing it closer to home, there are in the 20th Century
four major examples of deliberate Islamic genocide that fulfil
Revelation 13:15 in appalling detail.

It is often overlooked that the first genocide of the
20th Century was the slaughter of between 600,000 and
950,000 Armenians and the deportation of another 800,000
for their lack of faith in Muhammad.[268] Armenia was renowned
as the first nation in the world to accept Christianity as the
state religion and by the 10th Century its capital, Arni, was
called 'the city of a thousand and one churches'. However,
the Muslims invaded in the 11th, ruling until the end of the
19th Century, when the Armenians began to agitate for an
end to the Ottoman Empire's special taxes on Christians.
Sultan Abdul Hamid responded by massacring 100,000
'infidels' between 1895 and 1896 and another 30,000 in 1909,
inciting his people in the mosques with fabricated claims the

---

266 *Negationism in India: Concealing the Record of Islam*, The Voice of
India, http://koenraadelst.bharatvani.org/books/negaind/ch2.htm, 4 Jul,
2011.
267 *Story of Civilization*, Vol.1, New York; Our Oriental Heritage,
1972, p. 459.
268 Efraim Karsh, *Islamic Imperialism - A History*, New Haven &
London; Yale University Press, 2007, p. 118.

                                 Slouching Towards Bethlehem

Armenians were about to attack. The Armenians were offered the alternative of Islam or death and the victims were usually slaughtered according to Islamic rites.[269]

In 1913, the Sultan was overthrown and his successors, a triumvirate of what was called the Young Turks, Mehmed Talaat, Ismail Enver and Ahmed Djemal, sought to create a Muslim entity that extended to the Caspian Sea. To achieve this, on April 24, 1915, they ordered the complete extermination of the Armenian Christians.[270]

The Turkish army began by disarming and executing all the men, in one instance driving 5,000 into a cave to be suffocated.[271] They then sent the women and children and the elderly on the infamous 'death marches'. Young children were sometimes spared to be adopted by Turkish families, coerced into denouncing Christianity and becoming Muslims. Of the over one million Armenians on the marches, it is estimated seventy five percent perished en route, those surviving the ordeal then being herded into the desert without water, thrown off cliffs, burned alive or drowned in rivers.[272]

Hitler was hugely encouraged by the whole world's refusal to help the Armenians. When he conquered Poland, he told Reichsmarschall Hermann Goering and his commanding generals:

---

269 Vahakn N. Dadrian, *The History of the Armenian Genocide,* Oxford; Berghah Books, 1995, pp. 148-149.

270 In 1855, in the midst of a major revival when hundreds of thousands came to Christ, an 11 year old Russian boy called Efim Klubniken predicted this genocide and the time when it would begin, enabling many to flee. Among those who reached America was the Shakarian family whose story is told in *The Happiest People On Earth,* written by Demos Shakarian with John and Elizabeth Sherrill, Hodder & Stoughton Religious, 1977.

271 Robert Fisk, *The Great War For Civilisation (The Conquest of the Middle East),* London; Fourth Estate, 2005, p. 398.

272 www.historyplace.com/worldhistory/genocide/armenians.htm, 11 Feb, 2004.

Thus for the time being I have sent to the East only my
"Death's Head" units with the orders to kill without pity
or mercy all men, women and children of Polish race
or language. Only in such a way will we win the vital
space that we need. Who still talks nowadays about the
Armenians?[273]

A second major fulfilment through Islam was in 1971 when
the West Pakistani army massacred at least one and a quarter
million Bengalis in what became Bangladesh, the men executed
being identified as non-Muslim by lack of circumcision.[274]

The human death toll over only 267 days was incredible.
Just to give for five out of the eighteen districts some
incomplete statistics published in Bangladesh newspapers
or by an Inquiry Committee, the Pakistani army killed
100,000 Bengalis in Dacca, 150,000 in Khulna, 75,000 in
Jessore, 95,000 in Comilla, and 100,000 in Chittagong.
For eighteen districts the total is 1,247,000 killed. This was
an incomplete toll, and to this day no one really knows the
final toll.[275]

Koenraad Elst again:

Nandan Vyas (*Hindu Genocide in East Pakistan*, Young
India, January 1995) has argued convincingly that the
number of Hindu victims in the 1971 genocide was
approximately 2.4 million, or about 80% [Vyas compared
population figures for 1961 and 1971]… [However,]
taking into account a number of Hindu children born to
refugees in India rather than in Bangladesh, and a possible
settlement of 1971 refugees in India, it is fair to estimate
the disappeared Hindus at about 2 million.[276]

---

273 At Obersalzberg on August 22, 1939. Record published by *The New
York Times*, 24th Nov, 1945, p. 7, col. 2.
274 *Death By Government*, Rummel, p. 323.
275 Rummel, p. 331. See also www.hawaii.edu/powerkills/SOD.
CHAP8.HTM, 7 Mar, 2009.
276 http://koenraadelst.bharatvani.org/articles/irin/genocide.html, 4
Jul, 2011.

                              Slouching Towards Bethlehem

A third major fulfilment began in Africa's largest country, Sudan, in 1983. Although the media today report hundreds of thousands killed in its western region of Darfur since February 2003, Sudan's Islamic government actually began killing twenty years earlier, attacking all in southern Sudan and the Nuba Mountains who were opposed to the imposition of Sharia Law. Now led by Omar al-Bashir, an army officer who seized power in a 1989 coup, the National Islamic Front had by 1998 already killed or starved 1.9 million Christians, animists, and moderate Muslims.[277] Thankfully, the slaughter has at last come to an end with the creation of the Republic of Southern Sudan in July, 2011, and its recognition by the United Nations as the 193rd member state.

I was going to leave out the fourth major fulfilment, the Iran-Iraq War (1980-88) in which it is estimated one million died,[278] because all were Muslim and the issues were complicated by Western support for Iraq's aggression. However, its primary cause was the controversy between Shi'ite and Sunni concepts of Muhammad's successors with mullahs on both sides promising Paradise to the young combatants if they were to die as 'martyrs'. It should therefore be recognised as a war between two competing images of the beast.

Isolated Incidents or Recurring Outbreaks?

Along with suicide-bombings and the highly visible beheading of hostages, examples such as these 'holy wars' are often written off as isolated incidents of extremist, fundamentalist or Islamist behaviour, as abhorrent to true Muslims as to everyone else. This is perfectly understandable, given that many Muslims

---

277 Millard Burr, *Quantifying Genocide in Southern Sudan and the Nuba Mountains 1983-1998*, www.occasionalwitness.com/content/ documents/Working_DocumentII.htm, 17 Mar, 2012. Also www. ushmm.org/conscience/alert/darfur/pdf/darfur.pdf, 17 Mar, 2012.
278 http://necrometrics.com/20c300k.htm#Iran-Iraq, 18 Feb, 2012.

today are gracious and loving people who actually live out
the Qur'anic verse upholding tolerance:

> There is [or, Let there be] no compulsion in religion
> (Sura 2:256)[279]

However, one complication often not understood by those
of us in the West is that the Qur'an's revelations must be
understood in their particular timing i.e. when exactly each
was received by Muhammad. According to the principle of
naskh, or 'abrogation', new revelations override previous
revelations. They must all therefore be read in the light of
Islamic history.

Dr Mark Gabriel was an Egyptian Muslim scholar who
earned his Ph.D. and taught Islamic history at Al-Azhar
University in Cairo, the highest centre of Islamic learning. At
the age of 36, he became a follower of Jesus,[280] having found
Islam's history ...

> ...from its commencement to date, to be filled with
> violence and bloodshed without any worthwhile ideology
> or sense of decency. I asked myself "What religion would
> condone such destruction of human life?"[281]

Dr. Gabriel explains that Sura 2:256 was received in about 622
A.D. when Muhammad and his followers were still a minority
and fleeing from Mecca.[282] While calling others to treat him and
his followers with tolerance, this did not make Muhammad a

---

279   Pickthal and Yusafali, www.cmje.org/religious-texts/quran/
verses/002-qmt.php, 17 Sep, 2011.
280   www.arabicbible.com/testimonies/gabriel.htm, 22 Aug, 2011.
281   *Against the Tides in the Middle East,* International Academic Centre
for Muslim Evangelism in South Africa, published under the name
Mustafa, 1997, pp. 20-21.
282   Mark Gabriel, *Jesus and Muhammad (Profound Differences and
Surprising Similarities),* Lake Mary, Florida; Charisma House, 2004, p.
125. See also Section J, *Jihad - The Holy War of Islam and Its Legitimacy
in the Qur'an,* Ayatullah Morteza Mutahhari, www.al-islam.org/short/
jihad, 9 Mar, 2009.

                                    Slouching Towards Bethlehem

peace-maker. Four years later in Medina, when he gained the ascendancy, he expelled two Jewish tribes and exterminated the third, the Banu Quraiza. All the men, numbering between seven and eight hundred, were beheaded, while the women and children were sold into slavery. The Prophet kept the most beautiful widow, Rihana, as his concubine because she refused to marry him.[283]

In 630 A.D., he received a fresh revelation which "abrogated" the earlier revelation against compulsion, enabling him to break a peace treaty and capture Mecca:

> Then, when the sacred months have passed, slay the idolaters [*lit.* those who associate or make the same, i.e. polytheists or Christians who associate Jesus with God] wherever ye find them, and take them (captive), and besiege them, and prepare for them each ambush. But if they repent and establish [Muslim] worship and pay the poor-due [i.e. obligatory alms], then leave their way free. Lo! Allah is Forgiving, Merciful. (Sura 9:5)[284]

Some argue that this only applied to those who were a military threat to Muhammad and his followers[285] but since he and they then set out to conquer the world, they must have felt very threatened. Like Ibn Khaldun in the 14th Century and Osama bin Laden in the 21st Century, many Muslims hold that this famous 'Verse of the Sword' is the last word on the subject.

Whether the Qur'an is being misapplied or not, what is indisputable is that millions have died in the last hundred years, not in isolated incidents but in recurring outbreaks of Islamic *jihad*, or holy war. Pursued by many Islamic groups such as the Chechen mujahideen, the Muslim Brotherhood,

---

283 Sir William Muir, *The Life of Mahomet*, New Delhi; Voice of India, 1992.

284 Pickthal, www.cmje.org/religious-texts/quran/verses/009-qmt.php, 17 Sep, 2011.

285 For example, Robert Wright on http://evolutionofgod.net/q/koran, 17 Sep, 2011.

National Islamic Front, al-Qaeda, Al-Aqsa Martyrs' Brigade, Hamas and Hezbollah, jihad is a form of emperor worship. It is aimed at furthering Islam's divine 'universal mission', in Ibn Khaldun's words, 'to gain power over other nations', whether in Sudan or Spain, Algeria or London, Baghdad or New York, Bali or Lebanon, Yemen or Moscow. This is especially the case in Israel, for reasons we will consider next.

We see too that within Islam the phenomenon of emperor-worship is often centred around an ayatollah, imam or mullah who wants his followers to fight the megalomania of the Iranian Shah's Peacock Throne (Ayatollah Khomeini), the 'Russian atheists' in Afghanistan (Taliban's Mohammed Omar) or 'U.S. infidels' in Iraq (Muqtada al-Sadr). In an ironic and tragic twist, as mentioned above, Islam contains two competing antichrist regimes, Sunnis and Shi'ites, which foster the unrelenting suicide bombings of each other's mosques and shrines in Iraq and Pakistan.

As inevitably as the secular and atheistic political movements or Hinduism, Buddhism, Shintoism or Christian political cults do, the Islamic movements always elevate one man who comes to be seen as the embodiment of their state or movement, his thoughts as the only 'true' thoughts, until he has begun to receive the worship that is due only to Christ. We will consider this soon.

Islam and Israel

The people of Israel in the land of Israel will always be the prime target of militant Islam. In most reports of Islamist attacks anywhere in the world, there are two recurring stated motivations: to support the Palestinians' struggle against Israel and to strike all who support Israel, usually held to be Christian nations on new crusades. Al-Qaeda's official mission statement is headed, 'Jihad Against Jews and Crusaders'.[286]

To properly comprehend this, consider again Islam's basic assumption: 'There is but one God and Muhammad is His Apostle (lit. *rasoul,* messenger)'. Since Allah has 'abrogated' the revelations made to Moses, the Jews have been set aside by Him; since He has also 'abrogated' the revelations made through Jesus and the apostles, Christians have been too. Islam being the third monotheistic faith therefore sees Judaism and Christianity as waning while the crescent moon can only wax, until the whole earth is Islamic.

Imagine Islamic consternation, then, in 1948 when Israel suddenly became a sovereign nation again. Allah could not be resurrecting Israel, so it had to have been the work of Satan:

> ...an attempt by Jews to do something that was not legitimate: to seek political independence and that in the midst of what the Arabs regard as their own territory. This was for Islam and the Arabs the ultimate affront.[287]

Repeated attempts to destroy the fledgling nation, 'the little Satan', including all-out wars in 1948, 1967 and 1973, have all failed. Islamic militants have therefore also turned their attention to Israel's primary military supporter, 'America, the great Satan'. However, according to the hadith of al-Bukhari, Muhammad taught that Muslims will continue to fight the Jews until the Day of Resurrection:

> By this time, Muslims would have killed all the Jews but one. This one Jew would hide behind a rock, and the rock would say to the Muslims, "There is a Jew hiding behind me. Come and kill him".[288]

Given that the Jews, secular or religious, will never worship

---

286 www.fas.org/irp/world/para/docs/980223-fatwa.htm, 28 Oct, 2008.
287 Ronald Nettler, *Islam and the Minorities: Background to the Arab-Israeli Conflict,* Jerusalem, 1978, p. 11.
288 Mark A. Gabriel, *Islam and The Jews: The Unfinished Battle,* Lake Mary, Florida; FrontLine 2003, p. 115.

Muhammad (i.e. the Muslim's image of the first beast, which is their Islamic empire), the second beast (i.e. the spirit of antichrist) will continue to cause them to be killed, right up to the end.

'O Little Town …'

Lastly, consider the Bethlehem of our title. Situated just 8 kilometres or 5 miles south of Jerusalem, it used to be one of the oldest Christian communities in the world but 'the little town' of Christmas carols has now become predominantly Muslim.

Protected as Christian even by Muslim invaders from 637 A.D. until the end of the Ottoman Empire in 1918, in 1948 the population of approximately 9,000[289] was still 85% Arab Christians.[290] Ironically, with the rebirth of the Jewish state in 1948, Bethlehem came under Jordanian rule and, with the ensuing influx of Palestinian Muslims, by 1998 its population of some 22,000 were 60% Muslim.[291] Captured by the Israelis in 1967, Bethlehem was handed over in 1995 to the Islamic Palestinian Authority and by 2016, Bethlehem's mayor Vera Baboun reported, the professing Christian population had shrunk to 12%.[292]

Our Christmas carol looks fondly back 2,000 years:

> O little town of Bethlehem, how still we see thee lie!
> Above thy deep and dreamless sleep, the silent stars go by.
> Yet in thy dark streets shineth the everlasting Light;
> The hopes and fears of all the years are met in thee to-night.[293]

---

289 www.palestineremembered.com/download/VillageStatistics/Table%20I/Jerusalem/Page-056.jpg, 20 Oct, 2011.
290 Andrea Pacini, *Socio-Political and Community Dynamics of Arab Christians in Jordan, Israel, and the Autonomous Palestinian Territories*, Oxford; Clarendon Press, 1998, p. 282.
291 Ibid.
292 https://www.timesofisrael.com/christians-worry-silent-night-may-soon-refer-to-their-community-in-bethlehem/, 16 May, 2020..
293 Phillip Brooks, 1868.

However, as W.B. Yeats points out, it did not stay 'still':

> The darkness drops again; but now I know
> That twenty centuries of stony sleep
> Were vexed to nightmare by a rocking cradle,
> And what rough beast, its hour come round at last,
> Slouches towards Bethlehem to be born?

Obviously, Yeats was speaking metaphorically but I believe the metaphor is now particularly apt.

The Coming of the Mahdi

In the light of what we have seen about the spirit of antichrist, surely one of the most disturbing Islamic teachings is the prediction of the soon-appearing of the Mahdi (Arabic, *al Masih*, lit. the Guided One). This 'Lord of the Age' is to set up a world government. While acknowledging Jesus, or Isa in Arabic, as a messiah and that He will return, both Sunnis and Shi'ites believe He is coming back as a Muslim to work alongside the Mahdi and to rebuke Christians for worshipping Him. It is therefore the Mahdi for whom they are now waiting.

While also believing in the Antichrist (Arabic, *al-Masih ad-Dajjal*, lit. the False Messiah), they see him as the Mahdi's main opponent and, incidentally, as being blind in his right eye.

The Mahdi is to be a descendant of Muhammad and reign from either Damascus or the city of Kufah in Iraq[294] for a number of years (either five, seven, eight, nine, ten, nineteen, twenty, forty or seventy)[295] before Jesus returns for the Day of Judgement.

With this in mind, consider now how the President of Iran, Mahmoud Ahmadinejad, finished his address at the General Assembly of the United Nations, on September, 17, 2005:

---

294 www.islamicweb.com/history/mahdi.htm, 6 Jul, 2011.
295 http://dlserver.yasinmedia.com/v87/English_Page/books_en_html/
books/An%20Overview%20of%20the%20Mahdis%20Government/3.
htm#_Toc172189858, 6 Jul, 2011.

Dear friends and colleagues,
From the beginning of time, humanity has longed for the day when justice, peace, equality and compassion envelop the world. All of us can contribute to the establishment of such a world. When that day comes, the ultimate promise of all Divine religions will be fulfilled with the emergence of a perfect human being who is heir to all prophets and pious men. He will lead the world to justice and absolute peace.
O mighty Lord, I pray to You to hasten the emergence of Your last repository, the promised one, that perfect and pure human being, the one that will fill this world with justice and peace.[296]

Ahmadinejad is a Shi'ite so he is expecting the reappearance of the Hidden or Twelfth Imam.[297] However, in this instance, he is also speaking for the vast majority of Sunnis because they too eagerly await the Mahdi as 'a perfect human being', bringer of world-wide peace and God's 'last repository'.

We will study this more closely later in this series when we come to Revelation chapters 16, 19 and 20.

---

296 www.mohammadmossadegh.com/news/mahmoud-ahmadinejad/united-nations-speech/, 6 Jul, 2011.
297 Over the two hundred and forty years following the death of Muhammad, all eleven successors were executed or assassinated by rivals. The twelfth, a child of five when his father was poisoned in 872 A.D., went into hiding and never reappeared. Most Shi'ites, also known as Twelvers, believe like Ahmadinejad that God has been hiding him until the day he will appear to usher in the End Times. This has led to some like Messianic Jewish writer Joel Richardson and Glen Beck, the high-profile Mormon commentator, describing them as a doomsday cult.

  Slouching Towards Bethlehem

13
'Satan's Century'
Summary of 20th Century Emperor Worship

On January 26, 1995, an editorial in *The New York Times*, noting the fiftieth anniversary of the liberation of survivors of World War II's death camps, observed:

> At its worst, this has been Satan's century. In no previous age have people shown so great an aptitude, and appetite, for killing millions of other people for reasons of race, religion or class.[298]

We know from John's vision of the two beasts that these appalling events are not accidental or coincidental – they are the predictable outcomes of emperor worship and we who are Christians have been far too slow to recognise the significance of the phenomenon revealed by John.

Stalin, Hirohito, Mussolini, Hitler, Mao Zedong, Kim Il Sung, Pol Pot, Hoxha and Ceausescu were obvious 20th Century god-emperors in the political realm. Each of these also came to an end in the 20th Century.

The most likely empire to produce the next great manifestation is Islam as it spreads and grows in followers, wealth, influence and militancy. While at the moment we all benefit from the division between the Sunnis and the Shi'ites, if their promised Mahdi appears, he is likely to unite them and what then?

---

298 www.nytimes.com/1995/01/26/opinion/remembering-auschwitz. html, 22 Aug, 2011.

Wild at Heart

Lastly, before we consider the secular perspective of all these regimes, let us remember the overview of John's revelation: these two entities are beasts.

Reading about or watching the adulation of leaders like Hitler, as described by Albert Speer ('the surge of rejoicing, the ecstasy reflected in so many faces… The mass exultation… the worship of the masses'[299]), it is easy to confuse it with other cultural phenomena such as football crowds or rock concerts. We freely name as 'idols' our heroes of sport, music or entertainment, and they often are, especially to the 'groupies' who, like the temple prostitutes of old, ignore God's standard of purity.

However, John's two beasts are not athletic or entertaining, nor like the cute, redeemable beast of Disney's *Beauty and the Beast*[300] or the soft-hearted *Shrek*[301] but wild, merciless brutes. When the Lord returns, all of the natural animal kingdom will lose its carnivorous aggression, for all to enjoy (Isa 11:6-9), but He will destroy these two spiritual creatures on that day (Rev 19:20).

Accordingly, a major defining characteristic of both the feral state and the antichrist spirit, and it is readily seen in all of these empires despite their very different ideologies, is their underlying and often murderous aggression:

> And it was given to him (the spirit of antichrist) to give breath to the image of the beast (the feral state or empire), so that the image of the beast (the emperor) would even speak and cause as many as do not worship the image of the beast to be killed (Rev 13:15)

---

299 Albert Speer, *Inside The Third Reich*, New York and Toronto: Macmillan, 1970, p. 85.

300 Walt Disney Picture's much-loved animated musical of 1991 was based on an 18th Century French fairytale, *La Belle et la Bête*.

301 *Shrek* won DreamWorks Animation the first-ever Academy Award for Best Animated Feature in 2001.

  Slouching Towards Bethlehem

That they are not always murderous is clear in the following verses, where we see opponents being allowed to live but not to trade:

> …and he provides that no one will be able to buy or to sell, except the one who has the mark, either the name of the beast or the number of his name (Rev 13:17)

Given the importance of this mark, we will devote the whole of our next study to that.

Jesus said of the Holy Spirit that "when He comes… He will glorify Me, for He will take of Mine and will disclose it to you" (John 16:13-14). Notice, the Holy Spirit extends the kingdom of God by glorifying 'the man Christ Jesus' (1 Tim 2:5), by disclosing or revealing Him, His love and His reward.

As the counterfeit, the spirit of antichrist also glorifies a man, whichever antichrist is current, but by deceiving and coercing. Accordingly, antichrist regimes will always be aggressive and seek to dominate as many people as they can.

Emperors are most glorified not by having their character revealed – that is often kept carefully concealed – but by the size of their empires. The boundaries are usually natural barriers such as seas, rivers, deserts and mountains but where there are none, emperors build walls or fortifications against counter-attack.

The Roman emperors, for example, extended their empire as far as they could to the east, to the North Atlantic Ocean, and to the south, to the deserts of Arabia and Sahara. To the west, they tried to invade for hundreds of years but were held back by the Parthians, while beyond the northern border of the rivers Rhine and Danube were the 'barbarians', the Goths, Vandals and Huns.

We saw earlier the appalling death toll in the 12th and 13th Centuries of the Mongolian Khans' conquests, some 30 million men, women and children, but consider now how many lands they conquered: at its greatest extent, their empire stretched from the Pacific in the east to the Mediterranean and Baltic Seas in the west and the Arabian in the south.

Coming to the 20th Century, we saw the truly staggering number of deaths caused by the emperors Stalin, Hirohito, Mussolini, Hitler and Mao. Consider now the aggression of each of these men – not one of them was content within their boundaries.

Hitler openly wanted more *lebensraum*, literally 'living space', for the Germans; Mussolini wanted a piece of North Africa, invading Abyssinia, today's Ethiopia; Hirohito wanted the Greater East Asia Co-Prosperity Sphere and invaded even the South Pacific; Stalin and Mao wanted nothing less than the global demise of capitalism and triumph of Marxism-Leninism.

All of them had to be restrained and resisted by the armed forces of their intended victims.

Lastly, Islam. In the light of the often genocidal Islamic invasions over the last fourteen hundred years, we should not be at all surprised at the smouldering aggression observable in our daily news today. While every instance should be considered on its own merits, we should not simply accept the frequent Islamic justification of it being defensive warfare against victimisation.

Let us be very clear – this spirit will never be content with a democratic government. We will consider how to respond in our conclusions.

What Fills the Heart?

Every culture has its salutes and battle cries to motivate its warriors. In Jesus' phrase:

> The mouth speaks out of that which fills the heart
> (Matt 12:34)

Of course, men often fight to protect each other in their small platoons rather than for only the empire. For example, in about 1380, the Ottoman Empire created an elite fighting force called the Janissaries, to be loyal foremost to the emperor or Sultan:

> At first Janissaries may have been recruited from war prisoners. Later, they were recruited by systematic abduction of Christian youths from their families in the devshirmeh ['child levy'] system, which raised them as soldiers from a young age (as young as 8 but as old as 20) in special academies. They were forced to convert to Islam, as non-Muslims were not allowed to bear arms. ... [They] lasted until about 1826, when their many revolts and increasing ineffectiveness led to the abolition of the corps.[302]

Although fighting for the Ottomans, many of these young men carried quotations from the gospels into battle as lucky charms,[303] and their battalions were close-knit communities, effectively their only family.

However, salutes and battle cries often spell out the true nature of the regime.

The Romans formally greeted their emperors with *"Ave Caesar!"* (*ave* is Latin for 'Be well' or 'Long live') which the Nazis adapted to *"Heil Hitler!"* for everyone to wish him success; *"Sieg heil!"* ('Long live victory!') looked forward to the success of his empire.

---

302 www.mideastweb.org/Middle-East-Encyclopedia/janissary.htm, 8 Mar, 2012.
303 www.theottomans.org/english/campaigns_army/index_3.asp, 8 Mar, 2012.

The Russian soldiers' battle cry was *"Za Rodinu! Za Stalina!"* ('For Motherland! For Stalin!') and the Japanese, *"Tenno Haika! Banzai!"* ('Long live the Emperor! [May he live] Ten thousand years!').

The cry of Islamic jihadists and suicide bombers, *"Allahu akbar!"*, means 'Allah is the greatest!'[304] and affirms Muhammad's claim that his revelation of God is superior to all others.

These salutes and battle cries therefore plainly reveal the specific antichrist being worshipped.

Some require a closer look, such as the conquistadors' cry when they attacked the Incas, as we saw earlier: *"Santiago y cierra, España!"* ('Saint James and attack, Spain!'), or simply *"Santiago"*, as they sought protection from St. James, the patron saint of Spain.

Contrast these with the battle cries of the early Christians. Rather than pour out the libation or burn incense to the emperor, they often laid down their lives in the Roman circuses crying out: *"Maranatha! Hallelujah!"*

Hallelujah is a Hebrew call for all who hear to praise the Lord.[305] Maranatha is Aramaic and means 'Come, O Lord!', spoken in trust that He will put everything right when He returns.[306] John therefore finishes the Book of Revelation:

> He who testifies to these things says, "Yes, I am coming quickly." Amen. Come, Lord Jesus.
> The grace of the Lord Jesus be with all. Amen. (Rev 22:20-21)

---

304 www.islamic-dictionary.com/index.php?word=allahu%20akbar, 8 Mar, 2012.
305 Kittel & Friedrich, *Theological Dictionary of the New Testament* (abridged by Geoffrey Bromley), Grand Rapids, Michigan; William B. Eerdmans Publishing Co, 1990, pp. 563-564.
306 Ibid., p. 43.

14

Totalitarianism
The Secular Perspective

Although John's vision gives us the big picture to help us recognise the underlying pattern of emperor worship, not just in our time or nation but throughout all generations and in all nations, secular scholars naturally refuse it. Preferring their own perspective of this phenomenon, they call it totalitarianism, and seek to distinguish the modern form from older forms. For example, popular encyclopaedia *Encarta 96* begins with a definition:

> Totalitarianism – in political science, a system of government and ideology in which all social, political, economic, intellectual, cultural and spiritual activities are subordinated to the purposes of the rulers of the state.

The article then goes on to claim that this is peculiar to our times:

> Several important features distinguish totalitarianism, a form of autocracy peculiar to the 20th century, from such older forms as despotism, absolutism and tyranny. In the older forms of autocracy people could live and work in relative independence, provided they refrained from politics. In modern totalitarianism, however, people are made utterly dependent on the wishes and whims of a political party and its leaders. The older autocracies were ruled by a monarch or other titled aristocrat who governed by a principle such as divine right, whereas the modern totalitarian state is ruled by a leader, or dictator, who controls a political party...

It attributes this control to the dark side of technology:

> Total subjection of the individual became possible only

through advanced science and industrial technology. Among the decisive, technologically conditioned features of totalitarian dictatorships are a monopoly of mass communications, a terroristic secret-police apparatus, a monopoly of all effective weapons of destruction, and a centrally controlled economy...

It then identifies this economy's ability to control who can 'buy or sell':

> The centrally controlled economy enables the totalitarian dictatorship to... control the workers and make them dependent on the government. Without a work permit none can work. Work permits can be withdrawn for offences such as objecting to foul working conditions...

Although *Encarta* is right to say that totalitarian regimes in our times have used modern political means and more efficient policing due to modern technology, it fails to recognise the ages-old continuity. In fact, any modern political movement, irrespective of whether it is left or right-wing, can just as surely as any of the ancient regimes produce a single, autocratic leader. When we come to our next study regarding the mark of the beast, we will see that the older forms of autocracy just as surely controlled the ability of its subjects to buy and sell.

Emperor-worship did not die out over the ages; it has continued to afflict the human race for thousands of years. However, it is only occasionally noticed by modern secular thinkers. One was Friedrich Nietzsche.

Friedrich Nietzsche (1844-1900)

Some fifty years before Hitler came to power, German existentialist philosopher Friedrich Nietzsche dreamed of humans becoming *ubermenschlich* (over or superhuman) and inspired Hitler's Aryan racism. He also proclaimed the 'death of God' and inspired many liberal theologians. They, however, do not seem to have read on to his chilling prediction of the inevitable outcome of that 'death' – that the state would become *'the new idol'*:

> A state is called the coldest of all cold monsters.
> Coldly it lies also, and this lie creeps from its mouth: "I, the state, am the people…
> On earth there is nothing greater than I: it is I who am the regulating finger of God" – thus roars the monster.[307]

Like Hobbes, Nietzsche sees the State as having a life of its own but he recognises it as 'the coldest of cold monsters' or reptilian. He also hears it uttering the 'arrogant words and blasphemies' of John's first beast (Rev 13:5-6).

Nietzsche goes on to predict that 'all of the earth will worship him' (Rev 13:8):

> And not only the long-eared and the short-sighted fall on their knees!
> Ah, even in your ears, you great souls, it whispers its gloomy lies!
> Ah, it finds out the rich hearts which willingly lavish themselves!
> Yea, it finds you out too, you conquerors of the old God!
> Weary you became of the conflict, and now your weariness serves the new idol!

Having rejected 'the old God', the people rejoice, only to find that the State has now become 'the regulating finger of God' on earth. However, as Hitler demonstrated, it promises something for everyone:

> Everything will it give you, if you worship it, the new idol;
> Thus it purchases the lustre of your virtue, and the glance of your proud eyes.[308]

Astonishingly prescient.

---

307 *Thus Spake Zarathustra,* Discourse I, 11, Wordsworth Edition Ltd, 1997, pp. 45-46.
308 Ibid.

Hannah Arendt (1906-1975)

In 1951, this German-Jewish political theorist published her controversial *The Origins of Totalitarianism* which examined the imperialism and antisemitism of Stalin's Communists and Hitler's Nazis. It was controversial because her critics saw them as very different in origins and nature but she identified the commonality of the two empires:

> The totalitarian attempt at world conquest and total domination has been the destructive way out of all impasses… Wherever it has ruled, it has begun to destroy the essence of man…
>
> The trouble is that our period has so strangely intertwined the good with the bad…Without the fictitious world of totalitarian movements, in which with unparalleled clarity the essential uncertainties of our time have been spelled out, we might have been driven to our doom without ever becoming aware of what has been happening.

In other words, we have at last seen evil unmasked:

> And if it is true that in the final stages of totalitarianism an absolute evil appears (absolute because it can no longer be deduced from humanly comprehensible motives), it is also true that without it we might never have known the truly radical nature of Evil…
>
> The subterranean stream of Western history has finally come to the surface… This is the reality in which we live.[309]

In the light of John's vision, we know she was essentially correct but, without his perspective, her analysis of 'our period' failed to recognise both the historical pattern of human sinfulness and its supernatural inspiration. Indeed, she explicitly denied any demonic influence and, ten years later, she reworked her conclusion:

---

309 *The Origins of Totalitarianism,* San Diego; Harcourt, Brace, Jovanovich, 1973, Preface to the first edition, viii-ix.

> I changed my mind and do no longer speak of "radical
> evil" [but rather of the "banality of evil"]… It is indeed
> now my opinion that evil is never "radical", that it is only
> extreme and that it possesses neither depth nor demonic
> dimension. It can overgrow and lay waste the whole world
> precisely because it spreads like a fungus on the surface.
> It is "thought-defying", as I said, because thought tries to
> reach some depth, to go to the roots, and the moment it
> concerns itself with evil, it is frustrated because there is
> nothing. That is its "banality". Only the good has depth
> and can be radical.[310]

Arendt had changed her mind in 1961, after covering the trial of Adolf Eichmann in Jerusalem. Until then, she had been sure that anyone willingly participating in totalitarian regimes must be ideologically committed, encouraged by propaganda and coerced by the state's brutality against dissenters. Listening to Eichmann, she decided that he might never have even read *Mein Kampf* and that he was simply thoughtless and selfish.[311]

However, as Jesus told Peter, this is all Satan needs to be able to operate in any of us:

> "…for you are not setting your mind on God's interests, but man's" (Matt 16:23)

Neil Postman, George Orwell & Aldous Huxley

In the foreword to his 1985 book, *Amusing Ourselves to Death*, educator and social critic Professor Neil Postman agrees with Arendt regarding our thoughtlessness and the greatest threat to our global future:

> We were keeping our eye on *1984*. When the year

---

310 Quoted by Idith Zertal, *Israel's Holocaust and the Politics of Nationhood,* Cambridge Middle East Studies 21, Cambridge University Press, 2005, p. 156.
311 *Eichmann in Jerusalem: A Report on the Banality of Evil,* London; Penguin Classics, 1992.

came and the prophecy didn't,[312] thoughtful Americans
sang softly in praise of themselves. The roots of liberal
democracy had held. Wherever else the terror had
happened, we, at least, had not been visited by Orwellian
nightmares.

But we had forgotten that alongside Orwell's dark vision,
there was another – slightly older, slightly less well-known,
equally chilling: Aldous Huxley's *Brave New World*.[313]
Contrary to common belief even among the educated,
Huxley and Orwell did not prophesy the same thing.
Orwell warns that we will be overcome by an externally
imposed oppression. But in Huxley's vision, no Big
Brother is required to deprive people of their autonomy,
maturity and history. As he saw it, people will come to
love their oppression, to adore the technologies that undo
their capacities to think.[314]

Professor Postman further contrasted the two visions:

What Orwell feared were those who would ban books.
What Huxley feared was that there would be no reason
to ban a book, for there would be no-one who wanted to
read one. Orwell feared those who would deprive us of
information. Huxley feared those who would give us so
much that we would be reduced to passivity and egoism.
Orwell feared that the truth would be concealed from
us. Huxley feared the truth would be drowned in a sea
of irrelevance. Orwell feared we would become a captive
culture. Huxley feared we would become a trivial culture,
preoccupied with some equivalent of the feelies, the orgy
porgy, and the centrifugal bumblepuppy.

As Huxley remarked in *Brave New World Revisited*,[315] the

---

312 George Orwell, *1984*, London; Secker & Warburg, 1949. Orwell
was the pen-name of Eric Blair (1903-1950).
313 Published in 1932 by Chatto & Windus, London. Huxley (1894-
1963) wrote it in response to H.G. Wells's *Men Like Gods* (1923) and *The
Sleeper Awakes* (1910).
314 *Amusing Ourselves to Death: Public Discourse in the Age of Show
Business,* Penguin, 1985, Foreword.
315 www.huxley.net/bnw-revisited/index.html, 8 Mar, 2012.

                                    Slouching Towards Bethlehem

civil libertarians and rationalists who are ever on the
alert to oppose tyranny "failed to take into account man's
almost infinite appetite for distractions". In *1984*, Huxley
added, people are controlled by inflicting pain. In *Brave
New World*, they are controlled by inflicting pleasure.
In short, Orwell feared that what we hate will ruin us.
Huxley feared that what we love will ruin us.
This book [Postman's] is about the possibility that Huxley,
not Orwell, was right.[316]

Postman's book title plays on the thought that 'a-musing' means literally 'without thinking' and that this can be fatal. He had come to the same conclusion as Arendt but from an entirely different vantage point and analysis. He observes how the media today deliberately create images of political leaders to impact and entertain rather than to inform us (if you like, images of the image of the beast) because that is all we may have time and capacity to absorb. Politicians therefore now routinely engage image-managers, Postman highlighting ex-U.S. President Richard Nixon's claim that he lost the 1960 election to John F. Kennedy because he was sabotaged by the make-up artists.

Without detracting from Postman's main thesis on the power of the media, I believe he has overlooked the third possibility altogether – that both Huxley and Orwell were half-right. The Book of Revelation describes two major spiritual forces that have always afflicted us on the earth but will even more in time to come: one is called "Babylon the Great, the mother of harlots" (Rev 17:1-6), who is as seductive as Huxley describes, while the other, the spirit of antichrist, is as coercive as Orwell feared.

Huxley was also half-wrong because, as we will see, the Scriptures predict that there is yet to come at least one more coercive, talking and worship-demanding 'image of the beast'.

---

316 Postman, Ibid.

Winning the War on War?

Joshua S. Goldstein is Professor Emeritus of International Relations at American University in Washington, D.C. In 2011, his book, *Winning the War on War: The Decline of Armed Conflict Worldwide,*[317] notes:

> Despite the gory headlines, the decade since 9/11 has been the most peaceful worldwide in the past century…[318]
> In fact, the last decade has seen fewer war deaths than any decade in the past 100 years, based on data compiled by researchers Bethany Lacina and Nils Petter Gleditsch of the Peace Research Institute Oslo. Worldwide, deaths caused directly by war-related violence in the new century have averaged about 55,000 per year, just over half of what they were in the 1990s (100,000 a year), a third of what they were during the Cold War (180,000 a year from 1950 to 1989), and a hundredth of what they were in World War II. If you factor in the growing global population, which has nearly quadrupled in the last century, the decrease is even sharper. Far from being an age of killer anarchy, the 20 years since the Cold War ended have been an era of rapid progress toward peace…
> If the world feels like a more violent place than it actually is, that's because there's more information about wars -- not more wars themselves. Once-remote battles and war crimes now regularly make it onto our TV and computer screens, and in more or less real time. Cell-phone cameras have turned citizens into reporters in many war zones.[319]

There is no doubt Professor Goldstein is correct regarding war deaths over the last decade or two, as little comfort as that may be to the relatives of the two million killed during this time in Sudan.[320] In fact, if he had included the 84 million

---

317 New York, Dutton/Penguin, 2011.
318 http://winningthewaronwar.com/ 15 Sep, 2011.
319 www.foreignpolicy.com/articles/2011/08/15/think_again_war?page=full, 15 Sep, 2011.
320 Millard Burr, *Quantifying Genocide in Southern Sudan and the*

                    Slouching Towards Bethlehem

Chinese killed *in peacetime* between 1949 and 1987 by Mao and the Communist Chinese government,[321] he could have shown an even more dramatic decrease in violent deaths since then.

Harvard psychology professor Steven Pinker argues similarly in his book, *The Better Angels of Our Nature (Why Violence has Declined)*.[322] Taking his title from Abraham Lincoln's phrase[323] and trusting that mankind's innate goodness will prevail over our inner badness, Professor Pinker argues that:

> The key to explaining the decline of violence... is to understand the inner demons that incline us toward violence (such as revenge, sadism, and tribalism) and the better angels that steer us away. Thanks to the spread of government, literacy, trade, and cosmopolitanism, we increasingly control our impulses, empathize with others, bargain rather than plunder, debunk toxic ideologies, and deploy our powers of reason to reduce the temptations of violence.[324]

As nice as that would be, unfortunately the professors are determinedly secular. While mankind is clearly spreading government and cosmopolitanism, we have yet to see how open the Islamic governments (57 of the 193 nations in the

---

Nuba Mountains 1983-1998, www.occasionalwitness.com/content/documents/Working_DocumentII.htm, 17 Mar, 2012. Also www.ushmm.org/conscience/alert/darfur/pdf/darfur.pdf, 17 Mar, 2012.
321   See earlier chapter: 10 The Bitter Fruit.
322   New York; Viking, 2011.
323   Speaking as the United States was about to plunge into Civil War, Lincoln finished his inaugural speech in March, 1861, with the hope of better days: "We are not enemies, but friends. We must not be enemies. Though passion may have strained, it must not break, our bonds of affection. The mystic chords of memory, stretching from every battlefield and patriot grave to every living heart and hearthstone all over this broad land, will yet swell the chorus of the Union, when again touched, as surely they will be, by the better angels of our nature." http://www.bartleby.com/124/pres31.html, 12 Jan, 2012.
324   http://stevenpinker.com/publications/better-angels-our-nature, 10 Oct, 2011.

United Nations) will be to 'debunking toxic ideologies' and 'reducing the temptations of violence'. What if instead, they still want to follow the 7th Century example of Muhammad as the perfect Muslim?

And what of John's second beast, the spirit of antichrist? Despite Professor Pinker's talk of angels and demons, neither seem to have even noticed it yet.

In 1943, also speaking at Harvard, Winston Churchill predicted:

> The empires of the future are the empires of the mind[325]

Despite the confident claims of secularism, that 'religious considerations should be excluded from civil affairs or public education',[326] there will always be two issues to be addressed: ideological and spiritual.

I believe what we are watching at the moment is a relatively peaceful bisecting of the world into two primary ideologies backed by opposing spiritual forces: one is based entirely on our Judaeo-Christian heritage, though not usually acknowledged as such; the other on Muhammad's misinterpretation of that.

Accordingly, on one side, there is the phenomenal spread of liberal democracy, Francis Fukuyama's 'end of history', as mentioned earlier in the section on The Eleventh Horn. It remains to be seen how, or if, this will be outworked in Russia and China. As will be considered in the chapter *The Hidden Kingdom*, it is my belief that liberal democracy is on the side of the angels. Again despite secularism's loud claims of ownership, this has been quietly established by the Spirit of God through His people, Jews and Christians, over the last three and a half thousand years.

On the other side, we see the modern-day resurgence of Islam, empowered by the discovery of the Middle East's oil fields. Among the blossoms of the Arab Spring, dictators in

---

325   Speech at Harvard University, September 6, 1943.
326   *American Heritage Dictionary of the English Language*, 2004.

                                     Slouching Towards Bethlehem

Tunisia, Egypt, Libya and Yemen have fallen, and those in Syria and Bahrain are threatened, but what fruit will grow? The winners are likely to be more Islamist, due in large part to the West's helping the dictators to suppress Islamism, as we saw when the Shah of Iran was toppled. While it is possible that moderate or modern Islam may win out over fundamentalism, even apparently moderate Turkish and Egyptian democracies have so far produced increased antagonism towards Israel and the West.

Let us be clear. In this decade, Islam has gained most of its ground without overt armed conflict. With or without it, in Muslim thinking this is the predicted, inevitable, growth of *dar al-Islam* (house of submission) which is to overcome and absorb *dar al-harb* (house of war) i.e. all territory not under Islam. In this way alone, they promise, peace will come to the earth. Meanwhile, within *dar al-Islam*, all questioning of Muhammad's credentials is considered blasphemous and can be fatal.

Islam also has spiritual backing but, tragically, from John's second beast, the spirit of antichrist.

It is, of course, possible that both of these primary ideologies, liberal democracy and Islam, may resolve their own internal divisions and remain simply two differing world-views. However, given that both expect to win the whole world, it seems to me that the true believers are like boxers who have retired to their corners to be refreshed and coached before recommencing the bout.

We will consider this grand finale later in this series when we come to the end of the beasts.

15

John's Metaphors
The Two Beasts

Returning to our text, Revelation 13:1-15, let us recap what we have established so far about the two beasts:

(i) The first beast, 'out of the sea' (v. 1), is the principality and power of the Gentiles. This spiritual entity has 'seven heads' because it was manifest in the six Gentile empires which ruled over the ancient nation of Israel from about 2000 B.C. to 70 A.D. — Egypt, Assyria, Babylon, Medo-Persia, Greece and Rome. It will manifest again as the seventh Gentile empire in the last 'hour' before Jesus returns.

(ii) The seventh and last head of this beast has 'ten horns with ten diadems' (v. 1) which means it consists of "all the nations", or Gentiles, of the earth and they will ultimately unite into one earthly power to fight against Israel.

(iii) It is a wild beast because it is the good institution of God, the State, gone bad. Instead of upholding and enforcing justice as His servant, in these societies it has become self-aggrandising and unjust.

(iv) The fatal sword-wound on 'one of his heads' (v. 3), the sixth, was inflicted by the resurrection of Jesus when He received "all authority in heaven and on earth" in the time of the Romans. The first beast now only survives to fulfil the prophecies but any not understanding that will continue to marvel at the beast's endurance and give it too much value or worth, thereby worshipping it.

(v)   The second beast (and the eleventh horn) rises 'out of the land' (v. 11) and is the spirit of antichrist. Its goal is not just to oppose but to replace Christ. This spirit causes people to make an image of the first beast which can breathe and speak (v. 15), i.e. it is a living image.

(vi)   This image of the first beast is any deified leader and has appeared in many times and places over the last two thousand years. In John's day, the Roman emperors were worshipped with incense and libations or drink offerings but, since to worship means to accord ultimate worth, any leader to whom we accord ultimate worth or loyalty above God is being worshipped.

(vii)   The image is accompanied by supernatural signs so that the people worship this image of the first beast as if it is Christ. The signs include 'fire out of heaven' (v. 13), a real spiritual experience that counterfeits the manifestation of the Holy Spirit.

(viii)   The two beasts' allotted time period, 'forty-two months' (v. 5), is "the times of the Gentiles", Elijah's metaphorical "three years and six months" of drought and Israel's 'partial hardening'. It is therefore actually the last 2,000 years. During this time, the beasts have been allowed to physically overcome and kill the saints (v. 7) while the saints overcome by persevering in their faith 'even unto death'.

(ix)   The two beasts' overcoming of the saints can be seen throughout the 2,000 years of church history, not only in the secular state's persecution of believers but also in the use of the power of the state by any church, whether Roman Catholic, Eastern

Orthodox, Protestant or Reformed.

(x)   In the last one hundred years alone, the image of the first beast has been the secular political leaders from both the Left and the Right – Communist in Russia, China, North Korea and Cambodia, and Fascist in Italy and Germany.

(xi)   It has also appeared as the leaders of religious empires and kingdoms as in Japan, Nepal and Tibet.

(xii)   Even within Islam which purports to abhor all idolatry, the image is created and worshipped – their second article of faith, that Muhammad is God's Apostle, asserts his is the last word on every issue, abrogating the New Testament and Jesus Himself. His successors are therefore the image of the beast in each generation. The outworking can be seen today in Islamic militancy throughout the Middle East, North Africa, the ex-Soviet republics and South East Asia, and increasingly in Europe and the U.S.A.

(xiii) What secular historians and sociologists call totalitarianism is the phenomenon of emperor worship. They rarely recognise or acknowledge its essentially spiritual, demonic inspiration so they often believe we as humans have evolved past the point of its being a danger in the future.

(xiv)   Visionary writers and thinkers such as Friedrich Nietzsche, H.G. Wells, W.B. Yeats, Aldous Huxley and George Orwell all ended up fearing for our future and, in the case of Nietzsche and Yeats, foresaw a spiritual desolation.

(xv)   We are now seeing an ideological division of the world between liberal democracy and Islam. This exactly corresponds to the opposite outworking of our

Judeao-Christian heritage, as inspired by the Spirit of God, and Muhammad's heresy of that, inspired by John's second beast, the spirit of antichrist.

16

'Antichrist is Coming'
Ready or Not

There is one particular antichrist coming, among and following all of these, who will be *the* Antichrist. In his first letter, John tells us more about him:

> Children, it is the last hour; and just as you have heard that antichrist is coming, even now many antichrists have arisen…
> (1 John 2:18)

The *New International Version* (*NIV*) has this as 'the antichrist is coming' while some translations capitalise the word 'antichrist' – 'you have heard that Antichrist is coming'.[327] These make better sense than the NASB's lower case 'antichrist' as this is a title as well as a description, just as Christ is, and in this instance, the context clearly implies the title.

So, when John wrote this between 85-95 A.D.,[328] the disciples had already 'heard that Antichrist is coming'. Although Paul does not use the name 'antichrist', some forty years earlier he reminded the Thessalonians how he had talked to them about a future 'man of sin' who will meet his end at the Lord's return (2 Thess 2:5 & 8) and we will consider that passage soon.

Here, however, John adds that in addition to the final Antichrist, there were already many lesser antichrists in the 1st Century, making themselves obvious by their apostasy.

As we have just considered, many leaders since, such as the Caesars, Hirohito, Stalin, Mao, Mussolini, Hitler, Kim Il Sung, Pol Pot and Ayatollah Khomeini, have also qualified

---

327 For example, *New English Bible, Amplified*, William Barclay's translation, *The Message*.
328 *Zondervan NASB Study Bible*, p. 1829.

   Slouching Towards Bethlehem

for the name 'antichrist'. We saw that *anti* means 'instead of' or 'in place of' and these leaders have all sought, whether knowingly or unknowingly, to take the place in the hearts of their followers which is due only to Jesus Christ. That is why they have often been thought to be the final antichrist, even though they could not be him, as we will see.

John explains further in his second letter:

> For many deceivers have gone out into the world, those who do not acknowledge Jesus Christ as coming in the flesh. This is the deceiver and the antichrist…
> Anyone who goes too far and does not abide in the teaching of Christ, does not have God; the one who abides in the teaching, he has both the Father and the Son (2 John 7 & 9)

We know then that every true spiritual leader, prophet or teacher can be recognised by how truly they 'abide in the teaching of Christ', i.e. their faithfulness to the New Testament teaching about Jesus of Nazareth who came as God 'in the flesh' (e.g. 1 Tim 3:16, 1 John 4:2) and who will come again 'in the flesh', but this time to judge the world (e.g. Acts 1:11, 2 Tim 4:1). If any spiritual leader denies Jesus' incarnation, no matter how apparently profound his teaching and though he may not be as bad as the Antichrist, he is to be regarded as a deceiver and an antichrist. Accordingly, James warns us all:

> Let not many of you become teachers, my brethren, knowing that as such we shall incur a stricter judgment [i.e. greater accountability] (Jas 3:1)

John adds a specific test:

> 1. Beloved, do not believe every spirit, but test the spirits to see whether they are from God; because many false prophets have gone out into the world.
> 2. By this you know the Spirit of God: every spirit that confesses that Jesus Christ has come in the flesh is from God;
> 3. and every spirit that does not confess Jesus is not from God; and this is the **spirit** of the antichrist, of which you have heard

that it is coming, and now it is already in the world (1 John 4:1-3,
emphasis added)

Though the Antichrist is yet to come, the spirit that will
motivate him was already motivating these others. In this
instance, John is applying the test not to teaching but to
prophecy. This is essential because, according to Deuteronomy
13:1-5, *false prophets can be perfectly accurate and with signs
following* so all prophets and all prophecy must be tested for
their underlying theology.

Jesus spells out how we can recognise the activity of the
Holy Spirit who inspires all true prophecy:

He shall glorify Me (John 16:14)

This really is the simplest of tests: their attitude to Jesus Himself.
Do they accept Him as He presented Himself or do they try to
present 'another Jesus' or represent themselves as 'another Jesus'?

The Final Antichrist

All of the political leaders identified earlier qualified for the
name 'antichrist' but not for 'the Antichrist', because he will
still be in power when Jesus returns. Like John, Paul warns
us that we must judge every spirit and every message we hear
but he prophesies *there will be an end:*

1. Now we request you, brethren, with regard to the coming of
our Lord Jesus Christ, and our gathering together to Him,
2. that you may not be quickly shaken from your composure or
be disturbed either by a spirit or a message or a letter as if from
us, to the effect that the day of the Lord has come.
3. Let no-one in any way deceive you, for it will not come until
the apostasy comes first, and the man of lawlessness is revealed,
the son of destruction…
8. Then that lawless one will be revealed whom the Lord will
slay with the breath of His mouth and bring to an end by the
appearance of His coming (2 Thess 2:1-8)

The final antichrist will be simply, literally, blown away by the Lord Himself on His return. Puff.

Paul also warns of a falling away, 'the apostasy' (v. 3), which is to precede the Second Coming. Apostasy is the state of turning away from the message of Jesus so this confirms John's warning that we not follow those who 'go too far and do not abide in the teaching of Christ' (2 John 9). Likewise, the Lord's youngest brother Jude urges us to 'contend for the faith which was once for all delivered to the saints' (Jude 3).

Writing to Timothy, Paul adds:

> 1. But the Spirit explicitly says that in later times some will fall away from the faith, paying attention to deceitful spirits and doctrines of demons,
> 2. by means of the hypocrisy of liars seared in their own conscience as with a branding iron,
> 3 men who forbid marriage and advocate abstaining from foods which God has created to be gratefully shared in by those who believe and know the truth.
> 4. For everything created by God is good, and nothing is to be rejected if it is received with gratitude;
> 5. for it is sanctified by means of the word of God and prayer.
> (1 Tim 4:1-5)

Notice, some of the falling away includes forbidding marriage and re-establishing food laws.

I believe that 'the apostasy' included the Dark Ages when, as we saw, our largest body of professing believers, the Roman Catholic Church, was murderously rampant and some smaller Protestant denominations were not much better. While Jude urges us to 'contend for the faith', tragically some tried to enforce their version of the faith, as if any free-will trust *could* be enforced. In an over-reaction, some have become so liberal as to have abandoned any vestige of 'the faith'. Thankfully, that time may be almost over as both coercive and overly-liberal regimes of Christianity are dying out.

Both the Catholic and Orthodox[329] Churches explicitly forbade marriage to its clergy, male and female, and the Catholic Church taught 'abstaining from foods'. However, the food laws are now gone and in October, 2009, Pope Benedict encouraged married Anglican priests who converted to Catholicism to remain both as priests and married.[330] They will not be allowed to become bishops, which is very odd because the Scriptures say bishops are to be married and to have raised children (1 Tim 3:1-5 in *KJV*). Still, we can hope for further moves to revert to the Biblical faith in which Peter, the brothers of Jesus and all of the apostles except Paul and Barnabas were married (1 Cor 9:5).

Returning now to 2 Thessalonians, Paul is explicit – despite any teachings or prophecy to the contrary, Jesus will not return until the Antichrist, 'the man of lawlessness' and 'the son of destruction', is first revealed. He then spells out the 'anti-ness' of the last antichrist – this man is 'against Christ' and wants to be 'instead of Christ':

> 4. who opposes and exalts himself above every so-called god or object of worship, so that he takes his seat in the temple of God, displaying himself as being God.
> 5. Do you not remember that while I was still with you, I was telling you these things?
> 6. And you know what restrains him now, so that in his time he may be revealed.
> 7. For the mystery of lawlessness is already at work; only he who now restrains will do so until he is taken out of the way
> (2 Thess 2:4-7)

Verse 6's comment about the Antichrist being restrained or held back by 'he who now restrains' has been interpreted in several very different ways and will be properly considered in

---

329 The Orthodox regulate that bishops must not be married while priests can but only before being ordained.
330 http://visnews-en.blogspot.com/2009_10_20_archive.html, 14 Jun, 2011.

a later study in this series. For now, let us begin with what is unambiguous, that God has an appointed time for this man, that there will be both a revelation and an end of the final antichrist:

> 8. And then that lawless one will be revealed whom the Lord will slay with the breath of His mouth and bring to an end by the appearance of His coming;
> 9. that is, the one whose coming is in accord with the activity of Satan, with all power and signs and false wonders.
> (2 Thess 2:8-9)

This man's life and times will be ended by the most momentous event in history, the Second Coming of Christ. The Antichrist's reign therefore must immediately precede that as he will not die as all the others have done. Instead, he will be slain by 'the breath of His mouth'. As fearful as the Antichrist may be to us, the last battle will not be anything like an even contest – Jesus in all of His glory has only to say the word and the man will be brought to his knees before His throne to be judged.

Matthew, Chapter 24

We now come to Mathew 24. As Dr Derek Prince comments, if we compare eschatology (the study of end-times) to our body's skeleton, this passage is the spinal column by which every other bone maintains its rightful place. It is here that Jesus gives us an overview of the "signs of the times" we are to expect.

In Matthew 23, He had just been warning Israel that their behaviour would trigger the complete desolation of their beloved city, Jerusalem, and the Temple. Then:

> 1. Jesus came out from the temple and was going away when His disciples came up to point out the temple buildings to Him.
> 2. And He said to them, "Do you not see all these things? Truly I say to you, not one stone here will be left upon another, which will not be torn down."

3. As He was sitting on the Mount of Olives, the disciples came
to Him privately, saying, "Tell us, when will these things happen,
and what will be the sign of Your coming, and of the end of the
age?"
4. And Jesus answered and said to them, "See to it that no one
misleads you.
5. "For many will come in My name, saying, 'I am the Christ', and
will mislead many.
6. "You will be hearing of wars and rumors of wars. See that you
are not frightened, for those things must take place, but that is
not yet the end.
7. "For nation will rise against nation, and kingdom against
kingdom, and in various places there will be famines and
earthquakes.
8. "But all these things are merely the beginning of birth pangs.

Notice, Jesus places the onus on every one of us to avoid being
misled (v. 4). Also, that we need to trust His promise that no
matter how painful the inevitable deceptions, wars, famines
and earthquakes, He will come! As in the birth of a child (v. 8),
the pain will afterwards be quickly forgotten.

However, the pain will be great:

9. "Then they will deliver you to tribulation, and will kill you, and
you will be hated by all nations because of My name.
10. "At that time many will fall away and will betray one another
and hate one another.
11. "Many false prophets will arise and will mislead many.
12. "Because lawlessness is increased, most people's love will
grow cold.
13. "But the one who endures to the end, he will be saved.

In verses 10-12, Jesus is spelling out the apostasy that Paul also
predicts to the Thessalonians. Despite all of this, He assures
us that the gospel would continue to spread, from Jerusalem
to the whole world:

14. "This gospel of the kingdom shall be preached in the whole
world as a testimony to all the nations, and then the end will
come.

                                    Slouching Towards Bethlehem

New Zealand is at the uttermost parts of the earth from Israel and the first recorded sermon preached here was on Christmas Day in 1814. As for "all the nations" in-between, this is more difficult as "the whole world" uses 7,117 living languages.[331] Papua New Guinea alone has had 841 languages, 820 of which are still in use while 21 have become extinct.[332] However, for the first time in all of recorded history, it is becoming possible to preach in every one of them or by using trade languages.[333]

Since v. 14 is our Lord's answer to the disciples' question regarding His return and "the end of the age" (v. 3), then v. 15 is very significant. Remember, the capitalisation is to indicate a direct quote from the Old Testament, in this instance from the Book of Daniel:

> 15. "Therefore when you see the ABOMINATION OF DESOLATION which was spoken of through Daniel the prophet, standing in the holy place (let the reader understand)
> 16. then those who are in Judea must flee to the mountains…"

Some believe Jesus was referring to the destruction of the Temple by the Romans in 70 A.D., as we will consider soon. I do not believe He was as this was to follow the gospel being preached to the whole world and that is only now being fulfilled. However, that means about now we should be looking for this particular sign, "the abomination of desolation… standing in the holy place", and as Mark adds, 'where it should not be' (Mark 13:14).

Notice, it specifically affects everyone living in Judea (v. 16) and since, according to 1st Century Judaism, there was only one holy place in Judea, the Temple Mount in the centre of Jerusalem, we should continue to watch what is happening

---

331 www.ethnologue.com/home.asp, 6 Mar, 2020.
332 www.ethnologue.com/show_country.asp?name=PG, 6 Mar, 2020.
333 Besides preaching, in 2011 the United Bible Societies reported that the complete Bible is now available in 469 languages, the New Testament in 1,231 and at least one book in 2,527. www.biblesociety.org/?page_id=207, 18 Jul 2011.

there. For any who may not know, after two thousand years, Israel recaptured this area from the Jordanians in the Six Day War of 1967 but handed it back to the Islamic authorities.

What follows "the abomination of desolation" will be horrendous:

> 21. "For then there will be a great tribulation, such as has not occurred since the beginning of the world until now, nor ever will.
> 22. "Unless those days had been cut short, no life would have been saved; but for the sake of the elect those days will be cut short.

We are not told here *how* those days will be cut short but we can infer it will be by the return of the Lord Himself, as spelled out by Paul:

> 6. For after all it is only just for God to repay with affliction those who afflict you,
> 7. and to give relief to you who are afflicted and to us as well when the Lord Jesus will be revealed from heaven with His mighty angels in flaming fire (2 Thess 1:6-7)

Affliction of the saints will only be relieved when the Lord returns. Accordingly, He warns us to be especially careful of what evil-doers will be doing at that time:

> 23. "Then if anyone says to you, 'Behold, here is the Christ', or 'There He is', do not believe him.
> 24. "For false Christs and false prophets will arise and will show great signs and wonders, so as to mislead, if possible, even the elect.
> 25. "Behold, I have told you in advance." (Matt 24:21-25)

After v. 25's summation, from verse 26 to the end of the next chapter, 25, the Lord speaks of His coming to put right every wrong so this warning of the "false Christs and false prophets" with "great signs and wonders" (v. 24) is the last, ultimate, climax of evil. They are the antichrists, as we have seen from John's first and second letters and Revelation 13 and also the final Antichrist, as described by Paul in 2 Thessalonians.

So, what exactly is "the abomination of desolation" that will be "standing in the holy place", "where it should not be"?

17

"The Abomination of Desolation"
Recognising The Pattern

As I see it, this is the most important event and sign preceding the Second Coming and, since there has always been much debate about it, we need to examine it properly.

Firstly, then, what is "the abomination of desolation"? Randolph Tasker[334] defines it as:

> A description of some act of profanity which Jesus tells His disciples will be the sign that they must leave Jerusalem and escape to the hills. The key to its meaning, the reader of Mark xiii. 14 and Matt. xxiv. 15 is told, is to be found in Daniel in the Hebrew expression *siqqus somem* [or *shiqquts shamem*], which probably means the 'abomination which causes horror'. The LXX [the Septuagint or Greek translation] rendering *to bdelygma tes eremoseos*, 'the abomination that causes desolation' is followed in the Gospels. No certain conclusions have been reached regarding the meaning of the term *bdelygma* in this context. It has been identified with antichrist (cf. 2 Thes. ii.1-4); and the fact that the original text of Mark xiii. 14 could be translated 'standing where he ought not', gives plausibility to this view. It has also been regarded as a profanation of the Temple by the erection of an idol, similar to that perpetrated by Antioches Epiphanes; and the expression 'stand (neuter) in the holy place' in Matt. xxiv. 15 is in keeping with this. Others regard the expression as prophetic of the desecration wrought by the Roman army previous to the destruction of Jerusalem…[335]

---

334 Emeritus Professor of New Testament Exegesis at the University of London.

335 Ed. F.F. Bruce and J.I. Packer, *The New Bible Dictionary*, London; IVF Press, 1962, p. 5.

Notice, Professor Tasker covers a range of fulfilments, from Antiochus Epiphanes in 167 B.C. to Titus's legions in 70 A.D. onto the future, final Antichrist.

In support of the 70 A.D. fulfilment, F.F. Bruce adds:

> When the temple area was taken by the Romans, and the sanctuary itself was still burning, the soldiers brought their legionary standards into the sacred precincts, set them up opposite the eastern gate, and offered sacrifices to them there, acclaiming Titus as *imperator* (victorious commander) as they did so. The Roman custom of offering sacrifice to their standards had already been commented on by a Jewish writer as a symptom of their pagan arrogance, but the offering of such sacrifice in the Temple court was the supreme insult to the God of Israel. This action, following as it did the cessation of the daily sacrifice three weeks earlier, must have seemed to many Jews, as it evidently did to Josephus, a new and final fulfilment of Daniel's vision of a time when the continual burnt offering would be taken away and the abomination of desolation set up.[336]

Regarding Antiochus Epiphanes, an unknown Jewish historian[337] in the 2nd or 1st Century B.C. wrote:

> Now on the fifteenth day of Chislev, in year 145 [of the Seleucid era i.e. 167 B.C.], 'the abomination of desolation' was set up on the [Temple's] altar of burnt offerings (1 Maccabees 1:54, *NEB with Apocrypha*)

This was 'an altar to Zeus Olympias (the Greek equivalent of the Syrian god Baal Shamem)'[338] on which pigs and other

---

336 F.F. Bruce, revised by David F. Payne, *Israel and the Nations: The History of Israel from the Exodus to the Fall of the Second Temple*, Illinois; IVF Press, 1997, p. 226.

337 These events occurring between the end of the Old Testament and the beginning of the New are recorded in 1 and 2 Maccabees, Jewish history books considered non-canonical by Jews and Protestants but included in their canon by Roman Catholics and Orthodox Christians.

338 *The New Oxford Annotated Bible*, Apocrypha, p. 205.

---

unsanctioned animals were offered. Antiochus also set up a statue of himself as Zeus.[339] Most today therefore accept this is what Daniel was predicting. Others like N.T. Wright build on this, arguing that the Roman invasion in 67 A.D. was 'a re-enactment of the Maccabaean crisis'. He cites three prophecies of Daniel (9:26-7, 11:30-32 and 12:11) which 'deal with the destruction and desolation of the sanctuary at the hands of pagans, and in each case they highlight the cessation of the regular sacrifices'. In this view, the abomination is defined as pagan idolatry, the prophecies have all been outworked as apocalyptic metaphors and there will be no future fulfilment.[340]

Others see only a future fulfilment, as taught by Irenaeus in 185 A.D., because these two events 'do not match the details in the 'abomination of desolation' texts which are required for fulfilment'.[341] Another view defines the second abomination as the setting up of the Roman standards but also includes a future fulfilment in the final Antichrist.[342]

As I see it, all of these scholars are mostly correct, only falling short when they assume a sole fulfilment or limit themselves to two or three. In the previous study in this series, I noted that there are at least six instances of abominations that have caused, or will cause, Israel to become desolate, two before Daniel in the 6th Century B.C. and four after him.[343] At the time of this prediction by Jesus in 30 A.D., there had already been three with three more to come. Often not recognised, it is this multiplicity of occurrences and fulfilments that helps us establish a clearer definition from the pattern. It is also often not recognised that the Crucifixion of Jesus was the fourth

339   http://virtualreligion.net/iho/antiochus_4.html, 6 Aug, 2011.
340   *Jesus and the Victory of God*, Minneapolis; Fortress Press, 1996, pp. 511-512.
341   Randall Price, http://focusonjerusalem.com/AbominationofDesolation.htm, 26 May, 2010.
342   For example, Robert Jamieson, A. R. Fausset and David Brown, http://www.abomination-of-desolation.com, 26 May, 2010.
343   *Dancing in the Dragon's Jaws*, p. 108.

fulfilment and directly led to the fifth.

Definition and Context

The confusion comes from us failing to fully define the term – 'some act of profanity' is true but not concise enough – and from us not considering the historical context of Daniel's prophecies. After all, Daniel was living in the aftermath of one instance – Jerusalem, the Temple and the people of Israel *had already been made desolate* by the Babylonians in 586 B.C. That is why he was praying:

> 17. "So now, our God, listen to the prayer of Your servant and to his supplications, and for Your sake, O Lord, let Your face shine on Your desolate sanctuary.
> 18. "O my God, incline Your ear and hear! Open Your eyes and see our desolations and the city which is called by Your name… (Dan 9:16-18)

Notice, he describes the Temple as "Your desolate sanctuary" (v. 17) and asks God to end the "desolations" of his people Israel and of Jerusalem (v. 18).

And this was actually the *second* instance in Jewish history of an abomination that caused desolation, as we will see.

The first instance, in about 1050 B.C, is also not mentioned by any of the above commentators. However, almost five hundred years afterwards, in about 600 B.C., God told Israel they needed to learn from it so that they would understand what He was about to do again:

> 11. "Has this house, which is called by My name, become a den of robbers in your sight?
> 12. "Behold, I, even I, have seen it," declares the LORD. "But go now to My place which was in Shiloh, where I made My name dwell at the first, and see what I did to it because of the wickedness of My people Israel." (Jer 7:9-12)

Notice v. 11? Jesus Himself quoted it, to remind Israel of this prophecy when He cleansed the Temple in 30 A.D. (Matt 21:13) and *He wants us to likewise make the connections.*

So what were these abominations that caused desolation?

Let us begin by establishing a clearer definition with three parts:

(i) The Hebrew expression 'abomination' describes anything morally disgusting or horrible, especially idolatry

While used of sexual immorality (e.g. Lev 18:22, Deut 23:18) and injustice (Deut 25:16), it was especially used of idols:

> 25. "The graven images of their gods you are to burn with fire; you shall not covet the silver or the gold that is on them, nor take it for yourselves, or you will be snared by it, for it is an abomination to the LORD your God.
> 26. "You shall not bring an abomination into your house and, like it, come under the ban; you shall utterly detest it and you shall utterly abhor it, for it is something banned."
> (Deut 7:25-26)

This is the essential issue of Judaism, and monotheism, applying the first two of the Ten Commandments: "You shall have no other gods" and "You shall not make an idol… (to) worship them or serve them" (Exo 20:3-4). We see the term again when the godly king Josiah tried to clean up Jerusalem in about 622 B.C. by destroying the high places…:

> …which Solomon the king of Israel had built for Ashtoreth the abomination of the Sidonians, and for Chemosh the abomination of Moab, and for Milcom the abomination of the sons of Ammon… (2 Kin 23:13)

Solomon had compromised for the sake of the wives he had taken for political alliances (1 Kin 11:1-8). Ashtoreth was the love and fertility goddess of the Phoenicians in Sidon. Called Ishtar by the Assyrians and Babylonians, she was also known as Astarte, Aphrodite or Venus by the Greeks and Romans,[344] and her worship included 'sacred' male and female prostitution (2 Kin 23:7). Chemosh, the chief god of the Moabites, was called Milcom or Molech by the Ammonites and was the fire god to whom they sacrificed their children [345] as had the earlier Canaanites (Deut 18:10).

These idols were an abomination to God as was Israel's worship of them.

Paul reiterates this in the New Covenant (Gal 5:20, Col 3:5) and summarises:

> Therefore, my beloved, flee from idolatry (1Cor 10:14)

It is also the final point of John's first letter:

> Little children, guard yourselves from idols (1 John 5:21)

(ii) An abomination that 'makes desolate' (Hebrew *shiqquts shamem*)

This is the tipping point or last straw, the one that pushes God beyond all endurance. Historically, this was committed by both Israel and their Gentile enemies.

When committed by Israel, God responded by removing His glory or manifest presence from their midst. With His protection gone, their enemies were allowed to defeat them and to desecrate His dwelling place so that everything was left 'desolate'.

We see this in Daniel chapter 8, but it requires some background. In about 550 B.C. (v. 1), Daniel had a vision of a very powerful goat with one large horn defeating a ram. As he watched, he saw the goat's large horn broken off and being replaced by four horns (v. 8), out of one of which came a little fifth horn which grew until it dominated 'the Beautiful Land'

---

344 *Smiths Bible Dictionary*, www.bible-history.com/smiths/A/ Ashtoreth/, 11 Aug, 2011.

345 Ibid., www.bible-history.com/smiths/M/Molech/, 11 Aug, 2011.

---

i.e. Israel (v. 9). The angel Gabriel then interpreted the vision (vv. 20-22) as foretelling that the Greek empire (the goat) would defeat the Medo-Persian empire (the ram), after which the large horn (Alexander the Great) would be broken off and replaced by four (his four generals). Towards the end of the reign of one of the four (the Seleucids) would come a fifth (the infamous Antiochus Epiphanes). Thus Daniel foresaw the terrible events of 167 B.C.:

> 11. It [the little horn] even magnified itself to be equal with the Commander of the host; and it removed the regular sacrifice from Him, and the place of His sanctuary was thrown down. (Dan 8:11)

This fifth horn, Antiochus IV Epiphanes, ruled from 175 to 163 B.C. and his blasphemy was obvious even in the name he gave himself, Epiphanes or 'God (i.e. Zeus) made manifest'. In 167 B.C., he desecrated the Temple and stopped the offerings prescribed by the Law of Moses.

Now comes the important verse for our purposes. Daniel sees *why* God allows this to happen:

> 12. And on account of transgression the host [i.e. Israel's army] will be given over to the horn [i.e Antiochus Epiphanes] along with the regular sacrifice [i.e. the Temple worship]; and it will fling truth to the ground and perform its will and prosper (Dan 8:12)

It is Israel's transgression that causes God to give over their army to be defeated and to allow the ensuing desecration and desolation of the Temple. Daniel goes on:

> 13. Then I heard a holy one speaking, and another holy one said to that particular one who was speaking, "How long will the vision about the regular sacrifice apply, while the transgression causes horror [Heb. *shamem,* makes appalled or desolate], so as to allow both the holy place [the Temple] and the host [Israel's army] to be trampled?" (Dan 8:13)

Again, it is Israel's "transgression" that so appals or horrifies God that He allows both their Temple and their army to be "trampled" underfoot, or despised by the Gentile army.[346]

(iii) In these desecrations, Israel's enemies set up their own "abominations of desolation"

We see this in Daniel 11:31 where Gabriel predicts Antiochus's actions:

> 30. "For ships of Kittim will come against him; therefore he will be disheartened and will return and become enraged at the holy covenant and take action; so he will come back and show regard for those who forsake the holy covenant.
> 31. "Forces from him will arise, desecrate the sanctuary fortress, and do away with the regular sacrifice. And they will set up the abomination of desolation."

Here it is the Seleucid soldiers who set up the abomination of desolation.

Now, with this clearer definition, we can identify five instances in Israel's past, which will enable us to consider a possible sixth, future and final instance. They were:

(i)   in approximately 1050 BC, Israel's use of the Ark of the Covenant as an idolatrous talisman which led to the destruction and desolation of the sanctuary at Shiloh by the Philistines

---

346   The angel's reply is "2,300 evenings and mornings" (Dan 8:14) which is 1,150 days of "the regular sacrifice" of evening and morning burnt offerings, or just over three years. 1 Maccabees 1 records an undated decree forbidding Jewish burnt offerings (vv. 44-45) and soon after, 'on the fifteenth day of Kislev in the [Greek] year 145 (i.e. 167 B.C.), the "abomination of desolation" was set up on the altar' (v. 54). Ten days after that, 'on the twenty-fifth day of Kislev' the Greek pagans began offering their sacrifices on it (v. 59) and exactly three years later, 'on the twenty-fifth day of Kislev, in the [Greek] year 148 (i.e. 165 B.C.)…, on the anniversary of the day when the Gentiles profaned it, on that very day, it was rededicated' (vv. 52-54). So, while we have no exact timing for this desolation, we do know it was just over three years. The date is still celebrated today as the Festival of Hannukah or Dedication (John 10:22).

(ii) in 586 BC, Israel's use of the First Temple to excuse their idolatry and immorality led to the Babylonians sacking the Temple, Jerusalem and the land of Israel and the seventy year desolation

(iii) in 168 BC, Israel's renouncing of the Abrahamic covenant led to the Seleucid Greeks under Antiochus Epiphanes desecrating the Second Temple and its being desolate for three years

(iv) in 30 A.D., the crucifixion of Jesus of Nazareth. His body being the true Temple which the others all foreshadowed, this was the worst desecration of all and was committed by both Jews and Gentiles

(v) in 70 A.D., after forty years of grace for Israel to reconsider Jesus, His words and His resurrection, the Romans sacked the Second Temple and Jerusalem, leaving Israel, the people and the land, desolate until the 20th Century.

Details of each of these are in the *Appendix: Five Abominations of Desolation.*

What then could be the next or sixth?

The Sixth and Last "Abomination of Desolation"

In about 50 A.D., Paul wrote of a particular man who will be confronted by the returning Lord Himself. The prediction is in his second letter to the Thessalonians which is sometimes called Paul's mini-apocalypse. As mentioned earlier, while he does not use the terms 'antichrist' or "abomination of desolation", he does describe a future leader, 'the man of sin' (KJV) or 'lawlessness' with all of the Antichrist's characteristics:

> 3. Let no one in any way deceive you, for it [the day of the Lord] will not come unless the apostasy comes first, and the man of

Notice, there is first an apostasy (v. 3), a falling away of the people of God, in this instance, *of believers in Jesus*. Jesus confirms this, as we saw above, in Matthew 24:10 and 13.

Secondly, the 'man of lawlessness' will 'take his seat in the temple of God, displaying himself as being God'. Some have taken this literally, to mean there will be another temple, the Third Temple, built on the Temple Mount in Jerusalem.[347] Others take it spiritually or metaphorically – that since all believers as 'living stones' make up 'a spiritual house' (1 Pet 2:5), the Antichrist will be the leader of an apostate church. This is usually taught as a Pope of the Roman Catholic Church with apostate Protestant churches regathering under his leadership.[348]

However, as I see it, Jesus was much more specific than this:

At that time, there was only one possible "holy place" where any abomination could stand and that was on the Temple Mount in Jerusalem. His warning is also specific to those who

---

347 For example, Hal Lindsey, *The Late, Great Planet Earth,* Grand Rapids; Zondervan, 1970, p. 98; Randall Price, *The Coming Last Days' Temple*, Eugene, Oregon; Harvest House Publishers, 1999.
348 For example, Ellen G. White, *The Great Controversy*, chapter 3, www.ellenwhite.info/books/ellen-g-white-book-great-controversy-gc-03. htm, 25 Jul, 2011.

are nearby, in Judea. The question therefore should be asked, what is standing there now and what could be in the future? We will consider that next.

Notice, this also fulfils the third characteristic of the five historical abominations of desolation – that each was in the land of Israel.

The fourth characteristic was that the ensuing desolation was brought about by those who were not God's people but allowed or brought in by Him as agents of judgement, i.e. the Philistines, the Babylonians, the Seleucids and the Romans. As I see it, this has been the impact of Islam on the Middle East. Even T.E. Lawrence, the famous 'Lawrence of Arabia', saw the deadening effect of the Ottoman Empire, the last Caliphate which ended in defeat in the First World War.[349] Islamism is now having a similar effect wherever it is growing in Europe, as we will consider soon.

Lastly, each of the five had a blasphemous outcome, where an idol or emperor was worshipped instead of the God of Israel. This could be very easily fulfilled by Islam bringing forth the Mahdi.

As for this final abomination of desolation being the sixth, it would be particularly appropriate since six is the number of man, man having been created on the sixth day (Gen 1:26-31). This would mean the ultimate fallen man, 'the man of sin', will be brought to an end by the return of 'the last Adam, the second man' (1 Cor 15:45-47), the only truly righteous Son of Man, to establish the new Creation.

---

349   He wrote, for example, of Palestine: 'The sooner the Jews farm it all the better: their colonies are bright spots in a desert.' David Garnett, ed., *Letters of T.E. Lawrence*, New York; Doubleday, 1938, p. 71. On the anniversary of the Balfour Declaration, he told the *Jewish Guardian*, "Speaking entirely as a non-Jew, I look on the Jews as the natural importers of Western leaven so necessary for countries of the Near East." November 28, 1918, cited in Sir Martin Gilbert, *Churchill and the Jews*, London; Simon & Shuster, 2007, p. 51.

'Standing in the Holy Place'

The Arabic name for Jerusalem, *Al-Quds*, means literally, 'the Holy'.

Today, the Temple Mount is occupied by the Dome of the Rock, a Muslim building which encircles a large rock in the ground. It is not a mosque but a shrine to venerate the place where not only Abraham came but, they believe, Muhammad ascended to heaven. Although he never reached Jerusalem, Muslims believe he did, flying there from Mecca one night in 621 A.D. on a winged steed. Alongside the Dome, there is a much smaller dome marking the spot where he then leapt up into heaven.

Nearby is the mosque, *Al-Aqsa* or the Farthest Mosque, named after a reference in the Qur'an:

> Glory to (Allah) Who did take His servant for a Journey by night from the Sacred Mosque to the farthest Mosque, whose precincts We did bless, in order that We might show him some of Our Signs: for He is the One Who heareth and seeth (all things). (Surah 17:1)[350]

The 'Sacred Mosque' is in Mecca and since the Qur'an never mentions Jerusalem, some believe the 'Farthest Mosque' was in Medina. However, the accepted idea today that it was in Jerusalem comes from a *hadith*, which is 'a report of the sayings or actions of Muhammad or his companions, together with the tradition of its chain of transmission'[351]:

> Thabit Al-Bunani reported on the authority of Anas that the Prophet said, "I was brought al-Buraq, an animal white and long, larger than a donkey but smaller than a mule, whose stride was a distance equal to the range of its vision.
>
> I mounted it and came to Jerusalem, and tied it to the

---

350 Yusufali, www.cmje.org/religious-texts/quran/, 17 Sep, 2011.
351 Unknown origin but good definition. More details on www.encyclopedia.com/topic/hadith.aspx, 9 Mar, 2012.

ring used by the Prophets. After entering the Mosque, and praying two rakats in it, I came out and Gabriel brought me a vessel of wine and a vessel of milk. I chose the milk, and Gabriel said, 'you have chosen the true religion' We were then taken to heaven..."[352]

While Muhammad was there in Jerusalem, they believe, 'Abraham, Moses, Jesus and other prophets... gathered together to pray behind him'.[353] Notice the position attributed to Muhammad.

Five years after he died, in 637 A.D. the Muslim armies did reach Jerusalem, capturing it from the Byzantines and building a wooden mosque there. Fifty five years later, in 692 A.D., Abd al-Malik ibn Marwan, the fifth Umayyad Caliph and ruler of Damascus, built a more permanent mosque and the Dome of the Rock.[354] The Oxford University archaeological guide is very apt:

> Abd al-Malik's building spoke to Jews by its location, to Christians by its interior decoration.[355]

To proclaim his new religion's superiority, he took permanent possession of the only Jewish holy place on the earth. His message to Christians is also still there, in stone and Arabic script – the teachings and prophecies of Muhammad are inscribed all around the interior:

> There is no god but God. He is one. He has no associate...
>
> Muhammad is the servant of God and His messenger...
>
> O People of the Book [i.e. Christians], do not go to excess [or, exaggerate] in your religion, and do not say of God anything but truth. The Messiah, Jesus son of Mary, was

---

352 www.islamicparty.com/alaqsa/enter.htm, 6 Aug, 2011.
353 www.noblesanctuary.com/HISTORY.html, 8 Aug, 2011.
354 www.islamicparty.com/alaqsa/chapone.htm, 8 Aug, 2011.
355 Jerome Murphy-O'Connor, *The Holy Land: An Oxford Archaeological Guide From Earliest Times to 1700*, 4th ed. (1998), p. 85.

only a Messenger of God. The Messiah, and a Word of God bestowed on Mary, and a Spirit from God. So believe in God, and do not speak of a Trinity; it is best for you to refrain … God alone is the One worthy of worship: glory to God, exalted beyond having a son… [Surah 4:171]

It befits not (the Majesty of) God that He should take unto Himself a son…[Surah 19:35]

Praise be to God, who has not begotten a son, nor has a partner in His dominion…[17:111]

Whoever rejects the Signs of God [i.e. Muhammad's words], lo! God is swift at reckoning. [3:19][356]

As can be seen, Muhammad's primary disagreement with Jesus is His identity. Jesus described Himself as God's "only begotten Son" (John 3:16), explaining:

> 22. "For not even the Father judges anyone, but He has given all judgment to the Son,
> 23. so that all will honour the Son even as they honour the Father. He who does not honour the Son does not honour the Father who sent Him." (John 5:22-23)

We are therefore to honour Jesus "even as", or in the exact same way that, we honour the Father; if we do not, we are not properly honouring the Father. However, Muhammad set himself spectacularly against this, according to al-Bukhari:

> The Messenger of Allah (peace be upon him) said: "Shall I inform you about the gravest of all major sins?" We said: "Certainly, O Messenger of Allah." He said: "Ascribing partners to Allah, and disobeying parents."[357]

Muhammad taught that the New Testament had been

---

356 Bruce Lawrence, *The Qur'an: A Biography*, Sydney; Allen & Unwin, 2006, pp. 64-69.
357 http://islamtruth4all.blogspot.com/2011_01_01_archive.html, 8 Aug, 2011.

---

corrupted by Christians to justify their sin of *shirk*, the most heinous sin in Islam, that is the associating of anyone with God as an equal partner. *Shirk* comes from an Arabic verb, to share, hence the Dome of the Rock's spelling out of 'God has no associate', 'Jesus was only a messenger', 'do not speak of a Trinity', 'God has not begotten a son, nor has a partner in His dominion' etc.

Muhammad is also prophesying against the Hebrew prophet Zechariah who predicted the Crucifixion in exactly these Messianic terms:

> "Awake, O sword, against My Shepherd,
> And against the man, My Associate,"
> Declares the LORD of hosts.
> "Strike the Shepherd that the sheep may be scattered…"
> (Zech 13:7)

Jesus Himself quoted this prophecy several times when He was about to see it fulfilled (Matt 26:31, Mark 14:27, John 10:11-16).

We see then that the Dome is not only denouncing the Old and the New Testaments, Jews and Christians, but it is seen to be a monument to the spirit of antichrist:

> Who is the liar but the one who denies that Jesus is the Christ?
> This is the antichrist, the one who denies the Father and the Son
> (1 John 2:22)

And it has been 'standing in the holy place', 'where it should not be', for the last fourteen hundred years.

What then if the Mahdi was to step forward tomorrow, enter the Dome of the Rock and announce that he had come at last?

Summary of "the Abomination of Desolation"

We see then that:

(i) The Hebrew expression 'abomination' describes anything morally horrible, especially idolatry.

(ii) An 'abomination that causes desolation' (Heb. *shiqquts shamem*, Grk. *bdelygma tes eremoseos*) is the tipping point or last straw, the one that pushes God beyond all endurance. Historically, this was committed by both Israel and their Gentile enemies.

(iii) The result of each of Israel's 'abominations of desolation' was that God finally withdrew from them, i.e. His glory departed. With His protection gone, Israel's army was defeated, the land was trampled down by their enemies and His sanctuary was desecrated and left desolate.

(iv) In these desecrations, Israel's enemies set up their own 'abominations of desolation'.

(v) In Israel's history there have been five. The first was in about 1050 B.C., when the last straw of Israel's transgressions was the elders' using the ark of the covenant as an idolatrous talisman. The outcome was the destruction and desolation of the sanctuary at Shiloh.

(vi) The second was in 586 B.C. Israel were using the Temple to excuse their idolatry which led to the sacking and desolation of the First Temple, Jerusalem and the land of Israel for seventy years.

(vii) In 167 B.C., many were renouncing the Abrahamic covenant, leading to Antiochus Epiphanes' desecration of the Second Temple and its remaining desolate for three years.

(viii) The fourth, in 30 A.D., was the rejection and crucifixion of Jesus of Nazareth. His body being the true Temple which all the others foreshadowed, this was the worst desecration of all and was committed by both Jews and Gentiles. There was no immediate punishment and on the third day, our heavenly Father vindicated Jesus as the Christ by raising Him from the dead.

(ix) In 70 A.D., after forty years of grace for Israel to reconsider Jesus, His words and His resurrection, the Romans sacked the Second Temple, Jerusalem and the land of Israel and left them desolate. Israel, the people and the land, were not restored until the 20th Century.

(x) The sixth is yet to come. We cannot be dogmatic as to what that will be but we can see a pattern established in the previous five to help us consider how that fits with Jesus' warning and Paul's prediction.

(xi) The sixth appears to be a particular man, the Antichrist, which would be perfectly appropriate as six is the number of man. Thus the ultimate 'man of sin' will be confronted and judged by Jesus returning as the ultimate, righteous Son of Man.

(xii) This leads us to consider Islam, whose founding prophet, Muhammad, openly claimed to stand in the place of Christ. It is the most enduring and largest manifestation of the spirit of antichrist in human history and has already subdued one third of "all the nations", fulfilling Daniel 7:24.

(xiii) Muhammad's followers today occupy the only possible Jewish 'holy place' on earth, the Temple Mount in Jerusalem. Their shrine there already explicitly denies the teaching of Jesus, the Twelve and Paul regarding the identity of Jesus as Son of God.

(xiv) Muslims, both Sunni and Shi'ite, are longing for the emergence of an antichrist leader, the Mahdi, to take charge of the entire Islamic empire, to retake the land of Israel and annihilate every last Jew, and to judge the rest of us who have rejected Muhammad. This man could fulfill all the prophecies regarding the Antichrist.

18

Reviewing and Interpreting
Revelation 13:1-15

The vision of Revelation 13 identifies invisible, spiritual, principalities and power structures which every generation has to face politically, to a degree determined by the time and place or culture:

(i) The **first beast**, 'out of the sea', is the power of the state which in its largest form is a multinational empire.

(ii) The **second beast**, 'out of the land', is the spirit of antichrist.

(iii) Whenever the state or empire becomes the ultimate power in the lives of its citizens, its emperor becomes an antichrist, not necessarily by overtly opposing Jesus but by replacing Jesus as the exact image of the only true God to be obeyed and served.

(iv) The **first beast** has seven heads because it manifests in the seven consecutive Gentile empires enslaving or ruling over Israel from its inception as a nation. "Five have fallen, one now is and one is to come", as seen from the 1st Century, refers to Egypt, Assyria, Babylonia, Medo-Persia, Greece and Rome with the last yet to be fully manifest with its ten horns.

(v) The **second beast** causes people to worship the current empire, which is the first beast, and its living image, which is its emperor. 'Worship' does not require them to believe the emperor is the Creator but merely to accord him first place or ultimate worth in their lives and decisions. This image is worshipped and served instead of God and His Christ, hence every manifestation of this phenomenon is an antichrist.

(vi) Later, in Revelation 16:13, we see that, at last, **the second beast** will have a final manifestation as 'the false prophet', a particular individual who will only rule for a brief time, 'one hour', immediately before the Second Coming of Jesus. We will consider the end of both beasts properly later in this series.

In considering the deceptions of 'the spirit of antichrist' and human antichrists, we saw that:

(i) Antichrists are often political leaders of which 'the Antichrist' will be the last, 'the false prophet' who will be brought to his end by the return of Jesus Himself.

(ii) The spirit of antichrist can equally inspire political leaders to become religious figures and religious leaders to become dictatorial politicians. We Christians are not exempt, the latter being an official teaching of Roman Catholicism until late in the 20th Century and Protestantism between the 16th and 18th Centuries.

(iii) While in John's day, the Roman Caesars were content to be worshipped as one god among many, those inspired by the antichrist spirit may claim to be God's 'sole agent' (e.g. Muhammad and Hitler) and therefore the Messiah. All offer a counterfeit spirituality usually including 'another Jesus', 'a different spirit' and 'a different gospel'. Some theologians do too.

(iv) This demonic anointing is portrayed by John in Revelation 13 as 'fire from heaven' which counterfeits the Holy Spirit's coming on the Day of Pentecost.

(v) The secular world calls this phenomenon of emperor-worship Totalitarianism or Fascism.

Then and now:

(i)   For John's first hearers, this issue was unavoidable because of the Roman emperors' wanting to be worshipped.

(ii)   The worship was obvious then because it consisted of pouring out a libation of wine or burning incense while acknowledging Caesar as Lord. It is less obvious for us today as we need to first understand the Biblical concept of '*worth*-ship'. This can be seen in Jesus' teaching about us choosing to serve either God or mammon (Matt 6:24), i.e. that whatever we give ultimate worth and obedience to is the actual object of our worship. Besides having to choose between love of God or love of money, we will also be tempted to trust political leaders more than God.

(iii)   Regarding the 20th Century, we can now identify the spirit that caused the worship of political dictators such as Stalin, Hirohito, Mussolini, Hitler, Mao Zedong, Ceausescu, Hoxha and Pol Pot.

(iv)   In the 21st Century, there appears to be only one kind of leader still 'standing in the holy place' – Muhammad and his successors. He is worshipped either explicitly, as amongst the Sufis and many moderates, or implicitly, as amongst the followers of whoever is held to be his most accurate interpreter of the traditionalist or fundamentalist ayatollahs or imams, such as Ali Khamenei in Iran or Ali Sistani in Iraq.

(v)   While remaining alert to any other manifestations of the spirit of antichrist, at the moment we should familiarise ourselves with Islam, to identify its impact on all of our societies and respond appropriately, as will be considered in the next section.

We have considered most of Revelation chapter 13, unpacking

the symbolism of its metaphors as they would have been understood by John's original audience. We have seen that the whole vision was immediately relevant to them in the 1st Century A.D., laying bare the spiritual realities they were facing in their daily lives.

For those interested in interpretative approaches,[358] this confirms many aspects of the preterist view[359] of Revelation. However, we have also seen that what John saw did not cease in the 1st Century. In our brief survey of the 2,000 years of church history, we saw many confirmations of the historicist view[360] in that Revelation 13 has been fulfilled by both the Roman Catholic and the Protestant churches.

Then when we focused on the last 100 years, we found that Revelation 13 astonishingly, perfectly, explains the worst aspects of what *The New York Times* described as 'Satan's century' and the phenomenon of totalitarianism. This confirms many aspects of the idealist[361] interpretation but we

358   For detailed overviews of these approaches, see Merrill C. Tenney, *Interpreting Revelation*, London; Pickering & Inglis Ltd, 1958, pp. 135-146; Michael Wilcock, *The Message of Revelation*, Leicester; Inter-Varsity Press, 1975, pp. 23-24; Laurie Guy, *Making Sense of Revelation*, Oxford; Regent's Park College, 2009, pp. 5-13.

359   From the Latin *praeteritus*, 'that which has gone before'. Preterists see Matthew 24 as fulfilled by the destruction of Jerusalem in 70 A.D., and the Book of Revelation as describing 1st Century events. *Full preterists* see all of Revelation as fulfilled; *partial preterists* see up to chapter 19 as fulfilled, chapter 20 as started, and the rest as yet to come. See N. T. Wright's *Jesus and the Victory of God* (Minneapolis; Fortress Press, 1996); David Chilton's *The Days of Vengeance: An Exposition of the Book of Revelation* (Fort Worth; Dominion Press, 1990). Also F. F. Bruce, as we saw earlier in the section 'The Abomination of Desolation'.

360   *Historicists* believe that Revelation predicts the continuous unfolding of church history up until the Second Coming, e.g. that chapter 9 describes the Muslim invasion of Europe; chapter 13, the Roman Catholic Church and the papacy. Most of the Protestant reformers, such as Luther and Zwingli, held this view. See www.historicism.net.

361   *Idealists* believe that between specific messages for the 1st Century and predictions of the distant future, its visions reveal principles that

have ended up with precise applications or fulfilments. This is due to what can be called the typological interpretation of Revelation, i.e. the recognising of recurring types or patterns and thus establishing a more exact meaning for each of the metaphors John used.

This in turn enabled us to project the patterns revealed into the future, to consider what is likely to happen next. While justifying several aspects of the futurist[362] and dispensationalist[363] interpretations of Revelation, it also has given us a much more precise and secure basis for our predictions.

Where we have differed from all of these views has been in establishing a clear metaphorical meaning or essential content for the time period during which the antichrist spirit is allowed to 'wage war against the saints and to overcome them'. This 'forty-two months' (Rev 13:5), or 'a time, times and half a time'

---

are relevant to every age. They avoid literal fulfillments, accepting predictions only in the very general sense of good defeating evil. Early adherents include Origen and Augustine; more recently William Hendriksen, *More than Conquerors: An Interpretation of the Book of Revelation*, Grand Rapids, Michigan; Baker Book House, 1986.

362 *Futurists* believe that all of the visions from Revelation 4:1 onwards are yet to be fulfilled just before the Second Coming. The earliest adherent seems to be Irenaeus (ca. 130-202 A.D.) who taught about a literal three and a half year reign of the Antichrist and his seating himself in a rebuilt Temple in Jerusalem (*Against Heresies, Book V*, chap. xxv, para. 1 to chap xxvi, para. 1. www.columbia.edu/cu/augustine/arch/irenaeus/advhaer5.txt, 14 Mar, 2012). This view was apparently revived by Francisco Ribera (1537-1591) – see *Dictionary of Premillennial Theology*, ed. Mal Couch, Grand Rapids; Kregel Publications, 1996, p. 378.

363 *Dispensationalists* are *futurists* with the additional teaching of J. N. Darby (1800-1882) and the *Schofield Reference Bible* (Oxford University Press, 1909) that the church will be removed from the earth in what is known as 'the Rapture', either before or half-way through this period. See also: John F. Walvoord's *The Revelation of Jesus Christ*, Chicago; Moody Press, 1966; Tim LaHaye & Jerry Jenkins' sixteen book *Left Behind* series, Wheaton, Illinois; Tyndale House, 1995-2007. Chuck Missler also teaches this view in his *66/40* radio commentary series.

　　　　Slouching Towards Bethlehem

(Dan 7:25), is not a future to be awaited nor a past event to be recognised. Rather, we have established this spiritual and political phenomenon has been occurring for the last two thousand years, throughout all the "times of the Gentiles", the mystery of Elijah's drought and the partial hardening of Israel. This means we are coming to the end rather than the start of that time.

We have not properly considered the end of the two beasts or the dragon, leaving that for later in this series when we study Revelation chapters 16 and 19 and the battle of Har-Magedon.

Before then, in Book 3, we will turn to Revelation 13:16-18, the passage describing the infamous 'mark of the beast'. As we will see, this too is not just a future event to be awaited but was being imposed in John's day and has been occurring throughout the last two thousand years. What mark of the beast are we therefore facing today? And what will be coming tomorrow?

First, however, we need to complete our study of Revelation 13:1-15.

19

The Hidden Kingdom
What Has God Been Doing?

We saw in Book 1, *Dancing in the Dragon's Jaws*, that 'the great red dragon' of Revelation 12 is an invisible, malevolent, spiritual being who is at work on the earth. He is red because in ancient Jewish thinking, red was the colour of the dust of the earth (Adam, the name of the man made from the dust, means ruddy or red).[364] The dragon is great because he is 'the devil and Satan, who deceives the whole world' (Rev 12:10).

We also saw he has seven heads which, as the angel told John, symbolise "seven kings" or empires, of which "five have fallen, one is, the other is yet to come" (Rev 17:10). At the time of John's vision, about 95-96 AD, the dragon had already used five great Gentile empires (Egypt, Assyria, Babylon, Medo-Persia and Greece) to attack the woman of Revelation 12, which is the nation of Israel. He was then using the sixth (Rome) and was yet to inspire the seventh. These six heads therefore give an overview of the first two thousand years of Jewish history: each empire initiated massacres, in several instances genocidal, or tried to assimilate the woman to extinction to prevent the birth of her son, Messiah, before the sixth devoured Him.

In summary, God's answer to the fall of man was to create a nation to bring forth a new man, Messiah; Satan's response was to inspire other nations to thwart Him.

However, the birth, death and resurrection of Jesus of Nazareth perfectly fulfilled the plan of God so, having failed miserably and received a mortal wound for his troubles, the dragon changes tack. Vindictively, he still tries to destroy the woman, which explains the last two thousand years of

---

364 pp. 21 and 25

unrelenting antisemitism, but then attacks 'the rest of her children, who keep the commandments of God and hold to the testimony of Jesus' (Rev 12:17) i.e. the followers of Jesus of Nazareth, whether Jew or Gentile.

That was Revelation 12.

We have now seen in Revelation 13 that the dragon has been allowed to 'wage war against the saints and to overcome them' (v. 7). We have also seen his strategy to hinder the kingdom of God throughout the last two thousand years of Gentile history: he inspires the two beasts, i.e. the feral state and the spirit of antichrist, to divert the worship due to God and Messiah towards worship of empires and their emperors. In the process, he has killed hundreds of millions, some two hundred and seventy million in the last one hundred years alone.[365]

So, what has God being doing during all this time?

Apart from redeeming hundreds of millions as they have individually put their faith in Jesus, He too has been at work in the political realm, transforming whole nations structurally to resist the antichrist temptation. Many of us have not recognised this, even though we should have expected it because Jesus gave us parables explaining how the kingdom of God grows.

Consider, for example, the leaven which the woman 'hides' in three pecks of flour - it quietly permeates it all (Matt 13:33). Or the mustard seed - smallest of the Middle Eastern garden seeds, it becomes the biggest plant in the garden (Matt 13:31-32). Jesus adds that:

> "it… becomes a tree and THE BIRDS OF THE AIR come and NEST IN ITS BRANCHES" (Matt 13:32)

The capitals here signify He is quoting from the Old Testament but look at the original text. It is from Ezekiel where God says

---

365   Rummel's estimate plus Dikotter's latest research

of a twig of a cedar that represents the royal house of David:

> "On the high mountain of Israel I will plant it, that it may bring forth boughs and bear fruit and become a stately cedar. And birds of every kind will nest under it; they will nest in the shade of its branches" (Ezek 17:23)

Jesus is adapting this prophecy of the Davidic kingdom being restored after the Babylonian exile which includes the typological prediction: "birds of *every kind*". To a Jew, this meant not only clean birds but unclean birds (Lev 11:13-19).

Now think of the revelation made to Peter when he was commanded three times to kill and eat 'all kinds of four-footed animals and crawling creatures of the earth and *birds of the air*'. Initially horrified at this inclusion of unclean creatures, he was told, "What God has cleansed, no longer consider *unholy*" (Acts 10:11-16, emphasis added). He then became the first to preach the gospel to the Gentiles because, as he explained:

> "God has shown me that I should not call any man unholy or unclean" (Acts 10:28)

We see then that Ezekiel's vision was predicting that the kingdom of God, ruled over by the Son of David, would provide protection to both Jews and Gentiles.[366]

And so it has, not only spiritually but also politically - it has done so in the *essential values and structure of liberal democracy*. As Christians, we are called to:

> "Seek first His kingdom and His righteousness"
> (Matt 6:33)

It turns out this is far more profound than we may have realised. "His righteousness" means His way of doing *everything* and that includes political structures.

---

366 Details in *The Red Heifer's Ashes (Mysteries of Ancient Israel)*, pp. 60-62.

Slouching Towards Bethlehem

The Origin of Liberal Democracy

As seen earlier, a liberal democracy is defined as a country or state based on the liberty and equal rights of all citizens and governed by elected representatives. Winston Churchill famously observed:

> Many forms of Government have been tried and will be tried in this world of sin and woe. No one pretends that democracy is perfect or all-wise. Indeed, it has been said that democracy is the worst form of government except all those other forms that have been tried from time to time.[367]

Hitler and Mussolini only came to unbridled power because they were allowed to disable the inherent protections of democracy. Remember Mussolini's comparison as noted earlier:

> Fascism conceives of the State as an absolute, in comparison with which all individuals or groups are relative, only to be conceived of in their relation to the State. The conception of the Liberal State [i.e. democracy] is not that of a directing force, guiding the play and development, both material and spiritual, of a collective body, but merely a force limited to the function of recording results [i.e. elections]: on the other hand, the Fascist State is itself conscious and has itself a will and a personality - thus it may be called the "ethic" State…

Mussolini badly underestimated the extraordinary power of democracy - it is not 'merely a force limited to the function of recording results' but actually the best available system of checks and balances to restrain mankind's propensity to evil 'in this world of sin and woe'.

On the other hand, as also noted earlier, Francis Fukuyama overestimated that 'the universalisation of Western liberal

---

367 Speech in the House of Commons, *The Official Report*, House of Commons (5th Series), 11 November 1947, vol. 444, cc. 206-207.

democracy' had brought us to 'the end of history' because it is 'the end point of mankind's ideological evolution and… the final form of human government'. He was almost right but not because we cleverly evolved our ideology. Our modern democracy is simply the political structure closest to the Kingdom of God and therefore the best political defence we can have until Kingdom come, or rather, the King comes.

It really should be no surprise that the same Bible that helps us to clearly identify the issues of emperor-worship and totalitarianism also clearly identifies how best to face it. Its revelations have been slowly but surely proven true in our society. Contrary to popular belief, the ancient Greeks, while giving us the word 'democracy', did not give us what we enjoy today - the essential elements were all established long before, in the Judaeo-Christian revelation.

This is freely acknowledged by Jürgen Habermas who is described by the *Stanford Encyclopedia of Philosophy* as 'one of the most influential philosophers in the world'[368]:

> Universalistic egalitarianism, from which sprang the ideals of freedom and a collective life in solidarity, the autonomous conduct of life and emancipation, the individual morality of conscience, human rights and democracy, is the direct legacy of the Judaic ethic of justice and the Christian ethic of love. This legacy, substantially unchanged, has been the object of continual critical appropriation and reinterpretation. To this day, there is no alternative to it. And in light of the current challenges of a post-national constellation, we continue to draw on the substance of this heritage. Everything else is just idle postmodern talk.[369]

So, setting aside 'idle postmodern talk', let us consider more

---

368   http://plato.stanford.edu/entries/habermas/ 7 October, 2011.
369   Translation of an interview in 1999. Jürgen Habermas, *Time of Transitions*, Cambridge; Polity Press, 2006, pp. 150-151. My thanks to Jeff Talon for this.

carefully our extraordinary legacy and heritage which has given us freedom in all its glory.

Essential Elements

The five essential elements of liberal democracy are: the worth of every individual; the rule of law; the separation of powers; freedom of conscience and elected leaders.

(i) The worth of every individual.

Dismissed above by Mussolini as being only relative to an absolute State, it was divinely revealed to Adam and Eve: we are all created 'in the image of God' (Gen 1:27).

Accordingly, *every individual* is to be protected by all human government, as God later commanded Noah:

> 5. "Surely I will require your lifeblood; from every beast I will require it.
> And from every man, from every man's brother I will require the life of man.
> 6. "Whoever sheds man's blood, by man his blood shall be shed,
> For in the image of God He made man" (Gen 9:5-6)

Cain had refused to be his "brother's keeper", leaving God to deal with Abel's shed blood "crying out from the ground" for justice (Gen 4:9-10). God therefore spelled out to Noah His requirement that we not only love each other but also accept full responsibility to uphold justice.

This applies to us individually and corporately, as Paul explains:

> 1. Every person is to be in subjection to the governing authorities. For there is no authority except from God, and those which exist are established by God.
> 2. Therefore whoever resists authority has opposed the ordinance of God; and they who have opposed will receive condemnation upon themselves.
> 3. For rulers are not a cause of fear for good behavior, but for

In other words, our governments, in the administering of
justice, have the right to enforce obedience, if necessary by
using 'the sword' (v. 4). Remember, when Paul was writing
this, the 'governing authorities' were the Romans who used
that power to unjustly crucify Jesus, exile John, imprison and
ultimately execute Paul himself, as well as Peter, James and
many other believers.

However, despite all and any abuse of this power, God
knows we need an armed agency for justice within our
society so He continues to give that power to the governing
authorities. Our modern-day equivalent lethal weapon of
enforcement is the gun, so our police and armed forces have
a clear Biblical mandate:

Our part is to be subject to this authority and to ensure the
rightful use of it. Whenever this good entity, called Leviathan
by Hobbes, goes bad, or feral, as John describes, we are to be
"salt and light" (Matt 5:13-15). We are especially, always, to
speak up for the worth of every individual because we are all
made in the image of God.

This is why Christians were at the forefront of the abolition
of slavery in the British Empire, as well as historically caring
for the sick and handicapped, the poor and orphans, and for

the rights of unborn children and convicted prisoners.

(ii) The rule of law

This principle that no one is above the law is today popularly ascribed to 17th Century philosopher John Locke who argued against 'the divine right of kings'. It was actually spelled out by Moses over 3,000 years earlier. Here is the divine command to kings in the Torah, or Law of Moses:

> 18. "Now it shall come about when he sits on the throne of his kingdom, he shall write for himself a copy of this law on a scroll in the presence of the Levitical priests.
> 19. "It shall be with him and he shall read it all the days of his life, that he may learn to fear the LORD his God, by carefully observing all the words of this law and these statutes,
> 20. that his heart may not be lifted up above his countrymen and that he may not turn aside from the commandment, to the right or the left, so that he and his sons may continue long in his kingdom in the midst of Israel." (Deut 17:18-20)

All the kings of ancient Israel, even the hugely powerful David and Ahab, were called to account for violations (2 Sam 12:1-14, 1 Kin 21:18-19). In New Testament days, Herod was reprimanded by John the Baptist (Matt 14:3-4).

(iii) The separation of powers

This is often credited to the American Constitution which calls for an independent judiciary, free press and the separation of church and state - but it all goes back to the Mosaic Law.

While we are all made in the image of God, we are all also fallible and prone to corruption. As Solomon puts it:

> Behold, I have found only this, that God made men upright, but they have sought out many devices (Eccl 7:29)

In other words, we are all devious. Accordingly, all of our power structures have to be structured to address this fallibility and corruption of man in every role, just as they were in ancient Israel.

The rulers, the judiciary, the priestly educators and the prophets were autonomous but all answerable to God through each other. For example, Samuel, a prophet and judge, spoke out against the corruption of both Eli the high priest (1 Sam 3:11-20) and Saul the king (1 Sam 13:8-14). Hilkiah the high priest called Josiah the king back to the Law of Moses and he responded by seeking the word of God through Huldah the prophetess. On hearing her confirmation, he called all the elders and together they led the nation into remaking the covenant (2 Chron 34:14-31).

Today, this prophetic function is often exercised by our free press, such as Woodward and Bernstein's revealing of President Nixon's role in the Watergate scandal. Accordingly, all tyrannies seek to silence or control the media or 'fourth estate'.

(iv) Freedom of conscience

The 16th and 17th Century Puritan Pilgrims fled the European state churches of both Catholic and Protestant nations. Their principle of 'separation of church and state' was to prevent any denomination using the state to enforce their doctrines on all:

> The American concept of freedom of conscience is rooted in the Puritan's quest to practice their religion freely and their desire to promote religious tolerance… a revolutionary new idea of religious liberty, an idea that goes much beyond the Puritan vision of liberty for themselves alone… that freedom of conscience must be extended to people of all faiths and none… this deeply American idea of religious liberty…[370]

---

370   www.freedomforum.org/packages/first/Curricula/ EducationforFreedom/supportpages/L09-FreedomofConscience.htm, 30 Aug, 2012.

However, the Puritans had actually rediscovered and begun practising Paul's 1st Century teaching:

> ...for why is my freedom judged by another's conscience?
> (1 Cor 10:29)
>
> Who are you to judge the servant of another? To his own master he stands or falls; and he will stand, for the Lord is able to make him stand...
> The faith which you have, have as your own conviction before God (Rom 14:4 & 22)

This revelation was abandoned by the church when Constantine became a Christian in the 4th Century. As we saw earlier, the Roman Empire stopped compelling worship of the emperor but began compelling conversion to Christianity. The church ignored the teaching of Romans 14 and 1 Corinthians 8 and 10, consistently falling for the temptation of the spirit of antichrist until the Puritans again found the way of the Kingdom. Today, we take this freedom for granted but it was hard won and needs to be maintained.

(v) Elected leaders

Almost a thousand years before the Greeks' democracy of 6th Century B.C., the primary leadership of Israel in every circumstance, whether in the land or in exile, was representative elders in every village, city, tribe or in the Sanhedrin, their national assembly.

Here it is, in Deuteronomy:

> "Choose wise and discerning and experienced men from your tribes, and I will appoint them as your heads" (Deut 1:13)

Corrupt or abusive elders were publicly called to account by Ezekiel (Ezek 34:1-10) and Jeremiah (Jer 23:1-4). In New Testament times, every church was led by elders (Acts 14:23) who were recognised for their wisdom and experience

---

(1 Tim 3:4-7) but publicly corrected if necessary (1 Tim 5:19-20).

It is precisely these values and governing structures that are our best political protection and it is only in the dismantling or ignoring of these by the majority of its citizens that the spirit of antichrist can rise up in any nation. Conversely, it is in the promotion of these values and creation of these structures that the spirit of antichrist can be withstood.

'The Weapons of Our Warfare'

It may seem strange at first to think of opposing the spirit of antichrist by promoting particular values and structures but consider the weapons that Paul describes:

> 3. For though we walk in the flesh, we do not war according to the flesh,
> 4. for the weapons of our warfare are not of the flesh, but divinely powerful for the destruction of fortresses
> (2 Cor 10:3-4)

These spiritual weapons can destroy 'fortresses', or in the familiar words of the *King James Version*, 'pull down strongholds'. Paul's metaphor is an army invading an enemy's land, walled city by walled city, where the gates or walls need to be breached and the inhabitants taken captive.

So what exactly are the land, the fortresses, the weapons and the inhabitants that we are to wage war against, given that they are not 'of the flesh'?

Far too many Christians, if they think of these fortresses or strongholds at all, imagine them as satanic castles in the air. It may be they are reasoning that since Satan is 'the prince of the power of the air' (Eph 2:2), his fortresses must be somewhere out in the atmosphere. Some assume this from Daniel's revelation that angelic forces battle it out in the heavenly realm (Dan 10:13) but notice where Paul actually attacks these fortresses:

   Slouching Towards Bethlehem

They are in the human mind. The promised land is our souls, the fortresses are within us. They are 'speculations' and 'every lofty thing (lit. height) raised up' to withstand 'the knowledge of God' in us and our families, friends, communities and nations. We are supposed to pull down and destroy any wall in our minds that *keeps out truth* - any of our erroneous reasoning, imaginings, assumptions, traditions, opinions and ideas to which we mistakenly hold as if they accurately reflect reality. Of course, this is not to discount the fun or stimulation of works of fiction - remembering they are fictional ensures they do not become fortresses.

What are our weapons? Every word of truth and revelation. We are to 'speak the truth in love' (Eph 4:15).

The inhabitants of these fortresses? 'Every thought' (Greek *noema* - thought , purpose or plan). After Paul breached the walls, he sought to capture any rebel thought, purpose or plan disobedient to God's thoughts, purpose and plan, first in his own thinking and then in others.

All of these particular spiritual realities, both the structures and their residents, are in our minds and this warfare takes place inside us all as we grapple with the truth and seek to persuade others.

In regard to the antichrists of the 20th Century, no followers of Jesus should have fallen for the propaganda of Mussolini, Stalin, Hitler, Mao or Hirohito promoting the State as the highest authority and themselves as emperors to be worshipped. Instead, like Alexander Solzhenitsyn, Dietrich Bonhoeffer and many others, they should have argued for God and the values and structures of His kingdom as practised in liberal democracies.

In the 21st Century, we still need to remain alert, not only for new antichrists but because, I believe, we have yet to face the worst of Islam, not only in the Middle East but in almost every nation on earth now.

And it is not only about ideologies and thoughts - we face very real spiritual beings too:

> But the Spirit explicitly says that in later times some will fall away from the faith, paying attention to deceitful spirits and doctrines of demons (1 Tim 4:1)

Doctrines, i.e. teachings, are not all God's or mankind's ideas but can also be inspired by demons, and sometimes believers in those doctrines need to be set free from those demons (Acts 16:16-18, 2 Cor 11:4).

'Against the Spiritual Forces...'

Given the immensity of the principalities and powers of the nations, we each must trust in the only One able to deal with them:

> 10. Finally, be strong in the Lord and in the strength of His might.
> 11. Put on the full armor of God, so that you will be able to stand firm against the schemes of the devil.
> 12. For our struggle is not against flesh and blood, but against the rulers, against the powers, against the world forces of this darkness, against the spiritual forces of wickedness in the heavenly places.
> 13. Therefore, take up the full armor of God, so that you will be able to resist in the evil day, and having done everything, to stand firm (Eph 6:10-13)

Paul was not surprised or in any way dismayed by any of the spiritual forces we face. He reminds us to find our strength in God and to be prepared for 'the evil day' by putting on the only armour that *can* be of any use to us in the spiritual realm: truth, righteousness, readiness, faith, hope and the willingness to spread the word of God (vv. 14-17). This armour is *our developing character* and we cannot afford to create a chink in it by neglecting any part. We are therefore to pray, stay alert and persevere (v. 18). How to pray?

> 1. First of all, then, I urge that entreaties and prayers, petitions and thanksgivings, be made on behalf of all men,
> 2. for kings and all who are in authority, so that we may lead a tranquil and quiet life in all godliness and dignity.
> 3. This is good and acceptable in the sight of God our Savior,
> 4. who desires all men to be saved and to come to the knowledge of the truth (1 Tim 2:1-4)

Remember, Paul was writing this in a time when those in authority were often unjust and merciless and he himself had been wrongfully imprisoned. Daniel, seemingly powerless in exile in the heart of the Babylonian and Medo-Persian empires, was told that his entreaties and prayers for his people Israel were not only going to be answered but were also affecting the affairs of these empires (Dan 10:1-14, 20-21). Of course, Daniel was a man of unusual spiritual standing whose prayers were interspersed with prophecies and angelic visitations but so was Elijah and yet we are urged to emulate him:

> The effective prayer of a righteous man can accomplish much. Elijah was a man with a nature like ours, and he prayed earnestly… (Jas 5:16-17)

Who knows what God may want to do with any one of us in our time?

In the last one hundred years, we have seen the liberal democratic structure of the kingdom of God come in two very different ways: by armed conflict and prayer *and* by peaceful persuasion and prayer.

During WWII, the antichrist regimes of Hirohito, Mussolini and Hitler were brought to an end by the Allied armies and impassioned prayer. This is described by Norman Grubb's remarkable book *Rees Howells: Intercessor*,[371] and by Dr

---

371   London: Lutterworth Press, 1952, pp. 231-257.

Derek Prince in *Shaping History Through Prayer and Fasting.*[372] Many 20th Century Christian intercessors were inspired by Moses' intercession for Joshua to defeat the Amalekites (Exo 17:8-13) and Daniel's praying in the Babylonian, Medo-Persian and Greek empires (Dan 10:12-13, 20-21).

On the other hand, consider the recent peaceful transition of Nepal to democracy. After hundreds of years of rule by absolute monarchs believed to be the embodiment of Vishnu,[373] and therefore an antichrist regime, the king abdicated. This followed decades of pro-democracy agitation, under-girded by a Maoist Communist insurgency and a Christian revival.

Each situation then has to be faced in humility and prayer to determine how we should respond. In every case, however, all citizens need to be weaned away from disproportionate family, tribal or sectarian loyalties to initially democratic but ultimately *godly values and structures*. Our work as Christians is crucial.

In Murderous Regimes

There are times when we can only pray and endure or seek refuge in another country. Revelation 13 reveals that the spirit of antichrist is allowed its season:

> 7. It was also given to him to make war with the saints and to overcome them, and authority over every tribe and people and tongue and nation was given to him.
> 8. All who dwell on the earth will worship him, everyone whose name has not been written from the foundation of the world in the book of life of the Lamb who has been slain.
> 9. If anyone has an ear, let him hear.
> 10. If anyone is destined for captivity, to captivity he goes; if anyone kills with the sword, with the sword he must be killed. Here is the perseverance and the faith of the saints.
> (Rev 13:7-10)

---

372   New Kensington, PA: Whitaker House, 1973.
373   www.beliefnet.com/Faiths/Hinduism/2006/05/What-Is-A-Hindu-Kingdom.aspx, 6 Apr, 2010.

John saw himself as 'destined for captivity', during which he wrote the book we are now studying. He was also warning those wanting to fight the beast's sixth head that the Roman Empire would not be overthrown in their time. If his unbelieving compatriots had only understood this, they could have been spared the one million Jewish deaths of the Great Revolt of 66-70 A.D. against Nero, Vespasian and Titus.

Again, sixty years later, many more could have been spared by avoiding a false Messiah in their land:

> In 132 CE, Bar Kosiba organized a large guerrilla army and succeeded in actually throwing the Romans out of Jerusalem and Israel and establishing, albeit for a very brief period, an independent Jewish state. The Talmud (*Sanhedrin* 97b) states that he established an independent kingdom that lasted for two and half years.
>
> Bar Kosiba's success caused many to believe - among them Rabbi Akiva, one of the wisest and holiest of Israel's rabbis - that he could be the Messiah. He was nicknamed "Bar Kochba" or "Son of Star," an allusion to a verse in the Book of Numbers (24:17): "there shall come a star out of Jacob." This star is understood to refer to the Messiah.
>
> Bar Kochba did not turn out to be the Messiah, and later the rabbis wrote that his real name was Bar Kosiva meaning "Son of a Lie" - highlighting the fact that he was a false Messiah.[374]

Roman historian Dio Cassius recorded the response of the emperor:

> Hadrian sent against them his best generals. First of these was Julius Severus, who…did not venture to attack his opponents in the open at any one point in view of their numbers and their desperation, but by intercepting small groups. Thanks to the numbers of soldiers and his officers, and by depriving them of food and shutting them up, he

---

374   www.aish.com/jl/h/48944706.html, 14 Apr, 2010.

was able - rather slowly to be sure, but with comparatively
little danger - to crush, exhaust and exterminate them.
Very few of them in fact survived. Fifty of their most
important outposts and 985 of their most famous villages
were razed to the ground, and 580,000 men were slain in
various raids and battles, and the number of those who
perished by famine, disease and fire was past finding out.[375]

We too need to recognise our times, the time of the seventh
head with the ten horns, and hear what God Himself is calling
us to do in each situation in every nation. If the persecution
is inescapable, many being unable to flee Sudan or Zimbabwe
recently, our only option is 'the perseverance and the faith of
the saints'.

---

375   *Roman History,* LXIX, www.brainfly.net/html/books/diocas69.
htm, 14 Apr, 2010.

20

Islam
The Slouching Beast?

Earlier, we established that the most likely empire to produce the final antichrist and sixth abomination of desolation is that of Muhammad. We saw that Islam's end-time doctrines promote his welcome. We also saw that Islam has not remained within any territorial borders but, like the kingdom of God, has today permeated throughout all the nations.

How then should we respond as individuals? In five essential ways:

(i) Actively love Muslims and avoid being part of the problem

Despite the appearance in our Western media of hateful images of Muslims, most that I have met are culturally gracious. Edmund Burke once commented on the zealots of the French Revolution:

> By hating vices too much, they come to love men too little.[376]

Identifying Islam as the current antichrist regime, and the greatest of all time, creates a strong temptation for us to love Muslims too little. We must therefore be radically obedient to love our neighbours and our enemies and to do good to those who hate us (Luke 6:27).

One man wonderfully demonstrating this is Mazhar Mallouhi, a Syrian novelist who describes himself as a 'Sufi Muslim follower of Christ'. Despite much persecution

---

376   *The Oxford Dictionary of Political Quotations*, Oxford University Press, 1997, p. 67.

---

including imprisonment and exile, he has had remarkable success both in his personal testimony and in publishing throughout the Muslim world his culturally sensitive novels, Scripture portions and Biblical commentaries.[377]

Believers of all kinds are often better than their theology. We surely see this to be true among Christians and it is equally true of Muslims. One remarkable Muslim leader is 'the Gaza doctor', Izzeldin Abuelaish. This Palestinian infertility specialist was born and raised in the Jabalia refugee camp in Gaza but worked for decades in Israeli hospitals. Then, in January 2009, an Israeli shell landed on his house, killing three of his daughters and a niece. In his book, *I Shall Not Hate: A Gaza Doctor's Journey*, he writes:

> *What can you do?* You can do a lot. You can support justice for all by speaking out loudly to your family, friends, community, politicians and religious leaders. You can support foundations that do good work. You can volunteer for humanitarian organizations. You can vote regressive politicians out of office. You can do many things to move the world toward greater harmony…
> I know that what I have lost, what was taken from me, will never come back. But as a physician and a Muslim of deep faith, I need to move forward to the light, motivated by the spirits of those I lost. I need to bring them justice… I will keep moving but I need you to join me in this long journey.[378]

(ii) Be better informed

We need to hear the perspective of insiders. Earlier, I referred to Mahomed (a.k.a. Ed) Husain, whose autobiography *The Islamist* both humanises and details differing aspects of

---

377   Mazhar's story is told by Paul-Gordon Chandler in *Pilgrims of Christ on the Muslim Road (Exploring a New Path Between Two Paths)*, Lanham, Maryland; Rowan & Littlefield Publishers, 2007.
378   Random House, Canada, 2010. Emphasis in original.

Islam, and to Mark Gabriel who was an historian at Al Azhar University in Cairo. Another remarkable testimony is that of Bilquis Sheikh, a high-born Pakistani woman, whose book *I Dared to Call Him Father* is easy and inspiring to read.[379]

Dr Wafa Sultan is a Syrian-born psychiatrist and was named by *Time* magazine in 2006 as one of the world's 100 Most Influential People. She has written of *Obstacles in Liberating Islam*:

> As an Arab woman who suffered for three decades
> living under Islamic Sharia, it is clear to me that Islam's
> political ideology and Sharia must be fought relentlessly
> by Western civilisation to prevent its application in a free
> society. However, I have found myself fighting on two
> fronts. The first front is against Islamists, a daunting fight
> indeed, but the other front is one shaped by too many
> uninformed individuals who like to view themselves as
> open-minded "progressives"... Regarding themselves as
> tolerant, free-thinking individuals, they avoid questioning
> Muslims' harmful intentions...
> It is crucial for them to realise that Islam is based on an
> anti-liberal system. They need to awaken to the inhumane
> policies and practices of Islamists around the world. They
> need to realise that Islamism opposes the values they
> cherish. And equally important, they must not take for
> granted the respect for human rights and dignity that we
> experience... in the West today.[380]

She notes the unintended consequences:

> When Westerners make politically-correct excuses for
> Islamism, it actually suppresses and weakens my voice
> and that of others who are in this fight. Simply put,
> too many individuals and institutions stand in the way
> of overcoming Islamic political ideology. With their
> appeasing approach, they obstruct the pressing effort to
> modernise Islam.

---

379 Kingsway Publishing, Eastbourne, UK, 2001.
380 *Israel and Christians Today*, Auckland, Feb, 2010, p. 10.

> When I first immigrated to the U.S., I learned to my
> dismay that Islam has been labelled by many as "a religion
> of peace". But for me, as a Syrian who grew up in an
> Islamic country, a set of beliefs that insists that women are
> evil is an evil set of beliefs. A pious ideology that obliges
> non-Muslims to live as subjects under it as unequal is an
> immoral pious ideology...[381]

She also answered critics of her approach:

> People who avoid facing the gloomy facts regarding Islam
> have no moral authority to admonish liberated Arabs like
> me. Those who cannot confront Islamic doctrine boldly
> and will not allow themselves to question openly dreadful
> components of Islam are on the wrong side of this conflict.
> I have often been asked to soften and compromise my
> message. I refuse to do so. I believe the way to solve this
> Islamic predicament is to highlight and confront it in a
> most truthful and subsequently painful manner. As we
> all would agree, at times an acute disease must be treated
> aggressively rather than with a benign medicine like
> Aspirin.
> Lastly, I will carry on my mission because I love Muslims.
> I dream of a future when all Muslims, especially from
> the Middle East, who yearn for a better life outside their
> suppressive environment, can savour the taste of the
> freedom we all experience here in the U.S. This is not just
> Dr King's dream. This is a dream that should be granted to
> all humanity – including those in the Muslim world.[382]

This remarkable woman describes herself as a secularist, having
lost her faith in Muhammad in 1979 when, as a medical
student in Aleppo, she watched her professor being gunned
down by the Muslim Brotherhood while they shouted "God
is great!" Her book, *A God Who Hates*,[383] has been dismissed by
many Muslims as an emotional rather an intellectual decision

---

381   Ibid.
382   Ibid.
383   New York, St. Martin's Press, 2009.

                              Slouching Towards Bethlehem

but she has more than earned her right to be heard.

We can all stop making 'politically-correct excuses for Islamism'; we can all avoid being 'useful idiots'.

(iii) Recognise and encourage the differences between fundamentalism and modernism in Islam

Islam and Muslims are not a monolithic whole. Just as in Christendom, there are competing ideologies. In the simplest terms, some 85% are Sunnis while 15% are Shi'ites; Sunnis believe that Muhammad did not appoint a successor so they select one, a Caliph, while the Shi'ites believe he appointed as Imam his cousin Ali and his descendants. Most Shi'ites are Iranian, Iraqi or Palestinian. There are also Sufis, mystics who can be either Sunni or Shi'ite, who seek to experience God through meditation or dancing, like their famous whirling dervishes.

There is also a major division between fundamentalists and modernists. Fundamentalists seek to retain and apply Muhammad's 7th Century 'revelations' and mindset, as in Saudi Arabia's stoning of adulterers and amputation of thieves' hands. Saudi Arabia, home to Islam's holiest shrines of Mecca and Medina, is also home to a branch of fundamentalism called Wahhabism and followed by Osama bin Laden. Modernists, however, argue for adaptation to the 21st Century and even for the separation of Islam and the state. Some such as Dr. Zhudi Jasser, chairman of the American Islamic Forum for Democracy,[384] also do not accept the idea of the Twelfth Imam, denouncing it as coming from illegitimate hadith.

As can be seen from above, this is a major step away from the spirit of antichrist and it is essential this is encouraged.

---

384   http://aifdemocracy.org, 30 October, 2011. Dr. Jasser served as attending physician to the U.S. Congress and as a Lieutenant Commander in the U.S. Navy. His testimony to the Committee on Homeland Security on March 10, 2011, can be heard on www.youtube.com/watch?v=KpRgqDMrD4M, 30 Oct, 2011.

Canadian Paul Marek's grandparents fled from the Nazi occupation of Czechoslovakia. In 2006, he wrote a short essay, *Why The Peaceful Majority Is Irrelevant*, which was widely distributed on the internet. It was also published in a collection of 101 essays, *How to Achieve a Heaven on Earth*, other contributors being Barack Obama, Tony Blair, Martin Luther King Jr, Ted Turner, Al Gore and George W. Bush:[385]

> I used to know a man whose family were German aristocracy prior to World War Two. They owned a number of large industries and estates. I asked him how many German people were true Nazis, and the answer he gave has stuck with me and guided my attitude toward fanaticism ever since.
>
> "Very few people were true Nazis" he said, "but, many enjoyed the return of German pride, and many more were too busy to care. I was one of those who just thought the Nazis were a bunch of fools. So, the majority just sat back and let it all happen. Then, before we knew it, they owned us, and we had lost control, and the end of the world had come. My family lost everything. I ended up in a concentration camp and the Allies destroyed my factories."
>
> We are told again and again by 'experts' and 'talking heads' that Islam is the religion of peace, and that the vast majority of Muslims just want to live in peace. Although this unquantified assertion may be true, it is entirely irrelevant. It is meaningless fluff, meant to make us feel better, and meant to somehow diminish the specter of fanatics rampaging across the globe in the name of Islam. The fact is, that the fanatics rule Islam at this moment in history. It is the fanatics who march. It is the fanatics who wage any one of 50 shooting wars world wide. It is the fanatics who systematically slaughter Christian or tribal groups throughout Africa and are gradually taking over the entire continent in an Islamic wave. It is the fanatics who bomb, behead, murder, or honor-kill. It is the fanatics

---

385 *How to Achieve a Heaven on Earth*, ed. John E Wade II, Pelican Publishing Co Inc., 2010.

       Slouching Towards Bethlehem

who take over mosque after mosque. It is the fanatics who zealously spread the stoning and hanging of rape victims and homosexuals. The hard quantifiable fact is, that the "peaceful majority" is the "silent majority" and it is cowed and extraneous.

Although Marek does not identify the spiritual connection, he does recognise a striking similarity in the very different ideological regimes of the last 100 years:

> Communist Russia was comprised of Russians who just wanted to live in peace, yet the Russian Communists were responsible for the murder of about 20 million people. The peaceful majority were irrelevant. China's huge population was peaceful as well, but Chinese Communists managed to kill a staggering 70 million people. The average Japanese individual prior to World War 2 was not a war mongering sadist. Yet, Japan murdered and slaughtered its way across South East Asia in an orgy of killing that included the systematic killing of 12 million Chinese civilians; most killed by sword, shovel, and bayonet. And, who can forget Rwanda, which collapsed into butchery. Could it not be said that the majority of Rwandans were "peace loving"?

He concludes:

> History lessons are often incredibly simple and blunt, yet for all our powers of reason we often miss the most basic and uncomplicated of points. Peace-loving Muslims have been made irrelevant by the fanatics. Peace-loving Muslims have been made irrelevant by their silence. Peace-loving Muslims will become our enemy if they don't speak up, because like my friend from Germany, they will awake one day and find that the fanatics own them, and the end of their world will have begun. Peace-loving Germans, Japanese, Chinese, Russians, Rwandans, Bosnians, Afghans, Iraqis, Palestinians, Somalis, Nigerians, Algerians, and many others, have died because the peaceful majority did not speak up until it was too late. As for us who watch it all unfold, we must pay

attention to the only group that counts; the fanatics who threaten our way of life.

While some may fear this is Islam-bashing, Marek's point is actually that in *any* society, nation or belief system, it only takes a few, deeply dedicated to their cause, to harness the rest. He is simply illustrating the dictum: 'All that is necessary for evil to triumph is for good men to do nothing'.[386] Acclaimed British historian Sir Ian Kershaw also identified this phenomenon in Hitler's Germany, concluding of his vast research:

> The road to Auschwitz was built by hate, but paved with indifference.[387]

Hannah Arendt was similarly able to conclude of both the Fascists and the Communists:

> The success of totalitarian movements… showed [firstly] that the politically neutral and indifferent masses could easily be the majority in a democratically ruled country… [while it actually functioned] according to rules which are actively recognised by only a minority… [Secondly,] that democratic government had rested as much on the silent approbation and tolerance of the indifferent and inarticulate sections of the people as on the articulate and visible institutions and organisations of the country.[388]

Surely then we must do all we can to encourage the modernist movement among peace-loving Muslims, urging them to at least peacefully transition to the democratic protections described above.

---

386   Usually attributed to Edmund Burke but not documented anywhere.

387   *Popular Opinion and Political Dissent in the Third Reich: Bavaria 1933-45*, Oxford University Press, 1983, p. 277.

388   *Princeton Readings in Political Thought*, Princeton, New Jersey; University Press, 1996, p. 577.

(iv) Recognise the true significance of women

We saw in Revelation 12 that the dragon has three particular hatreds: for women, for Israel and for Christians.[389] As predicted in Genesis 3:15, this is due to the unique role of "the woman" in bringing forth "her seed", Jesus of Nazareth, to "bruise the serpent's head", i.e. destroy his kingdom. As the Seed of only the woman, Jesus was born without a human father; Israel as a nation was the wife of God to give Him birth.

After the dragon fails to prevent the woman, in both senses, from bringing forth Jesus, in his bitterness he continues to attack women in general[390] and the nation of Israel (Rev 12:13) as well as 'the rest of her children, who keep the commandments of God and hold to the testimony of Jesus' (Rev 12:17), i.e. Christians.

These three hatreds help us to unmistakably identify the spirit behind fundamentalist Islam, given its attitude towards women, Israel and Christians.

It is therefore no wonder that the best hope for modernising the Islamic nations is through the love and courage of their women. This is too big a subject to be addressed here except to say that we must do whatever we can do to encourage the empowering and educating of Muslim women.

(v) Remember that the only long-term answer is a supernatural encounter with the risen Jesus

He can somehow touch the hearts of His seemingly most implacable enemies, as Paul testified to King Agrippa:

> 9. "So then, I thought to myself that I had to do many things hostile to the name of Jesus of Nazareth.
> 10. "And this is just what I did in Jerusalem; not only did I lock up

---

389   *Dancing in the Dragon's Jaws*, p. 69.
390   See the author's *Because of the Angels (Unveiling 1 Corinthians 11:2-16)*, Auckland; Emmaus Road Publishing, 2002. Also *Woman at Risk Worldwide*, www.frontline.org.za/articles/women%20at%20orisk%20worldwide.htm, 23 May, 2012.

---

many of the saints in prisons, having received authority from the
chief priests, but also when they were being put to death I cast
my vote against them.
11. "And as I punished them often in all the synagogues, I tried
to force them to blaspheme; and being furiously enraged at
them, I kept pursuing them even to foreign cities.
12. "While so engaged as I was journeying to Damascus..."
(Acts 26:9-12)

Although not as sudden or dramatic as Paul's 'Damascus
road', a truly remarkable conversion in our day has been that
of Mosab Hassan Yousef. The eldest son of Sheikh Hassan
Yousef, one of the seven founders of the Palestinian Hamas
organisation, Mosab has left Islam to follow Jesus and his
memoirs are both inspiring and enlightening because he details
how his fundamentalist defences were penetrated.

Born in Ramallah in the West Bank, he grew up in a very
loving family. He still admires and respects his father as a
devout and compassionate imam who, he believes, has been
misled:

> What my father saw in those early days was the part of
> Islam that reflects love and mercy. What he didn't see,
> what he perhaps has never yet allowed himself to see, is
> the other side of Islam... And thirty five years later, I want
> to ask him: Do you remember where you started? You saw
> all those lost people, your heart broke for them, and you
> wanted them to come to Allah and be safe. Now suicide
> bombers and innocent blood? Is this what you set out to
> do?[391]

Beaten and imprisoned by the Israelis at age 18, Mosab became
disillusioned as over three years he also saw the brutality
of Hamas prison leaders torturing and killing their fellow-
Palestinians. He was spared because of his connections but he
began questioning what motivated them and the 'martyrdom

---

391 *Son of Hamas,* Carol Stream, Illinois; Tyndale House Publishers,
Inc., 2010, pp. 11-12.

operations' which were killing many civilians, including women and children:

> It was impossible for me to mentally reconcile the kindness and character of my father and his leadership with an organisation that carried out such things… I loved my father so deeply, and I admired so much about who he was and what he stood for… [but] he had obviously found a way to rationalise the idea that it was fine for somebody else to explode people into scraps of meat…My view of my father grew much more complicated.[392]

He decided to stand against this evil by helping Israeli intelligence prevent suicide bombings. In an interview much later, he explained, "against evil – not against Hamas, not against Palestinians."

Then one day in 1997, walking past Jerusalem's Damascus Gate, he was invited by a British tourist to a Bible study where he was given a New Testament. Captivated by the Sermon on the Mount, he was stunned to read Jesus' words: "I tell you, love your enemies and pray for those who persecute you, that you may be sons of your Father in heaven" (Matt 5:44-45):

> Never before had I heard anything like this, but I knew this was the message I had been searching for all my life. For years I had struggled to know who my enemy was, and I had looked for enemies outside of Islam and Palestine. But I suddenly realised that the Israelis were not my enemies. Neither was Hamas… I saw that enemies were not defined by nationality, religion or colour. I understood that we all share the same common enemies: greed, pride, and all the bad ideas and the darkness of the devil that live inside us.
> That meant I could love anyone. The only real enemy was the enemy inside me.[393]

---

392   Ibid., pp. 58-59.
393   Ibid., p. 122.

By 2001, he had concluded that:

> …with the big checks flowing from Iraq's ruthless dictator
> Saddam Hussein [US$10,000 to the family of anyone
> killed fighting Israel and US$25,000 to the family of every
> suicide bomber], Hamas found it had lost its monopoly
> on [religiously motivated] suicide bombings. Now the
> bombers also came from Islamic Jihad and the Al-Aqsa
> Martyrs Brigades, the secularists, the communists and
> the atheists. And they all competed with one another to
> see who could kill the most Israeli civilians… Now I saw
> it through Israeli eyes too. And even more importantly,
> I watched the mindless killing through the eyes of Jesus,
> who agonised for those who were lost. The more I read
> the Bible, the more clearly I saw this single truth: loving
> and forgiving one's enemies is the only real way to stop the
> bloodshed.
> Accelerating my departure from Islam was the hypocrisy I
> saw all around me. Islam taught that a devoted servant of
> Allah went straight to heaven… but suddenly it seemed
> that *anyone* killed by the Israelis, whether a nominal
> Muslim, a communist, even an atheist, was being treated
> as a holy martyr. The imams and the sheikhs told the
> families of the dead, "Your loved one is in heaven".
> Of course, the Qur'an didn't support their rhetoric but
> these leaders didn't seem to care. This wasn't about truth
> or theology; it was about lying to people for strategic
> advantage and political expediency.[394]

One of Mosab's Jewish Christian friends, Amnon, was
imprisoned for refusing military service:

> He was there because he refused to work with the Israelis;
> I was there because I had agreed to work with them.
> I was trying to protect Jews; he was trying to protect
> Palestinians… I thought that if we just had a thousand
> Amnons on one side and a thousand Mosabs on the other,
> it could make a big difference.[395]

---

394   Ibid., pp. 145-149. Emphasis in original.
395   Ibid., p. 207.

                                          Slouching Towards Bethlehem

Notice what first penetrated Mosab's fundamentalism – he knew it was wrong, no matter the Qur'an or his beloved father said, to target women and children and to torture and kill the innocent. As Paul says, it was written on his heart (Rom 2:14-15). When he decided to stand up and fight, not against people but whatever was wrong or evil, he began to love his enemies, befriending Jews and Christians and ultimately God Himself in Jesus Christ.

21
Conclusions

We have to learn how to respond in a variety of situations but at all times to recognise that we face spiritual principalities and powers. We are therefore:

(i) To trust in God and His ability to deal with every issue, situation and era. Our part is primarily to put on His spiritual armour, which is our developing godly character, and to respond as He leads.

(ii) In the geo-political world of democratic nations, to recognise, maintain and propagate the checks and balances which were ordained by God to deal with the fallibility and sinfulness of mankind. What we today call liberal democracy is actually an outworking of the Kingdom of God as revealed to Moses three and a half thousand years ago.

(iii) To understand the significance of five essential revelations:

(a) the worth of every individual, created in the image and likeness of God

(b) the rule of law for all

(c) the separation of powers including an independent judiciary and the free press or media

(d) freedom of conscience

(e) elected and accountable leaders.

(iv) To propagate the benefits of these as introduced or restored in the last hundred years, both by armed conflict, as in World War II, and by peaceful persuasion, as in Nepal.

(v)   If facing murderous persecution, to either flee or endure.

(vi) In peaceful lands, to respond to Islam and our Muslim neighbours by:

(a) loving them as ourselves so that we are not part of the problem

(b) being better informed both by personal interaction and by testimonies such as that of Mark Gabriel, Ed Husain, Bilquis Sheikh, Wafa Sultan and Mosab Hussein Youssef

(c) encouraging them to modernism rather than fundamentalism so that they may be open-minded enough to reconsider Jesus

(d) recognising the significance of Muslim women, to encourage their empowerment and education

(e) helping all to encounter our risen Lord, Jesus Christ.

Epilogue

No book on apocalyptic literature and modern culture would be complete without some reference to Bob Dylan, one of the West's preeminent poetic and prophetic voices.

In October, 1983, the most apocalyptic of all Dylan's albums, *Infidels*,[396] addressed in extraordinary metaphor the issues of Israel's bad press *(Neighbourhood Bully)*, the church's temptations *(Sweetheart Like You)*, humanism's self-adulation *(Licence to Kill)* and Satan's subtlety *(Man of Peace)*. He is setting to music Revelation chapters 12, 13, 19 and 21.

The opening track, however, was *Jokerman*, which not only describes the rise of the Antichrist but also delivers a devastating warning, replete with Biblical allusions, to the cynics, secularists and materialists of our age. Dylan begins:

> *Standing on the waters casting your bread*
> *While the eyes of the idol with the iron head are glowing.*
> *Distant ships sailing in through the mist,*
> *You were born with a snake in both of your fists while a*
> *hurricane was blowing.*
> *Freedom just around the corner for you*
> *But with the truth so far off, what good will it do?*
>
> *Jokerman dance to the nightingale tune,*
> *Bird fly high by the light of the moon,*
> *Oh, oh, oh, Jokerman.*

Nearly all of the speculation on the identity of the Jokerman, which ranges from Dylan himself to Abraham, Jesus and Ronald Reagan,[397] seems to completely overlook his defining characteristics and their Biblical basis, despite Dylan's careful references: the Jokerman is a mocker and a denizen of the

---

396 Columbia Records, New York.
397 For example, www.songmeanings.net/songs/ view/3458764513820552092/, 12 Sep, 2011.

---

night; he is a self-deluded narcissist and idolater and he will come to a bad end. All his scoffing will cease when he at last has to face the consequences of his choices – the coming of the Antichrist.

Ignoring the wisdom of God ('How blessed is the man who does not walk in the counsel of the wicked... nor sit in the seat of scoffers!' Psa 1:1), the worldly-wise Jokerman mocks everything that is holy.

From the opening lines, 'Standing on the waters, casting your bread while the eyes of the idol with the iron head are glowing', we see his messianic pretensions while he participates in an appalling Canaanite ritual. Their worship of Baal included sacrificing their children by placing them in the arms of an iron image with an internal fire. 'You were born with a snake in both of your fists' is Jokerman thinking he is as invincible as the demi-god Hercules who strangled two snakes while in his crib.

'Freedom just around the corner for you, but with the truth so far off, what good will it do?' Freedom cannot occur without the truth that sets us free (John 8:31-32) and mocking cannot take us there: 'a scoffer seeks wisdom and finds none' (Prov 14:6)

> *So swiftly the sun sets in the sky,*
> *You rise up and say goodbye to no one.*
> *Fools rush in where angels fear to tread,*
> *Both of their futures, so full of dread, you don't show one.*
> *Shedding off one more layer of skin,*
> *Keeping one step ahead of the persecutor within.*
>
> *Jokerman dance to the nightingale tune,*
> *Bird fly high by the light of the moon,*
> *Oh, oh, oh, Jokerman.*

Romans 13:12 urges us to 'lay aside the deeds of darkness and put on the armour of light'. The Jokerman, however, loves the night and sleeps during the day. In his self-confidence, he rushes in where even angels will not go. The only changes he thinks he needs are superficial but, like a snake, the shed skin only reveals the same snake and that will never satisfy his internal persecutor – his own conscience (Rom 2:14-15).

> *You're a man of the mountains, you can walk on the clouds,*
> *Manipulator of crowds, you're a dream twister.*
> *You're going to Sodom and Gomorrah*
> *But what do you care? Ain't nobody there would want to*
> *marry your sister.*
> *Friend to the martyr, a friend to the woman of shame,*
> *You look into the fiery furnace, see the rich man without any*
> *name.*
>
> *Jokerman dance to the nightingale tune,*
> *Bird fly high by the light of the moon,*
> *Oh, oh, oh, Jokerman.*

He can please all the crowds, taking every politically correct view, not worrying about society becoming like Sodom and Gomorrah (Luke 17:28-30) because he thinks it will never impact badly on him. He straddles all moral divisions, having both friends who will stand for right and friends who embrace the wrong.

'The fiery furnace and rich man without any name' comes straight from Jesus' warning (Luke 16:19-31) that all his fame and riches will mean nothing in the after-life.

> *Well, the Book of Leviticus and Deuteronomy,*
> *The law of the jungle and the sea are your only teachers.*
> *In the smoke of the twilight on a milk-white steed,*
> *Michelangelo indeed could've carved out your features.*
> *Resting in the fields, far from the turbulent space,*
> *Half asleep near the stars with a small dog licking your face.*
>
> *Jokerman dance to the nightingale tune,*
> *Bird fly high by the light of the moon,*
> *Oh, oh, oh, Jokerman.*

The Jokerman knows of the harshness of natural laws and the survival of the fittest but little of grace and forgiveness. Like Sartre's followers, he accepts the nausea of the outworking of his philosophy, seeing himself as unflinchingly heroic.

> *Well, the rifleman's stalking the sick and the lame,*
> *Preacher man seeks the same, who'll get there first is*
> *uncertain.*
> *Nightsticks and water cannons, tear gas, padlocks,*
> *Molotov cocktails and rocks behind every curtain,*
> *False-hearted judges dying in the webs that they spin,*
> *Only a matter of time 'til night comes steppin' in.*
>
> *Jokerman dance to the nightingale tune,*
> *Bird fly high by the light of the moon,*
> *Oh, oh, oh, Jokerman.*

The consequences, however, are most felt by the weak in society who are targeted by the compassionate with the gospel or the ruthless for exploitation. In an increasingly godless and lawless world, it is every man for himself and 'only a matter of time 'til night comes steppin' in'. In this vicious spiritual warfare, we will be caught in any falsehood that we tolerate.

Dylan's chilling conclusion:

> *It's a shadowy world, skies are slippery grey,*
> *A woman just gave birth to a prince today and dressed him in*
> *scarlet.*
> *He'll put the priest in his pocket, put the blade to the heat,*
> *Take the motherless children off the street*
> *And place them at the feet of a harlot.*
> *Oh, Jokerman, you know what he wants,*
> *Oh, Jokerman, you don't show any response.*
>
> *Jokerman dance to the nightingale tune,*
> *Bird fly high by the light of the moon,*
> *Oh, oh, oh, Jokerman.*

In a world where nothing is black and white, there suddenly appears the prince dressed in scarlet, the Antichrist. With the connivance of the religious authorities, he heats up the blade to brand his followers with the mark of the beast and this saviour of the orphans is not putting them in loving homes – they are being offered to Babylon, 'the great harlot' of Revelation, chapters 17 and 18.

It is about now that the Jokerman sees what has really been going on and that the outcome of his scoffing will be the loss of his soul.

So… who wants to be a Jokerman?

#

Five "Abominations of Desolation"

The First Instance – The Distress of Shiloh (c. 1050 B.C.)

When Israel first entered the Promised Land, they gathered at Shiloh to set up the Tabernacle (Josh 18:1) and it stayed there until Samuel's time (1 Sam 1:3), a period of about 450 years (Acts 13:19). Unfortunately, by this time Israel had descended into anarchy as 'every man did what was right in his own eyes' (Jud 21:25) so the Lord warns the high priest Eli, father of two corrupt priests:

> "You will see the distress of My dwelling…" (1 Sam 2:32)

He also warns Samuel:

> The LORD said to Samuel, "Behold, I am about to do a thing in Israel at which both ears of everyone who hears it will tingle" (1 Sam 3:11)

The Book of Judges describes their many sins over the 450 years but the worst, the tipping point or last straw, is when the elders of Israel use the ark of the covenant as an idolatrous talisman to fight the Philistines:

> "Let us take to ourselves from Shiloh the ark of the covenant of the LORD, that it may come among us and deliver us from the power of our enemies" (1 Sam 4:3)

They are looking to the ark of the covenant for help, *to the symbol rather than to God.* The result is an unmitigated disaster – the Lord withdraws His protection, 30,000 Israeli soldiers are killed including Eli's two sons, Eli himself falls and dies and the ark is captured by the Philistines. When Eli's daughter-in-law hears the news, she names her new-born son Ichabod, saying, "The glory has departed from Israel" (1 Sam 4:21).

Note the order of events:

(i)   Israel's sinning reached such a state that God finally withdrew; His glory departed from Israel.

(ii) With His protection gone, Israel's army was defeated, the holiest symbol of His presence, the ark of the covenant, was captured and their sanctuary at Shiloh was left desolate.

(iii) The Philistines then committed their own idolatrous abomination, taking the ark back to their temple of Dagon only to be themselves judged, city by city, until they sent it back to Israel (1 Sam 5:1-6:18).

Samuel then helped them to mend their ways. Within fifty years, David planned and Solomon built their magnificent Temple but almost 500 hundred years later…

The Second Instance – The Desolation of the First Temple (586 B.C.)

This second instance, in 586 B.C., is also not mentioned by any of the above commentators. In Jeremiah, chapter 7, we see that God sent Jeremiah to stand in the gate of the Temple to prophesy:

> 4. "Do not trust in deceptive words, saying, 'This is the temple of the LORD, the temple of the LORD, the temple of the LORD'"

Their words are 'deceptive' and self-deluding because they think it does not matter if they carry on sinning because they are God's people and still fellowshipping with Him in His house.

> 11. "Has this house, which is called by My name, become a den of robbers in your sight? Behold, I, even I, have seen it," declares the LORD

                                   Slouching Towards Bethlehem

Just as robbers think they are safe when they are hiding in their den, Israel think they are safe because they can hide in the Temple:

> 9. "Will you steal, murder, and commit adultery and swear falsely, and offer sacrifices to Baal and walk after other gods that you have not known,
> 10. then come and stand before Me in this house, which is called by My name, and say, 'We are delivered!' – that you may do all these abominations?

Their abominations are about to be judged:

> 13. "And now, because you have done all these things," declares the LORD, "and I spoke to you, rising up early and speaking, but you did not hear, and I called you but you did not answer,
> 14. therefore, I will do to the house which is called by My name, in which you trust, and to the place which I gave you and your fathers, as I did to Shiloh" (Jer 7:4-14)

This was their downfall, just as it was at Shiloh.

Ezekiel confirms Jeremiah's warnings. He is taken by the Spirit of God from his exile in Babylon to Jerusalem, to see the Temple, the city and the land of Israel about to be made desolate (Ezek 6:3-14) because of the many abominations Israel was committing there (Ezek 8:3-18). He sees Israel's armies being defeated (Ezek 9:1-11) and God's glory departing (Ezek 10:1-22).

Note the order:

(i)   Israel's sins multiplied beyond God's forbearance so that His glory departed.

(ii) With His presence and protection gone, Israel's army was defeated and their holiest place, the Temple, Jerusalem and the land of Israel were made desolate.

(iii) The Babylonians then committed their own idolatrous abomination, using the Temple's holy vessels at a blasphemous feast (Dan 5:3-4). This event triggered the famous 'writing on the wall' (Dan 5:5-28), the death of Belshazzar and the end of their kingdom (Dan 5:30-31).

The chroniclers of Israel also spell out this pattern in 2 Chronicles 36:

> 14. All the officials of the priests and the people were very unfaithful following all the abominations of the nations; and they defiled the house of the LORD which He had sanctified in Jerusalem.
> 15. The LORD, the God of their fathers, sent word to them again and again by His messengers, because He had compassion on His people and on His dwelling place;
> 16. but they continually mocked the messengers of God, despised His words and scoffed at His prophets, until the wrath of the LORD arose against His people, until there was no remedy.

Again, Israel's 'abominations' (v. 14) increased 'until there was no remedy' (v. 16).

> 17. Therefore He brought up against them the king of the Chaldeans who slew their young men with the sword in the house of their sanctuary...
> 19. Then they burned the house of God and broke down the wall of Jerusalem, and burned all its fortified buildings with fire and destroyed all its valuable articles.

God removes His protection, Israel's army is defeated (v. 17), their holiest place, the Temple, and Jerusalem are made desolate (v. 18) and the people are exiled.

Tragically, Israel *still* does not understand. In exile in Egypt, they attribute all their woes to their neglect of Ishtar, the Babylonian fertility goddess known as the Queen of Heaven, as recorded in Jeremiah 44:

> 17. "...we will certainly carry out every word that has proceeded from our mouths, by burning sacrifices to the queen of heaven and pouring out drink offerings to her, just as we ourselves, our forefathers, our kings and our princes did in the cities of Judah and in the streets of Jerusalem; for then we had plenty of food and were well off and saw no misfortune.

> 18. "But since we stopped burning sacrifices to the queen of
> heaven and pouring out drink offerings to her, we have lacked
> everything and have met our end by the sword and by famine."

So Jeremiah tries one last time:

> 21. "As for the smoking sacrifices that you burned in the cities of
> Judah and in the streets of Jerusalem, you and your forefathers,
> your kings and your princes, and the people of the land, did
> not the LORD remember them and did not all this come into His
> mind?
> 22. "So the LORD was no longer able to endure it, because of
> the evil of your deeds, because of the abominations which you
> have committed; thus your land has become a ruin, an object of
> horror and a curse, without an inhabitant, as it is this day"
> (Jer 44:21-22)

Verse 22 spells out exactly *how* abominations cause desolation:

(i)   Israel's "evil deeds" were "the abominations" that push
      God beyond endurance.

(ii) He removed His protection and allowed their enemies
      to make the Temple, Jerusalem and the land desolate.

(iii) Ezekiel saw the idols of the surrounding nations set
      up in the Temple (Ezek 8:3-16). Jeremiah therefore
      went on to prophesy that God will judge all those
      nations and their gods and will make them "desolate"
      too: Egypt (Jer 46:19, 25), Philistia (Jer 47:4), Moab
      (Jer 48:7-9), Ammon (Jer 49:2), Edom (Jer 49:17) and
      Babylon (Jer 50:2-3).

Daniel, then, was living in this time of the First Temple,
Jerusalem and the land lying desolate. In about 538 B.C., Daniel
reads Jeremiah's prophecy that "the desolations of Jerusalem"
were to last seventy years (Dan 9:1-2) so, having been captive
in Babylon since 605 B.C. (Dan 1:1), he prays for restoration.
He has not the slightest doubt as to what had happened –
God had fulfilled what Moses had prophesied would happen

if Israel became unfaithful:

> 31. "I will lay waste your cities as well and will make your
> sanctuaries desolate, and I will not smell your soothing aromas.
> 32. "I will make the land desolate so that your enemies who
> settle in it will be appalled over it.
> 33. "You, however, I will scatter among the nations and will draw
> out a sword after you, as your land becomes desolate and your
> cities become waste. (Lev 26:31-33)

Accordingly, Daniel prays:

> 11. "Indeed all Israel has transgressed Your law and turned aside,
> not obeying Your voice; so the curse has been poured out on
> us, along with the oath which is written in the law of Moses the
> servant of God, for we have sinned against Him…
> 13. "As it is written in the law of Moses, all this calamity has come
> on us; yet we have not sought the favor of the LORD our God by
> turning from our iniquity and giving attention to Your truth…
> 17. "So now, our God, listen to the prayer of Your servant and to
> his supplications, and for Your sake, O Lord, let Your face shine
> on Your desolate sanctuary" (Dan 9:11-17)

Daniel is answered by Gabriel who explains that Jerusalem and the Temple will indeed be rebuilt but made desolate again after the death of Messiah the Prince (Dan 9:26-27) which, as we know, happened in 70 A.D.

However, Gabriel had earlier told him of another desolation that would happen before then…

The Third Instance – Desolation of the Second Temple (167 B.C.)

Most commentators see this as the first instance of Daniel's 'abomination' prophecies being fulfilled. Most also recognise it as a type or foreshadowing of what they consider will be

the second and third but which are actually the fifth and sixth instances, as we will see.

Antiochus IV Epiphanes desecrated the Temple and it remained desolate for the three years:

> Harsh and utterly grievous was the onslaught of evil. For the temple was filled with debauchery and revelling by the Gentiles, who dallied with prostitutes and had intercourse with women within the sacred precincts, and besides brought in things for sacrifice that were unfit. The altar was covered with abominable offerings that were forbidden by the laws.[398]

'Sacred' prostitution was a normal feature of Greek worship, as it had been earlier among the Canaanites.

The abominations of Israel leading up to these abominations of the Gentiles included the corruption of the high priesthood and many renouncing the Abrahamic covenant:

> At that time there appeared in Israel a group of renegade Jews who incited the people. 'Let us enter into a covenant with the Gentiles round about,' they said, 'because disaster upon disaster has overtaken us since we separated ourselves from them'. The people thought this a good argument and some of them in their enthusiasm went to the king and received authority to introduce non-Jewish laws and customs. They built a sports stadium in the Gentile style in Jerusalem. They removed their marks of circumcision and repudiated the holy covenant. They intermarried with Gentiles and abandoned themselves to evil ways.[399]

Note the sports stadium link to circumcision – the Greek men raced nude so the Jewish men began having operations to remove 'their marks of circumcision' which was, of course, the sign of the Abrahamic covenant (Gen 17-9-14). The high priesthood was granted to the highest bidder and the winners outdid each other in foolishness and cruelty (2 Macc 4:7-8, 23-25), putting to death any who opposed them (vv. 39-50).

The historian concludes:

---

398   2 Maccabees 6:3-5, *NRSV with Apocrypha.*
399   1 Maccabees 1:11-16, *NEB.*

Very great wrath came upon Israel.[400]

'Wrath came upon Israel' is an expression often used of God's justice when the covenant has been broken (e.g. Num 16:46, 18:5; Deut 9:8, Neh 13:18). The historian explains:

> Now I beg my readers not to be disheartened by these calamities, but to reflect that such penalties were inflicted for the discipline of our race and not for its destruction. It is a sign of great kindness that acts of impiety should not be let alone for long but meet their due recompense at once. The LORD did not see fit to deal with us as He does with other nations… So, He never withdraws His mercy from us; though He disciplines His people by calamity, He never deserts them.[401]

See again the pattern:

(i)   Israel's transgression so horrified God that He withdrew from them.

(ii)   He gave over the host, Israel's army, to be defeated and allowed their holiest place, the Temple, "to be trampled" and profaned by their enemies.

(iii)   Antiochus then committed his own abominations in the temple. He not only offered a pig on the bronze altar to desecrate it, as mentioned earlier, he also set up a statue of Zeus with his own facial features. In other words, he became himself an 'abomination of desolation'. Just as Daniel had predicted: "he will exalt and magnify himself above every god and will speak monstrous things against the God of gods; and he will prosper until the indignation is finished, for that which is decreed will be done" (Dan 11:36), "yet he will come to his end, and no one will help him" (Dan 11:45).

---

400   1 Maccabees 1:64, *NRSV*
401   2 Maccabees 6:12-16, *NEB*.

The Maccabees then rose up to throw off the Seleucid yoke and to rededicate the Temple.

The Fourth Instance – The Crucifixion (30 A.D.)

None of the above scholars seem to have recognised the Crucifixion as an abomination that causes horror to God. However, as asked in our previous study,[402] what could be more horrible to God the Father than the rejection and execution of His only begotten Son?

When Jesus drove out the money-changers and traders from the Temple, He was challenged:

> 18. The Jews then said to Him, "What sign do You show us as your authority for doing these things?"
> 19. Jesus answered them, "Destroy this temple, and in three days I will raise it up."
> 20. The Jews then said, "It took forty-six years to build this temple, and will You raise it up in three days?"
> 21. But He was speaking of the temple of His body.
> (John 2:18-21)

In other words, His authority for cleansing the Temple was His ability to rebuild or restore every temple they could desecrate or destroy, including His own body. This is because Moses' Tabernacle at Shiloh and the First, or Solomon's, and Second Temples were all to foreshadow Jesus Himself, the Word become flesh who tabernacled among us (John 1:14).

This means that His crucifixion was desecrating and making desolate *the true Temple*, the flesh and blood of the perfect Man in whom 'all the fullness of God dwells in bodily form' (Col 2:9). There is also extraordinary irony in that, whereas at Shiloh and in Ezekiel's vision the glory of God left freely, in 30 A.D. they dragged *the glory of God* (Heb 1:3) *outside Jerusalem to crucify Him* (Heb 13:12).

Wonderfully, mercifully, for us all, this desolation was

---

402 *Dancing in the Dragon's Jaws*, p. 106.

overcome by His resurrection.

I must add a caution here, lest we repeat the appalling misjudgment of many over the last two thousand years. For example, John of Antioch (344-407 A.D.) was the Patriarch of Constantinople and one of the most famous preachers of all time. He was given the name Chrysostom, literally 'golden-mouthed', yet in a series of *Orations Against The Jews*, he was anything but:

> The Jews are the most worthless of all men. They are lecherous, rapacious, greedy. They are perfidious murderers of Christ. They worship the Devil. Their religion is a sickness. The Jews are the odious assassins of Christ and for killing God there is no expiation possible, no indulgence or pardon. Christians may never cease vengeance, and the Jew must live in servitude forever. God always hated the Jews. It is essential that all Christians hate them.[403]

This is racist, antisemitic nonsense – the entire early church was initially Jewish and led by Jews. Paul the great apostle had passionately hated Jesus and killed His followers (Acts 22:3-8). Did he really find 'there is no expiation possible, no indulgence or pardon' for Jews? He wrote:

> 15. It is a trustworthy statement, deserving full acceptance, that Christ Jesus came into the world to save sinners, among whom I am foremost of all.
> 16. Yet for this reason I found mercy, so that in me as the foremost, Jesus Christ might demonstrate His perfect patience as an example for those who would believe in Him for eternal life (1 Tim 1:15-16)

Rather than agree with Chrysostom, it is essential that all Christians not hate anybody, recognising that while Jesus' death was called for by Israel's leaders, it was undeniably

---

403 Michael Rydelnik, www.messiahpa.org/persecution.pdf, 3 Aug, 2011.

                    Slouching Towards Bethlehem

Gentiles, Roman soldiers, who crucified Him. This means that we all, Jews and Gentiles, are guilty of His death and it was for all of our sins that He died (1 Pet 3:18). Peter explains further:

> 22. 'Men of Israel, listen to these words: Jesus the Nazarene, a man attested to you by God with miracles and wonders and signs which God performed through Him in your midst, just as you yourselves know -
> 23. this Man, delivered over by the predetermined plan and foreknowledge of God, you nailed to a cross by the hands of godless men and put Him to death.
> 24. 'But God raised Him up again, putting an end to the agony of death, since it was impossible for Him to be held in its power. (Acts 2:22-24)

Notice, Peter begins with God's sovereignty. Jesus has always been the Passover Lamb of God, known and slain before the foundation of the world (1 Pet 1:19-20). With His "foreknowledge", God's "predetermined plan" was always to use this terrible sin both of "the men of Israel" (executing Jesus for blasphemy for claiming to be their Messiah) and of the "godless men" (the Roman soldiers) to save us all, if we will accept that He died for us.

This also means this "abomination of desolation", the Crucifixion of our Lord Jesus Christ, was set up by Jews and Gentiles simultaneously.

The Fifth – The Desolation of the Temple, Jerusalem and the Land (70 A.D.)

Despite the Crucifixion causing the ultimate horror in the heart of God the Father, astonishingly, God did not immediately withdraw from Israel. For reasons discussed in our earlier study, *Dancing in the Dragon's Jaws*, He gave them forty years to reconsider what they had done. Only then did He allow the host of Israel to be defeated by the Romans, Jerusalem to be sacked, the Second Temple to be desecrated and destroyed and the people to be scattered throughout all the nations where they remained for most of the last two thousand years.

Jesus had warned the leaders of Israel that they were "filling up the measure" of the guilt of their forefathers (Matt 23:32) in killing "the prophets and wise men and scribes" that God had been sending them (Matt 23:34). In killing even His Son (Matt 21:33-46), they would cause the desolation of their beloved city, Jerusalem (Matt 22:7), and of their marvellous Temple:

> 36. "Truly I say to you, all these things will come upon this generation.
> 37. "Jerusalem, Jerusalem, who kills the prophets and stones those who are sent to her! How often I wanted to gather your children together, the way a hen gathers her chicks under her wings, and you were unwilling.
> 38. "Behold, your house is being left to you desolate!"
> (Matt 23:36-38)

This desolation and subsequent exile of the entire nation was the decreed punishment, as Gabriel told Daniel:

> "On the wing of abominations will come one who [or, that] makes desolate [i.e. the Crucifixion], even until a complete destruction, one that is decreed, is poured out on the one who makes desolate [i.e. the nation of Israel]" (Dan 9:27, NASB)

I am clarifying the *NASB* here but the *NKJV* is clearer:

> "Upon the wing of abominations is one making desolate…"

The *New Revised Standard Version (NSRV)* has another perspective:

> "And in their place [i.e. the sacrifice and grain offering] shall be an abomination that desolates [i.e. the Crucifixion], until the decreed end is poured out upon the desolator [i.e. the nation of Israel]" (Dan 9:27, *NSRV*) [404]

---

404 The *NRSV* follows an emendation of the Hebrew text which reads

                                     Slouching Towards Bethlehem

And, according to Jesus, that "complete destruction" or "decreed end", the Divine punishment, was poured out in 70 A.D.:

> 20. "But when you see Jerusalem surrounded by armies, then recognize that her desolation is near…
> 22. because these are days of vengeance, so that all things which are written will be fulfilled.
> 23. "… There will be great distress upon the land and wrath to this people;
> 24. and they will fall by the edge of the sword, and will be led captive into all the nations; and Jerusalem will be trampled under foot by the Gentiles until the times of the Gentiles are fulfilled. (Luke 21:20-24)

"Until the times of the Gentiles are fulfilled" – as we saw in our earlier study, when Israel finally recaptured Jerusalem in the Six Day War in June, 1967, after two thousand years, it signalled a new era for Israel and our whole world.

Lastly, to finish this overview of 70 A.D., the Romans then set up their own "abomination of desolation". As we saw earlier from F.F. Bruce, the soldiers brought their legionary standards into the Temple court opposite the eastern gate and offered sacrifices to them there. He commented:

> This action, following as it did the cessation of the daily sacrifice three weeks earlier, must have seemed to many Jews, as it evidently did to Josephus, a new and final fulfilment of Daniel's vision of a time when the continual

---

"in their place" rather than the Masoretic Text's "on the wing of…".
Regarding the *NIV*'s perspective, Stephen R. Miller writes:
'The *NIV*'s translation would indicate that Antichrist will place some
kind of object ("abomination") in the temple precincts ("on a wing of
the temple") that will be offensive to the Jews and cause them not to
worship there ("causes desolation"). 'Of the temple' is placed in brackets
by the *NIV* translators, showing that it is not in the Hebrew text. The
NIV's interpretation… is possible but would seem unlikely since 'wing'
(kānāp) is not found elsewhere in the Old Testament referring to a part of
a building or building complex."
Daniel: New American Commentary, Nashville; Holman Reference,
1994, p. 272.

---

burnt offering would be taken away and the abomination of desolation set up.[405]

The Roman legions' standard-bearers, or *signiferi*, included the *imaginifer* who carried the *imago* or image, a three-dimensional beaten metal portrait of the emperor [406], so they brought their emperor-worship into the very heart of Jerusalem.

Unfortunately, I believe, this was not the 'final fulfilment of Daniel's vision'. However, before we press on to the sixth, let us note the pattern in the fifth:

(i)   after a forty year period of grace, God finally responded to Israel's fourth "abomination of desolation" in 30 A.D.

(ii)   in 70 A.D., He gave over Israel's army to be defeated, allowing the Second Temple, Jerusalem and the land of Israel to be made desolate by their enemies.

(iii)   the Romans then set up their own abominations, images of the emperor to be worshipped as he was throughout Asia Minor, especially in Pergamum as discussed earlier.

---

405   F.F. Bruce, revised by David F. Payne, *Israel and the Nations: The History of Israel from the Exodus to the Fall of the Second Temple*, Illinois; IVF Press, 1997, p. 226.

406   As can be seen on www.roman-empire.net/army/imaginifer.html, 6 Aug, 2011.

This, then, was the situation facing John and his 1st Century hearers when he wrote Revelation.

Summary of the Five Historical Instances

We can now summarise the essential characteristics of these actual instances as follows:

(i)   Each instance is the tipping point or last straw to God after a general apostasy or falling away from Him. It therefore begins with His people rather than with others.

(ii) Each involved the dwelling place of God: the sanctuary at Shiloh in 1050 B.C.; the First or Solomon's Temple in Jerusalem in 586 B.C.; the Second Temple in 167 B.C.; the flesh and blood body of Jesus of Nazareth in 30 A.D.; and the Second or Herodian Temple in 70 A.D.

(iii) Each instance was in the land of Israel rather than in any other nation.

(iv) Each ensuing desolation was brought about by those who were not God's people but allowed by Him as agents of judgement: the Philistines, the Babylonians, the Greek Seleucids and the Romans.

(v)   Each had a blasphemous outcome: in 1050 B.C., the Philistines placed the ark of the covenant in the temple of Dagon in Ashdod (1 Sam 5:1-2); in 586 B.C., Nebuchadnezzar put the vessels of the Temple in the temple of Nabu/Marduk in Babylon (2 Chron 36:7) and Belshazar used them at his blasphemous feast (Dan 5:3); in 167 B.C., Antiochus Epiphanes set up a pagan altar and an image of himself as Zeus in the Temple; in 30 A.D., Israel rejected Jesus as the 'image of the invisible God' (Col 1:15); and in 70 A.D., the Roman soldiers worshipped the image of their emperor as a god in the Temple precincts.

We can chart these as follows:

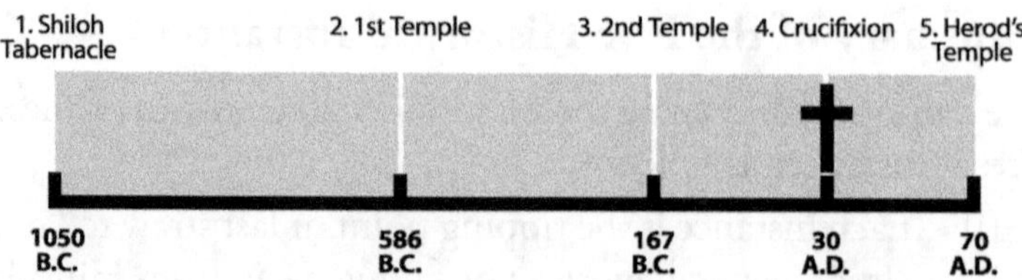

Figure (ii) - Timeline of the Abominations of Desolation

Could Jesus Have Meant One of These?

In 30 A.D., could Jesus have meant either of the last two or did He have one more in mind when He said:

> "Therefore when you see the ABOMINATION OF DESOLATION which was spoken of through Daniel the prophet, standing in the holy place (let the reader understand), then those who are in Judea must flee to the mountains" (Matt 24:15-16)

We have seen that Daniel the prophet accurately predicted at least three abominations of desolation: the transgression of Israel and the desecration by Antiochus Epiphanes in 167 B.C. (Dan 8:9-14; also in 11:31) as well as the Crucifixion in 30 A.D. and Titus's destruction of Jerusalem in 70 A.D. (Dan 9:26-27). Now we need to add another prediction from Daniel 12:11:

> "From the time that the regular sacrifice is abolished and the abomination of desolation is set up, there will be 1,290 days"

To which then is Jesus referring? 'Let the reader understand' means that Matthew (and Mark) was writing for a later audience including us. It will therefore take some searching out but since Jesus was predicting the future, it cannot be Antiochus Ephiphanes, which leaves us only three options:

Slouching Towards Bethlehem

(i) His crucifixion three days later

Matthew's account could be telling his readers/listeners that Daniel 9:26 and perhaps 12:11 are being fulfilled in 30 A.D. However, as I see it, there are two flaws in this view.

Firstly, Jesus was not crucified "in the holy place" but outside the city. Mark adds that the abomination would be 'standing where it should not be' (Mark 13:14). Malefactors were supposed to be executed outside the city so the Crucifixion was in the appropriate place for the crime of which He was accused (Num 15:35, Heb 13:12-13).

Secondly, there was no need in 30 A.D. for the disciples to "flee to the mountains" and they remained in Jerusalem just as Jesus had commanded them (Acts 1:4), nor was this the beginning of "a great tribulation" as described in the following verses, Matthew 24:17-22.

(ii) The destruction of Jerusalem forty years later

This clearly was "a great tribulation" and the disciples did need to flee as soon as they saw the Romans coming to besiege Jerusalem, as Jesus warned in Luke 19:41-44 and 21:20. However, by the time Romans broke through the walls and desecrated the Temple, it was too late for anyone to flee. Accordingly, some argue that the arrival of the Roman standards to surround Jerusalem fulfilled Daniel 9:26[407] but I do not see this as fulfilling 'standing in the holy place' either.

(iii) A fulfilment yet to come for those of us living now

There are a number of other prophecies that are clearly yet to be fulfilled, such as 2 Thessalonians 2:1-8:

> 1. Now we request you, brethren, with regard to the coming of our Lord Jesus Christ and our gathering together to Him,
> 2. that you not be quickly shaken from your composure or be

---

407 For example, Robert Jamieson, A. R. Fausset and David Brown, quoted on www.abomination-of-desolation.com, 26 May, 2010.

disturbed either by a spirit or a message or a letter as if from us,
to the effect that the day of the Lord has come.
3. Let no one in any way deceive you, for it will not come unless
the apostasy comes first, and the man of lawlessness is revealed,
the son of destruction,
4. who opposes and exalts himself above every so-called god or
object of worship, so that he takes his seat in the temple of God,
displaying himself as being God…
8. that lawless one will be revealed whom the Lord will slay with
the breath of His mouth and bring to an end by the appearance
of His coming

This 'man of lawlessness' will be brought to an end by the second coming of Jesus. It seems clear to me that there are no other viable alternatives – he is the last Antichrist and the final "abomination of desolation".

This returns us then to Daniel 12:11 and the 1290 days between the abolition of the regular sacrifices (the Crucifixion in 30 A.D. fulfilling the entire Old Testament sacrificial system) and the setting up of another abomination of desolation.

As has been shown in *Dancing in the Dragon's Jaws*, 1260 days (or 'forty two months', 'three years and six months' and 'a time, times, and half a time') is "the times of the Gentiles" and *a metaphor for the last two thousand years*. We took this from Jesus saying the end of this time period would be signalled by the Gentiles losing sovereignty over Jerusalem (Luke 21:24). Although Israel regained Jerusalem in the Six Day War of June 1967, we also saw that we cannot be dogmatic about that date because Moshe Dayan handed back the Temple Mount to the Muslim authorities. However, we do seem to be very close.

Identifying the 1260 days in this way means that the last abomination of desolation, the revealing of the Antichrist, will be '30 days' later and that he will be brought to an end '45 days' after that, as Daniel 12:12 has it:

As I see it, these two lunar time periods, one month and one and a half months, can be either literal or metaphorical. Remember, Daniel's '70th Week' was both. The first half was literal and fulfilled by Jesus' ministry of three and a half years while the second half was metaphorical i.e. the last 2,000 years, its meaning being foreshadowed by Elijah's literal drought on Israel. Accordingly, these two short time periods revealed by Gabriel to Daniel can be either. Personally, I think, I fervently hope, they will be literal and short as the reign of the Antichrist will not be pleasant:

"Unless those days had been cut short, no life would have been saved; but for the sake of the elect those days will be cut short." (Matt 24:22)

Bibliography

Books

Abuelaish, Izzeldin. 2010. *I Shall Not Hate: A Gaza Doctor's Journey,* Toronto: Random House

Anderson, Sir Robert. 1990. *Daniel in the Critics' Den,* Grand Rapids: Kregel Publications.

Andrews, Lewis M. Jr. 2004. *Tempest, Fire and Foe: Destroyer Escorts in World War II and the Men Who Manned Them,* Victoria, Canada: Trafford Publishing

Arendt, Hannah. 1973. *The Origins of Totalitarianism,* San Diego: Harcourt, Brace, Jovanovich

    -    1992. *Eichmann in Jerusalem: A Report on the Banality of Evil,* London: Penguin Classics

    -    1996. *Princeton Readings in Political Thought,* Princeton, New Jersey: Princeton University Press

Aron, Raymond. 2001. *The Opium of the Intellectuals,* Piscataway, New Jersey: Transaction Publishers

Azumah, John Alembillah. 2011. *The Legacy of Arab-Islam in Africa (A Quest for Inter-Religious Dialogue),* Oxford: Oneworld Publications

Barclay, William. 1957. *Letters to the Seven Churches,* London: SCM Press

Baynes, Norman H. 1942. Editor of *The Speeches of Adolf Hitler: April 1922-August 1939,* Vol. 1, New York: Oxford University Press

Belich, James. 1988. *The New Zealand Wars (and the Victorian Interpretation of Racial Conflict),* Auckand: Penguin

Bernières, Louis de. 1994. *Captain Corelli's Mandolin,* London: Secker & Warburg

Blaiklock, E.M. 1965. *Cities of the New Testament,* London: Pickering & Inglis

    -    1977. *Commentary on the New Testament,* London: Hodder & Stoughton.

Bloomfield, Arthur E. 1970. *The End of the Days (A Study Daniel's Visions),* Minneapolis: Bethany Fellowship Inc.

Bruce, F.F. 1962. *The New Bible Dictionary*, with J.I. Packer, London: IVF Press

-        1997. *Israel and the Nations: The History of Israel from the Exodus to the Fall of the Second Temple*, revised by David F. Payne, Illinois: IVF Press

-        2003. *The New Testament Documents: Are They Reliable*, 6th Edition, Downers Grove, Illinois: InterVarsity Press

Bullock, Alan. 1962. *Hitler: A Study in Tyranny*, Harmondsworth, UK: Penguin Books

Burleigh, Michael. 2001. *The Third Reich - A New History*, London: Pan Macmillan

-        2006. *Sacred Causes (Religion and Politics From European Dictators To Al-Qaeda)*, London: HarperPress

Carlé, Graeme. 2002. *Because of the Angels (Unveiling 1 Corinthians 11:2-16)*, Auckland: Emmaus Road Publishing

-        2011. *Dancing in the Dragon's Jaws*, Auckland: Emmaus Road Publishing

Cassirer, Ernst. 1946. *The Myth of the State*, New Haven: Yale University Press

Chandler, Paul-Gordon. 2007. *Pilgrims of Christ on the Muslim Road (Exploring a New Path Between Two Paths)*, Lanham, Maryland: Rowan & Littlefield Publishers, Inc.

Chang, Jung, with Jon Halliday. 2005. *Mao: The Unknown Story*, London: Jonathan Cape

Chilton, David. 1985. *Paradise Restored: A Biblical Theology of Dominion*, Fort Worth: Dominion Press

-        1990. *The Days of Vengeance: An Exposition of the Book of Revelation*, Fort Worth: Dominion Press

Conrad, Joseph. 2002. *Heart of Darkness*, Oxford: Oxford University Press

Crile, George. 2003. *Charlie Wilson's War: The Extraordinary Story of How the Wildest Man in Congress and a Rogue CIA Agent Changed the History of Our Times*, New York: Grave Press

Dadrian, Vahakn N. 1995. *The History of the Armenian Genocide*, Oxford: Berghah Books

Diamond, Jared. 1999. *Guns, Germs and Steel (The Fate of Human Societies)*, New York: W.W. Norton & Co.

Didion, Joan. 1990. *Slouching Towards Bethlehem: Essays*, New York: Farrar, Straus and Giroux

Dikötter, Frank. 2010. *Mao's Great Famine: The History of China's Most Devastating Catastrophe, 1958-1962*, New York: Bloomsbury and Walker Press

Durant, Will. 1972. *Story of Civilization*, Vol.1, New York: Our Oriental Heritage.

Elliot, Gil. 1972. *Twentieth Century Book of the Dead*, London: Allen Lane Penguin Press

Elliott, Mark. 1982. *Pawns of Yalta: Soviet Refugees and America's Role in Their Repatriation*, Champaign, Illinois: University of Illinois Press

Esposito, John L, with Dalia Mogahed. 2007. *Who Speaks For Islam? (What a Billion Muslims Really Think)*, New York: Gallup Press

Fest, Joachim. 2007. *Albert Speer (Conversations with Hitler's Architect)*, Cambridge: Polity Press

Fisk, Robert. 2005. *The Great War for Civilisation: The Conquest of the Middle East*, London: Harper Collins

Foster, Thomas. 1983. *Amazing Book of Revelation Explained*, Blackburn, Vic., Australia: Acacia Press

Fukuyama, Francis. 1992. *The End of History and the Last Man*, New York: Free Press

Gabriel, Mark A. 1997. *Against the Tides in the Middle East*, International Academic Centre for Muslim Evangelism in South Africa, first published as *Mustafa*.

    -        2003. *Islam and The Jews: The Unfinished Battle*, Lake Mary, Florida: FrontLine

    -        2004. *Jesus and Muhammad (Profound Differences and Surprising Similarities)*, Lake Mary, Florida: Charisma House

Gandhi, M.K. 1983. *An Autobiography (or The Story of My Experiments with Truth)*,

Harmondsworth, U.K.: Penguin Books

Garnett, David, 1938. Ed. *Letters of T.E. Lawrence*, New York: Doubleday

Gibb, Sir Hamilton. 1968. *Islam - A Historical Survey*, 2nd
edition, Oxford: Oxford University Press

Gilbert, Sir Martin. 2007. *Churchill and the Jews*, London: Simon
& Shuster

Goldstein, Joshua S. 2011. *Winning the War on War: The Decline
of Armed Conflict Worldwide*, New York: Dutton/Penguin

Goldingay, John E. 1989. *Daniel*, Word Biblical Commentary 30,
ed. John D.W. Watts, Dallas: Word Books.

Grubb, Norman. 1952. *Rees Howells: Intercessor*, London:
Lutterworth Press

Guy, Laurie. 2004. *Introducing Early Christianity: A Topical
Survey of Its Life, Beliefs & Practices,* Downers Grove, Illinois:
InterVarsity Press

-            2009. *Making Sense of the Book of Revelation,*
Oxford: Regent's Park College

Habermas, Jürgen. 2006. *Time of Transitions*, Cambridge: Polity
Press

Halliday, Jon with Jung Chang. 2005. *Mao: The Unknown Story*,
London: Jonathan Cape

Harries, Meirion and Susie. 1991. *Soldiers of the Sun - The Rise and
Fall of the Japanese Army*, New York: Random House

Heath, Gordon L. 2009. *A War with a Silver Lining: Canadian
Protestant Churches and the South African War (1899-1902),*
Montreal: McGill-Queen's University Press,

Hendriksen, William. 1986. *More than Conquerors: An
Interpretation of the Book of Revelation,* Grand Rapids: Baker
Book House

Hitler, Adolf. 1942. *The Speeches of Adolf Hitler: April 1922-August
1939*, Vol. 1, ed. Norman H. Baynes, New York: Oxford
University Press

Hochschild, Adam. 1999. *King Leopold's Ghost: A Story of Greed,
Terror and Heroism in Colonial Africa,* Boston & New York:
Mariner Books

Husain, Mahomed M. 2007. *The Islamist*, London: Penguin Books

Huxley, Aldous. 1932. *Brave New World*, London: Chatto &
Windus

Inoguchi, Capt. Rikihei with Cmdr. Tadashi Nakajima & Roger Pineau. 1994. *The Divine Wind: Japan's Kamikaze Force in World War II*, Annapolis: Bluejacket Books

Jenkins, Jerry B., with Tim LaHaye. 2000. *The Indwelling: The Beast Takes Possession*, Wheaton, Illinois: Tyndale

Johnson, Dennis E. 2001. *Triumph of the Lamb (A Commentary on Revelation)*, Phillipsburg, New Jersey: P & R Publishing Co.

Karsh, Efraim. 2007. *Islamic Imperialism - A History*, New Haven & London: Yale University Press

Kershaw, Sir Ian, 1983. *Popular Opinion and Political Dissent in the Third Reich: Bavaria 1933-45*, Oxford University Press

Khaldun, Ibn. 1969. *The Muqaddimah: An Introduction to History*, New Jersey: Princeton University Press

Koester, Craig R. 2001. *Revelation and the End of All Things*, Grand Rapids: Wm B. Eerdmans Publishing Co

Kubizek, August. 2006. *The Young Hitler I Knew (the Definitive Inside Look at the Artist Who Became a Monster)*, London: Greenhill Books

LaHaye, Tim, with Jerry B. Jenkins. 2000. *The Indwelling: The Beast Takes Possession*, Wheaton, Illinois: Tyndale

Lal, K.S. 1973. *Growth of Muslim Population in Medieval India*, Delhi: Research Publications in Social Sciences

Lane, Tony. 1996. *The Lion Concise Book of Christian Thought*, Oxford: Lion Hudson Plc.

Lawrence, Bruce B. 2006. *The Qur'an: A Biography*, Sydney: Allen & Unwin

Lawrence, T.E. 1938. *Letters of T.E. Lawrence*, New York: Doubleday

Lindsey, Hal. 1970. *The Late, Great Planet Earth*, Grand Rapids: Zondervan

Madden, Thomas F. 2006. *The New Concise History of the Crusades*, Lanham: Rowman & Littlefield Publishers, Inc.

Manchester, William. 1981. *Goodbye, Darkness: A Memoir of the Pacific War*, London: Michael Joseph

McQuaid, Peter. 1995. Editor of *Wartime Memories*, Auckland: Dolphin Publications Ltd.

Mogahed, Dalia, with John L. Esposito. 2007. *Who Speaks For Islam? (What a Billion Muslims Really Think)*, New York: Gallup Press

Mounce, Robert H. 1977. *The Book of Revelation*, The New International Commentary on the New Testament, ed. F.F. Bruce, Grand Rapids: Wm. B. Eerdmans Publishing Co.

Muggeridge, Malcom. 1934. *Winter in Moscow*, London: Eyre and Spottiswoode

\- 2005. *Conversion: The Spiritual Journey of a 20th Century Pilgrim*, Eugene, Oregon: Wipf & Stock Publishers

Muir, Sir William. 1992. *The Life of Mahomet*, New Delhi: Voice of India

Murphy-O'Connor, Jerome. 1998. *The Holy Land: An Oxford Archaeological Guide from Earliest Times to 1700*, 4th Edition, Oxford: Oxford University Press

Nettler, Ronald. 1978. *Islam and the Minorities: Background to the Arab-Israeli Conflict*, Jerusalem

Nietzsche, Friedrich. 1997. *Thus Spake Zarathustra*, Hertfordshire: Wordsworth Edition Ltd

Ohnuki-Tierney, Emiko. 2007. *Kamikaze Diaries (Relections of Japanese Student Soldiers)*, London: University of Chicago Press

Orange, Claudia. 1990. *An Illustrated History of the Treaty of Waitangi*, Wellington: Allen & Unwin

Orwell, George. 1949. *1984*, London: Secker & Warburg

Pacini, Andrea. 1998. *Socio-Political and Community Dynamics of Arab Christians in Jordan, Israel, and the Autonomous Palestinian Territories*, Oxford: Clarendon Press

Payne, David F. 1997. *Israel and the Nations: The History of Israel from the Exodus to the Fall of the Second Temple*, Illinois: IVF Press

Perkins, Pheme. 1988. *Reading the New Testament,* Mahwah, New Jersey: Paulist Press.

Pineau, Roger with Capt. Rikihei Inoguchi & Cmdr. Tadashi Nakajima. 1994. *The Divine Wind: Japan's Kamikaze Force in World War II,* Annapolis: Bluejacket Books

Pinker, Steven. 2011. *The Better Angels of Our Nature (Why Violence has Declined),* New York: Viking

Postman, Neil. 1985. *Amusing Ourselves to Death: Public Discourse in the Age of Show Business,* New York: Penguin

Powell, Barry B. 2007. *Classical Myth,* Fifth Edition, Upper Saddle River, New Jersey: Pearson Prentice Hall

Price, Randall. 1999. *The Coming Last Days' Temple,* Eugene, Oregon: Harvest House Publishers

Prince, Derek. 1973. *Shaping History Through Prayer and Fasting,* New Kensington, PA: Whitaker House

Princeton Readings in Political Thought, ed. Mitchell Cohen & Nicole Fermon, 1996. Princeton, New Jersey: Princeton University Press

Rashin, Alexander. 2003. *Why Didn't Stalin Kill All the Jews?* New York: Liberty Publishing House

Rees, Laurence. 2005. *Auschwitz: The Nazis and the Final Solution,* London: BBC Books

Richardson, Joel with Walid Shoebat. 2008. *God's War on Terror (Islam, Prophecy and the Bible),* Newtown, Pensylvania: Top Executive Media

Rummel, Rudolph. 1990. *Lethal Politics: Soviet Genocide And Mass Murder Since 1917,* New Brunswick, New Jersey: Transaction Publishers

　　　　　- 　　　　　1994. *Death By Government: Genocide and Mass Murder,* New Brunswick, New Jersey: Transaction Publishers

Russell, Bertrand. 1956. *Portraits from Memory and Other Essays,* New York: Simon & Schuster

Schlosser, Eric. 2001. *Fast Food Nation: The Dark Side of The All-American Meal,* Boston: Houghton Mifflin Harcourt

Shakarian, Demos with John and Elizabeth Sherrill. 1977. *The Happiest People On Earth,* London: Hodder & Stoughton Religious

Shakespeare, William. 1962. *Complete Works,* London: Oxford University Press

Sheikh, Bilquis. 2001. *I Dared to Call Him Father,* Eastbourne, UK: Kingsway Publishing

Shinya, Michiharu. 2001. *Beyond Death And Dishonour,* Auckland: Castle Publishing

Shirer, William. 1960. *The Rise and Fall of the Third Reich (A History of Nazi Germany),* New York: Simon & Shuster

Shoebat, Walid and Joel Richardson. 2008. *God's War on Terror (Islam, Prophecy and the Bible),* Newtown, Pensylvania: Top Executive Media

Shotter, David Colin Arthur. 2005. *Augustus Caesar,* 2nd edition, New York: Routledge

Speer, Albert. 1970. *Inside the Third Reich,* trans. Richard & Clara Winston, New York & Toronto: Macmillan

Spong, John Shelby. 1992. *Born of a Woman: A Bishop Rethinks the Birth of Jesus,* San Francisco: Harper
- 1996. *Liberating the Gospels: Reading the Bible with Jewish Eyes,* San Francisco: HarperCollins
- 1999. *Why Christianity Must Change or Die: A Bishop Speaks to Believers in Exile,* New York: HarperOne

Nakajima, Cmdr. Tadashi Capt. with Capt. Rikihei Inoguchi & Roger Pineau. 1994. *The Divine Wind: Japan's Kamikaze Force in World War II,* Annapolis: Bluejacket Books

Tenney, Merrill C. 1958. *Interpreting Revelation,* London: Pickering & Inglis Ltd

Wade, John E II. 2010. Ed. *How to Achieve a Heaven on Earth,* Gretna, Louisiana: Pelican Publishing Co Inc.

Wagener, Otto. 1985. *Hitler: Memoirs of a Confidant,* edited by Henry Ashby Turner Jr., Newhaven: Yale University Press

Walvoord, John F. 1966. *The Revelation of Jesus Christ,* Chicago: Moody Press

Wells, H.G. 1945. *The Last Books: The Happy Turning* and *Mind at the End of its Tether,* Rhinebeck, New York: Monkfish Book Publishing

White, Ellen G. 1974. *The Great Controversy,* Mountain View, California: Pacific Press.

Wilcock, Michael. 1975. *The Message of Revelation,* Leicester, England: InterVarsity Press

Williams, William. 1867. *Christianity Among the New Zealanders,* reprinted 1989, Edinburgh: The Banner of Truth Trust

Wright, N.T. 1992. *Who Was Jesus?* London: BPC Paperbacks Ltd.

-          1996. *Jesus and the Victory of God,* Minneapolis: Fortress Press

-          1999. With Marcus Borg, *The Meaning of Jesus (Two Visions),* New York: Harper Collins

Yousef, Mosab Hassan. 2010. *Son of Hamas,* Carol Stream, Illinois: Tyndale House

Zertal, Idith. 2005. *Israel's Holocaust and the Politics of Nationhood,* Cambridge Middle East Studies 21: Cambridge University Press

Books On-Line

Aquinas, Thomas (1225-1274). *Summa Theologiae,* www. newadvent.org/cathen/14663b.htm

Cassius Dio (150-235 AD). *Roman History,* http://www.brainfly. net/html/dio_cass.htm

Elst, Koenraad. *Negationism in India: Concealing the Record of Islam,* Voice of India. Available on http://koenraadelst. bharatvani.org/books/negaind/ch2.htm

Hobbes, Thomas (1588-1679). *Leviathan: The Matter, Forme and Power of a Common Wealth Ecclesiasticall and Civil,* http:// oregonstate.edu/instruct/phl302/texts/hobbes/leviathan-contents.html

Hadith, http://www.cmje.org/religious-texts/hadith/

Irenaeus (125-202 AD), *Against Heresies,* www.columbia.edu/cu/ augustine/arch/irenaeus/

Lucian of Samosata (125-180 AD) *The Passing Peregruis*, www.
    tertullian.org/rpearse/lucian/peregrinus.htm
Luther, Martin (1483-1536). *Works* IV, http://archive.org/details/
    worksofmartinlut009638mbp
Pliny Secundus (23-79 AD). *Epistles*, X.96, www.textexcavation.
    com/plinytestimonium.html
Plutarch (50-120 AD). *Lives of Noble Greeks and Romans*, http://
    ebooks.adelaide.edu.au/p/plutarch/lives/chapter48.html
Smith's Bible Dictionary, www.bible-history.com/smiths/
Stanford Encyclopedia of Philosophy, http://plato.stanford.edu/
Tacitus, Cornelius (56-117 AD). *Annals* XV.44, www.
    earlychristianwritings.com/tacitus.html
The Italian Encyclopedia, 1932, www.fordham.edu/halsall/mod/
    mussolini-fascism.html
Qur'an, http://www.cmje.org/religious-texts/quran/

Bible Translations

English Standard Version, 2001. Wheaton, Illinois: Crossway
New American Standard (NASB), 1970. La Habra, California: The
    Lockman Foundation
New English Bible with the Apocrypha (NEB), 1971. New York:
    Oxford University Press
New International Version (NIV), 1978. Grand Rapids, Michigan:
    Zondervan Bible Publishers
New King James Version, 1992. Nashville: Thomas Nelson
    Publishers
*New Oxford Annotated Bible (New Revised Standard Version with
    the Apochrypha)*, Augmented 3rd Edition, 2001. New York:
    Oxford University Press
Schofield Reference Bible, 1909. Oxford University Press
The Amplified Bible (Amp.), 1965. Grand Rapids, Michigan:
    Zondervan Bible Publishers
The Message, 2004. Eugene H. Peterson, Colorado Springs:
    NavPress
The New Testament, 1969. William Barclay, London: Collins
Zondervan (NASB) Study Bible, 1999. Grand Rapids, Michigan:
    Zondervan

Dictionaries & Encyclopaedia

American Heritage Dictionary of the English Language, 2004.
     Boston: Houghton Mifflin Harcourt
Cambridge History of the Bible, 1963. Cambridge University Press
Concise Oxford Dictionary, 1985. Oxford University Press
Dictionary of Premillennial Theology, ed. Mal Couch, 1996. Grand
     Rapids: Kregel Publications
Encarta 96, 1996. Buffalo, New York: Microsoft
Expository Dictionary of New Testament Words, W.E. Vine, 1975.
     London: Oliphants
NAS Exhaustive Concordance of the Bible, 1981. Nashville: Holman.
Princeton Readings in Political Thought, ed. Mitchell Cohen &
     Nicole Fermon, 1996. Princeton, New Jersey: Princeton
     University Press
The New Bible Dictionary, ed. F.F. Bruce and J.I. Packer, 1962.
     London: IVF Press
The New Oxford Annotated Bible, Augmented Third Edition. 2001.
     New York: Oxford University Press
Theological Dictionary of the New Testament, Kittel & Friedrich,
     abridged by Geoffrey Bromley, 1990. Grand Rapids,
     Michigan: William B. Eerdmans Publishing Co
The Oxford Dictionary of Political Quotations, 1997. Oxford
     University Press
The Zondervan Pictorial Encyclopedia of the Bible, ed. Merrill C.
     Tenney, 1977. Grand Rapids: Zondervan

Newspapers & Magazines

Israel and Christians Today, Auckland
New Zealand newsletter of the International Christian Embassy
     in Jerusalem (ICEJ)
The Evening Post, Wellington
The Guardian, London
The New York Times, New York
The Washington Post, Washington D.C.

Articles & Pamphlets

Bertrand Russell, *Why I am Not a Communist*. Essay published in *Portraits from Memory and Other Essays,* 1956. New York: Simon & Schuster

Islam and Christianity (as seen in the Bible), 1995. Discover Islam Centre, Manama, Kingdom of Bahrain

Instructions from the Secretary of State for War and Colonies, Lord Normanby, to Captain Hobson, recently appointed H.M. Consul awt New Zealand, concerning his duty as Lieutenant Governor of New Zealand…, dated 14 August 1839. Available on www.nz.com/new-zealand/guide-book/history/colonial.aspx

Millar Burrow, *The Origin of the Term "Gospel",* Yale University; *Journal of Biblical Literature,* Vol. 44, No. 1/2 (1925). Available on www.jstor.org/pss/3260047

Millard Burr, *Quantifying Genocide in Southern Sudan and the Nuba Mountains 1983-1998.* Available on www.occasionalwitness.com/content/documents/Working_DocumentII.htm

PBS article by L. Michael White, *The Antichrist: A Historical Puzzle.* Available on www.pbs.org/wgbh/pages/frontline/shows/apocalypse/antichrist/white.html

Woman at Risk Worldwide, available on www.frontline.org.za/articles/women%20at%20orisk%20worldwide.htm

Miscellaneous

Abraham Lincoln speech, 1861, quoted on http://www.bartleby.
com/124/pres31.html

Bill Bland, *The Cult of the Individual (1934-1952)*, quoted
on http://harikumar.brinkster.net/paper/march2003/
cultindividual.html

Interfax News Agency, Moscow, quoted by BBC Monitoring
Service, U.K.

J. V. Stalin: Works, Volume 12, quoted on http://harikumar.
brinkster.net/paper/march2003/cultindividual.html

Lion Feuchtwanger, *Moscow 1937* and *20 Letters to a Friend*.
Quoted on http://harikumar.brinkster.net/paper/march2003/
cultindividual.html

Pew Forum, http://pewforum.org/news/display.php?NewsID=18850

*The Cambridge History of China: Alien Regimes and Border
States, 907-1368*, 1994, quoted by Matthew White, http://
necrometrics.com/pre1700a.htm#Yuan

Winston Churchill speech, 1947. The Official Report, House of
Commons (5th Series)

Zhudi Jasser interview on www.youtube.com/
watch?v=KpRgqDMrD4M

Slouching Towards Bethlehem

A

The Revelation Series

Coming in 2025, the final in the series:

Kingdom Come
Justice For All

Graeme offers some extraordinary new insights into the two resurrections, Jesus' return, and how He will hold us and the whole world to account.

The Revelation Series

John's original audience was obviously meant to understand the Book of Revelation - it was 'unsealed' for them (Rev 22:10) - so what did he and they *already know*? Book 1, *Dancing in the Dragon's Jaws*, provides the breakthrough in understanding all of Revelation, not because of anything new but by simply reverting back to the mind of a 1st century Jewish teenager. Beginning with the vision of Revelation 12, Graeme shows how its images of a seven-headed dragon attacking a woman in labour is just Jewish History 101.

This key then unlocks five extraordinary Biblical mysteries including: Israel's survival, despite the attempts of six great Gentile empires to prevent the birth of Jesus the Messiah; Israel's 'partial hardening' and rebirth in 1948; 'the times of the Gentiles' and the metaphor of 'a time, times, and half a time'; the two comings of Elijah, and what is happening now before Jesus returns.

As Book 1 in this series of seven, it lays the essential foundation for understanding:

- The two beasts of Revelation 13 (Book 2)
- The mark of the beast and the 144,000 (Book 3)
- The two witnesses of Revelation 11 (Book 4)
- Armageddon and Babylon the Great (Book 5)
- The seven seals, trumpets, and bowls (Book 6)
- The Millennium, the Resurrection, Judgement Day and the new heavens and earth (Book 7, due out in 2025)

As Psalm 4:7 advises us

> The beginning of wisdom is: *acquire* wisdom;
> And with all your getting, *acquire* understanding.

Because of the Angels
Unveiling 1 Corinthians 11:2-16

This text has been largely lost to today's church because we have assumed it was just Paul's "cultural baggage" regarding veils but instead we have obscured it with ours. Although he was writing in Greek, he was not using Greek metaphors but instead explaining the Jewish revelation and meaning of 'heads', 'covering', the fall of Satan, and spiritual warfare.

Today more than ever, we need to regain this lost revelation of gender-differences and relationships as well as the origin of Satan and the mystery of the Nazarite vow.

The Red Heifer's Ashes
Mysteries of Ancient Israel

Considered by Orthodox rabbis to be the greatest mystery of the Law of Moses, this is a truly astonishing revelation of Messiah. Every detail is unfolded as the reader today follows a supernatural path through the whole Old Testament, just as the two disciples did on the road to Emmaus.

On that day in 30 AD when Jesus rose from the dead, He considered this was so important that He then repeated it for the whole Early Church in Jerusalem in what has to have been the greatest Bible study in history!

Eating Sacred Cows
A Closer Look at Tithing

Some testify that God has blessed them for tithing but some are disappointed, often too ashamed to speak openly in case they are 'letting God down'.

And what should we make of Malachi's rebuke of ancient Israel, "You are cursed for you are robbing God! Bring the whole tithe into the storehouse…" (Malachi 3:8–9)?

Graeme cites from other oddly overlooked tithing texts that instead show how God wants us to receive a revelation of His goodness in annual holidays and well as in being generous.

This revised version expands the much-loved original by 50%.

Born of the Spirit
A study guide for new & old believers

This Bible study is for all who want to develop their personal spirituality and is formatted for you to record your own answers. It will help you check the foundations of what Jude, the Lord's youngest brother, called 'the faith which was once for all delivered to the saints' (Jude 3).

It is also written to avoid all denominational allegiances so you can clearly see for yourself how God wants us to love, live, and learn.